I0129213

PEASANT EUROPE

First published in the 1930s, Tiltman's *Peasant Europe* strays from the normal look at Europe during this time period. While much of the continent is concerned with "problems of international relations, industry and the future of armaments", Tiltman goes a step further than most writers and speaks with the common peasant to uncover their day-to-day concerns. He finds that most simply want consideration and a reasonable standard of living for themselves and their children. Accompanying the text are full page photographs, most of which are taken by the author himself, which offer a candid look at peasant life.

THE KEGAN PAUL LIBRARY
OF ARCHAEOLOGY AND HISTORY

Jerusalem in History • *K. J. Asali*

Ancient Civilizations and Ruins of Turkey • *Ekrem Akurgal*

A Short History of the Saracens • *Ameer Ali*

Alexander the Great • *E. A. Wallis Budge*

The Technical Arts and Sciences of the Ancients • *Albert Neuburger*

A History of the Hebrew People • *Charles Foster Kent*

A History of the Jewish People, Vol. II • *James Stevenson Riggs*

A Short History of the Saracens • *Ameer Ali*

Discoveries in the Ruins of Nineveh and Babylon • *Austen H. Layard*

Annals of the Kings of Assyria • *E. A. Wallis Budge*

Jerusalem in History • *K. J. Asali*

Early Europe • *G. Hartwell Jones*

The Technical Arts and Sciences of the Ancients • *Albert Neuberger*

Excavations at Ur • *Sir Leonard Woolley*

Jewish Life in the Middle Ages • *Israel Abrahams*

The Mameluke or Slave Dynasty of Egypt, 1260-1517 • *William Muir*

On the Trail of Ancient Man • *Roy Chapman Andrews*

Peasant Europe • *H. Hessell Tiltman*

The Kingdom of Georgia • *Oliver Wardrop*

The Land of the Hittites • *John Garstang*

PEASANT LANDSCAPE
A pastoral valley in Czechoslovakia.

Peasant Europe

BY

H. HESSELL TILTMAN

Routledge
Taylor & Francis Group

LONDON AND NEW YORK

First published in 2005 by
Kegan Paul Limited

Published 2013 by Routledge
2 Park Square, Milton Park, Abingdon, Oxfordshire OX14 4RN
711 Third Avenue, New York, NY 10017, USA

First issued in paperback 2016

Routledge is an imprint of the Taylor & Francis Group, an informa business

© Kegan Paul, 2005

All Rights reserved. No part of this book may be reprinted or
reproduced or utilised in any form or by any electric, mechanical
or other means, now known or hereafter invented, including
photocopying or recording, or in any information storage or retrieval
system, without permission in writing from the publishers.

ISBN 13: 978-1-138-99483-6 (pbk)
ISBN 13: 978-0-7103-1155-9 (hbk)

British Library Cataloguing in Publication Data

Library of Congress Cataloging-in-Publication Data
Applied for.

CONTENTS

ILLUSTRATIONS

FOREWORD

WESTERN EUROPE, preoccupied with the problems of
international relations, industry, and the future of
armaments, is sometimes in danger of overlooking the
fact that more than half the entire population of that
Continent is composed of peasants. The immense
territories of this hundred millions of cultivators (outside the frontiers of the U.S.S.R.), whose bent backs till
the soil of the ocean of peasant-lands, stretch from the
Black Sea to the Baltic, forming a natural barrier between
East and West. The peoples who inhabit that land of
farmsteads—Poles, Ukrainians, Czechs, Slovaks, Hungarians, Southern Slavs, and the rest—together represent
the largest single unit in Europe, split by artificial
political walls, but united by the bonds of common interests
and, in war or peace, usually a common fate.

Those peasant territories remain to-day almost virgin
soil for the world's manufacturers, populated by millions
of potential customers clad in home-made clothing and
living on the produce of their soil.

In this immense region governmental neglect, oppressive taxation, the fall in world agricultural prices,
and political persecution in some of the most populous
of the areas concerned first called a halt to development
and then set the pendulum swinging back to conditions
reminiscent of the serf-states of a century ago. That
neglect and repression, unreported but nevertheless real,
existed before the oncoming agricultural crisis left the
peasant millions too poor to buy matches, salt, and oil—
the three essentials of village life—and will, unless the
course of history changes, continue to exercise their
baneful influence long after the world crisis has passed.

For generations the tillers of the soil, living far from "civilization", were content to remain the "dumb oxen" of humankind. To-day an awakening is in progress, born of a growing consciousness of human and racial rights and quickened by a peace settlement which, while ostensibly based upon the principles of self-determination, denied all freedom and security to whole peasant nations such as the Ukrainians and Croats, while in other areas, such as "Greater Rumania", minorities numbering millions were handed over, without consultation and against their wishes, to the care of nations a hundred years behind them in culture and development.

In the following pages are outlined the economic, political, and social conditions existing to-day in those peasant lands east and north of Vienna. *Peasant Europe* is based, not upon information thoughtfully revealed by the Press Bureaux maintained by governments, but on facts gathered during talks round the family tables of those who, born on the soil, "see with the eyes and speak with the tongue of the peasant"; and who demand, not opportunities for migration, but consideration and decent conditions for themselves, their children, and their neighbours' children.

In an area divided by political barriers into seven states, and inhabited by some fourteen races with individual histories and in differing stages of development, conditions naturally vary. The highly organized agriculture of Hungary and Czechoslovakia finds little echo in the dwarf-farms perched high up on the Bulgarian hillsides or in the poverty-stricken villages of Serbia and the Old Kingdom of Rumania. Similarly, the main preoccupations of the thoughtful peasants in Eastern Europe are not Fascism, the fear of war, or the world depression, but the police régimes and calculated repression from which millions of them—Ukrainians, Croats, Slovenes, Hungary's "Irredenta", the Bulgarians of the Dobruja, and other "Minorities"—suffer under the "uneasy peace".

These things, as I learned in those valleys and plains, occupy an even larger place in the thoughts of the peasant masses than the disastrous collapse of agricultural prices which heralded the worst agrarian depression in history. Out of them is coming a new unity and a revival of the dreams of that "Green International" of which the Bulgarian Stambuliski dreamed a decade ago.

In Yugoslavia, Macedonia, Rumania, and Poland I have met and talked with the leaders of peasant thought, whose aims and aspirations are outlined in these pages. Their names are suppressed—a necessary precaution in writing of ideals and ideas for which hundreds have died since 1919, and many more now languish in the prison-cells of the countries named.

For the same reason I make only collective and anonymous acknowledgment here to the many individual peasants who received me into their homes, and who there, at meetings often attended by whole village communities, told me the story of their lives.

I cannot forbear, however, a brief acknowledgment to the zeal and enterprise shown by the police authorities of three nations—Yugoslavia, Rumania, and Poland—in seeking to prevent any foreign observer from talking with the peasants, and thus learning the truth about the political and economic conditions which whole peoples are now enduring—conditions which, directly traceable to the peace settlements and the chauvinism and bad faith of the victorious governments, will remain a challenge to statesmanship and a menace to the peace of Europe until dramatic changes have been made, and justice returns to the peasant lands.

H. HESSELL TILTMAN.

London,
   April, 1934.

PEASANT EUROPE

CHAPTER I

THE "OTHER HALF OF EUROPE"

MEET the peasant lands.

Meet them on that peasant highway that winds northward from Bucarest, through Buzau and Focsani to Cernauti, better known by its old Austrian name of Czernowitz. Along that road have marched countless invaders pouring from the limitless lands of the north down to the Balkan plains ; the last the German-Austrian armies only a few years ago. Now peace reigns once more along that roadway, and there remains, to remind one of bygone wars, only a significant absence of large houses, destroyed and never rebuilt, and the raised mounds which mark the graveyards of the dead.

North of Buzau the road rises, until from its brink one can gaze out across the seemingly endless ocean of farmlands, stretching away to the horizon in every direction. That highway is as good an introduction as any to the land of the peasant millions, for there is no intruding civilization, and few villages, to disturb the picture of ageless calm—the landscape is empty save for the wayside shrines erected by the pious when the Turkish tide ebbed southward and the eternal peasant figures to right and left of it, men and women, tilling the soil.

Or meet the peasant hosts on the slopes of the Balkan mountains in Bulgaria, where little shepherd boys tend their flocks of sheep on the lofty hillsides, as unrecorded generations of Bulgar boys have done since the Romans swept across those hills and valleys.

It matters not which highway you choose as a gateway to peasant Europe as long as it carries you east of Vienna, for in everything that matters the peasant lands are a single unit. Political frontiers may run this way and that as each war swings the lines on the maps. They may, and sometimes do, represent racial distinctions which sharply divide one region from another. But they represent nothing else.

From the economic and social viewpoints, the peasant lands form one unit, with the same interests, the same ideals, and the same problems. There is a greater natural affinity between the Ukrainian peasant of Volhynia, living under Poland, and the Croatian peasant outside Osijek, living under Yugoslavia, than there is between the Birmingham engineer and the South Wales coalminer. For every one of those millions of peasants dwelling between the Black Sea and the Baltic, under whatever government he may be living at this moment, has been raised in the same stern world, remote from everything except the soil. All grow old in the eternal conflict between the cultivator and the weather.

The fact that there are few large-scale industries in Eastern Europe strengthens further the common bond. In the Western countries, such as France and Germany, the state can safeguard its peasants with the aid, or at the expense, of industry. But in the real peasant lands which stretch eastward from Vienna, Prague, and the frontiers of Germany until they merge into Asia, the peasant *is* the state.

The finances—even the survival—of nations like Poland, Hungary, Yugoslavia, Rumania, and Bulgaria rest upon the bent backs of the tillers of the soil. The peasants of those lands and Russia once grew the bulk of Europe's food ; before the days of Canadian wheat-elevators and frozen Australian mutton their power was supreme. Numbering more than half the entire population of our continent, their standard of living does much to condition the measure of prosperity enjoyed by the other half. Yet they labour and sweat, from dawn till dark, for a bare subsistence. Taxed to the hilt and cheated out of even the simulacrum of political power granted to them in some nations, and totally withheld in others, the peasants are at once the most industrious and the most pathetic of all Europeans.

United by the bonds of common interest, their force would be irresistible. From the Baltic to the Bosphorus, they hold the issues of peace and war in their own hands. And every interest which they have makes war for them a disaster—every interest save one! That is the all-powerful national consciousness.

In certain regions existing frontiers swallowed up whole peasant nations, and placed them under alien and despotic rule. Until treaty revision—or war—frees them, they will remain the sport of governments which sit firmly in power on the backs of the toiling millions, like the Old Man of the Sea, content to consult the interests and wishes of every class of the community except the one class from which is derived their power—the peasants.

Any hint of a separate policy dictated by the needs of those peasants must at once be suppressed at all costs. Hence the trepidation aroused by Stambuliski, the murdered Bulgarian peasant leader, and his dream of a "Green International". Hence also the Polish attempts to discredit Witos, probably the greatest peasant leader in Europe to-day, and the persecution meted out to that statesman and former Premier of Poland following the restoration of Pilsudski's power in 1926. There are few more dangerous occupations in Europe to-day than that of a spokesman of the slowly awakening peasant masses, and by that danger may truly be measured the fears of those who have battened upon the peasant in the past.

Only in Bulgaria, most democratic of Balkan states, and in Czechoslovakia can the peasants be said to control their own destiny. In every other State they are the serfs of governments which live on their labours, giving them in return the minimum degree of well-being necessary to avert revolution. Those governments gamble upon the two outstanding qualities of every true peasant, whatever his nationality—his conservatism and his patience. There are signs that the conservatism does not run as deep as once it did, and that the patience is becoming exhausted. Changes in the structure of agrarian Europe, dictated by economic considerations and by peace settlements which often outraged the principle of nationality, are teaching the peasants to think for themselves. In a thousand thousand villages these things are the subject of eager discussion. Strange ideas, revolutionary ideas, are abroad. Listening to village orators in Croatia, Macedonia, Bessarabia, and elsewhere in that ocean of farmlands, I found myself wondering what harvest the new and strange sowing of ideas will bring forth. For none can deny the power of peasant Europe when once awakening comes ; the cold figures speak too plainly to admit of doubt.

According to League of Nations figures, 82·4 per cent of the population of Bulgaria is engaged in agriculture, 75 per cent in Poland, 80 per cent in Rumania, 60 per cent in Hungary, 40 per cent in Czechoslovakia, and 80 per cent in Yugoslavia. About one hundred millions of men, women, and children in Eastern Europe, outside the frontiers of Soviet Russia, are peasants. Add to that total the Russian hosts west of the Urals and thirty millions of Ukrainians under the Soviet state, and the peasants living in Europe east of Vienna total one hundred and fifty millions !

Moreover, this vast world of the peasant, lying remote from railways and even roads—unseen and unchronicled —is growing in numbers and importance. The population of the Soviet Union is increasing by three million persons every year—*an increase equal to the whole of the rest of Europe combined*. The excess of births over deaths in Bulgaria is 14·8 per thousand inhabitants, in Hungary 9·9 per thousand, in Poland and Rumania 15 per thousand, and in Czechoslovakia 7·1 per thousand. In all those countries this annual increase in population is almost entirely confined to the peasant regions.*

* In August 1933 the Polish Government published figures showing a decrease of births, for the previous twelve months, of nearly 100,000—from 1,015,000 to 932,000. The natural rate of increase per thousand inhabitants in Poland for 1932, therefore, was rather less than the 15 per thousand recorded for the years up to and including 1931. It is too early to say whether this decrease will be maintained or whether it is due to special causes, such as the agricultural crisis and industrial depression.

THE WEALTH OF MODERN HUNGARY

Gathering the wheat harvest in a land where the big estates still survive.

"CONVERSATION PIECE" IN SLOVAKIA
Peasant girls of the Low Tatras in holiday dress.

Given more efficient health services, and especially aid during maternity, this annual growth in numbers would be very much greater. Bulgaria's increase, for instance, has taken place despite the highest death-rate from tuberculosis in all Europe; while the lack of medical facilities for the rural populations is reflected in the infant mortality rates, which vary from 197 deaths under one year (per thousand live births) in Rumania to 137 in Czechoslovakia and Bulgaria, and 106 in Austria.

The peasants of the seven predominantly agricultural nations of Eastern Europe—Austria, Bulgaria, Hungary, Poland, Czechoslovakia, Yugoslavia, and Rumania—produced in a recent year approximately 136,533,000 quintals of wheat, 89,000,000 quintals of rye, 51,000,000 quintals of oats, 127,600,000 quintals of maize, and 484,748,000 quintals of potatoes.*

Considerably more than half those mountains of food is grown by peasants owning "dwarf" farmsteads of up to twenty acres, often subdivided into as many separate strips of land. Their tools and their farming methods belong to the time of the Old Testament.

These dry figures concerning populations and harvests may not be "news" in the sense that Fleet Street knows news, but nevertheless they reveal the paramount importance of the peasant to Europe.

Without the strong right arms of these inarticulate millions there could be no war. Without the incomes derived from the corn, the vegetables, wine, tobacco, fruit, and livestock which they produce, Western Europe might live, but it could not prosper, as it discovered when the contraction of purchasing power in that region first became acute in 1929. That relationship will be even more important in the future than in the past, for the peasant millions represent the one undeveloped reservoir of human needs still existing in Europe. Short of everything which industry can produce, from farm tractors and kitchen ranges to hats and plates, the peasants lack

---

* One quintal equals 112 pounds.

only purchasing power to initiate the greatest industrial
boom of the twentieth century. One industrialist remembered that fact, and thereby built up the greatest shoe
manufacturing business in the world. His name was
Thomas Bata, and you may see his agencies, the posters
advertising his shoes, and the shoes themselves in the
most remote villages of Yugoslavia and other lands.
Another famous industrialist saw the golden opportunity
in the peasant. Henry Ford opened agencies for the sale
of farm tractors throughout Eastern Europe, and was
actually selling 2,000 machines a year in Rumania alone
when the agricultural crisis brought the wheels of trade
between peasant and manufacturer to a standstill. But it is
doubtful whether Ford would have achieved any real
success in the peasant regions while the system of smallholdings obtained. Every peasant may acquire the habit
of buying shoes instead of fashioning them himself out
of sheepskin. Every peasant family needs scythes, reaping-
hooks, and maybe even ploughs. But the tractor belongs
to the lands where the large estate still survives, or to
Russia, where the *kolhos* is in fashion. The "strip
farming" system which exists in most parts of Eastern
Europe, and the "dwarf holdings" upon which
countless families depend for the means of survival,
belong to the still-surviving era of hand cultivation.

From these smallholdings of from five to twelve
English acres which are almost universal in the peasant
lands, and have greatly increased in numbers since the
widespread land reforms which followed the war, springs
a special economic and social outlook. Indeed, they may
be said to express the fundamental line of demarcation
between the real peasant lands and those other nations
in which farming is merely one industry of many. The
true peasant is he to whom the soil is sacred and the
plough the symbol of life. The millions whose lives we
are considering are peasants not by any accident of fate,
but by desire.

Farming in Eastern Europe is, indeed, "a tradition,
a way of life, a civilization, and any attempt to regard it

merely from the cash aspect, essential as that aspect is, must fail".*

Within this region, bounded roughly by the frontiers of Germany and Switzerland on the west, and those of Soviet Russia and Turkey on the east and south, special conditions have always existed, sharply defining the real peasant countries from their more westerly neighbours. For five centuries the whole population has existed by and on the soil. As no new areas of fertile land remained to be brought under cultivation, the growing populations have during the past century pressed hardly upon the means of subsistence, and have been responsible for that "land hunger" which has always existed in the peasant lands right up to the land reforms following 1918, and which indeed, in certain countries such as Hungary and the Ukrainian regions of Poland, exists right up to to-day.

The pressure of population was responsible for three factors which dominate life in Eastern Europe. It forced the cultivation of inferior land which could only be worked where cheap labour was available in abundance and which yielded only a low standard of return—hence, partly, the low yield of crops in some of the countries under review. It was responsible for the importance of the small family farm of not more than twenty, and often less than ten, acres as the main unit of the distribution of land—a tendency greatly strengthened by the land reforms which followed the war, and, thirdly, it was responsible for the fact that agriculture was, and to a certain extent still is, undertaken as a means of providing families with food rather than as a source of gain.

The younger brothers worked on the plot inherited by the eldest brother, often without demanding money payment, and the women and children of the household took their share. The food requirements of the towns were mainly supplied from the estates of the big landowners. A peasant family, down to yesterday in Russia, reckoned its wealth not in terms of money, but in terms of grain and milk to fill so many "mouths", from grandparents downwards.†

---

* *World Agriculture* : An International Survey. Oxford Press, p. 134.
† *World Agriculture*, p. 146.

For a brief time following 1918, while high prices could be obtained for agricultural produce, conditions encouraged many "middle" peasants, owning their own land, to depart from this conception of farming. Many of them added to their acres, and employed machinery and even hired labour. To-day that class is the most heavily indebted of all, and such peasants consider themselves fortunate if they can supply their family with the means of life. The agricultural crisis has, within three short years, reintroduced the economics of the Russian *mir*. Villages are once more self-contained, living on what they produce. In many regions, as will be related in a later chapter, even salt and matches are unprocurable. In 1933, as in 1833, farming in Eastern Europe means, in all respects save one, the growing of food for the family.

That exception is necessitated by the tax-gatherer. The load of taxation placed upon the backs of the peasant-owners of land is immensely heavier, and more widely distributed, to-day than anything which faced the small-holders of a century ago. There are larger armies to be maintained, costs of government have risen, and new and improved methods of corruption have been devised. But for those taxes—on his land, his house, even his peasant-cart—the average agriculturist could forget money and conduct the few small transactions necessary for his low standard of comfort by barter in the local market-place.

Barter has, indeed, come back, and the most popular form of negotiable currency in both the Balkan countries and Poland is eggs. But the tax-gatherer forbids any such simple solution of the problems of poverty; whatever world prices may be, the peasant must grow for export, and must take the best price obtainable, in order to satisfy the demands of his government. Without the pressure of the tax-collector Europe's surplus of wheat would not be nearly as large as it is. A reduction of acreage is now being effected here and there; a further reduction might operate to the advantage of the world generally, but it would not assist the individual peasant to pay his taxes, usually levied at so much to each acre of ground *irrespective of whether that ground is producing food or not.*

In a very real sense, the more large estates that are split up, the more peasant farms created, the more the effects of the land system, economically viewed, remain the same. In Hungary, landless labourers employed on the large estates are sometimes permitted to cultivate extra land in their leisure time, on a basis of two-thirds of the crop for the landowner and one-third for themselves. In the Bukovina or Bessarabia, now incorporated in Greater Rumania, a wide redistribution of land, amounting to about 30 per cent of the total cultivated area, took place after the war. The peasants, whether Rumanians, Ukrainians, or of other racial origin, secured the means of production. That was all they did secure. To-day there is no actual starvation in those regions— a fact which, considering that they are entirely agricultural, is hardly surprising. But every peasant is working six months in each year for the tax-gatherer, and six months for himself.

Yet, if the land reforms have not, partly owing to world conditions and partly to the rapacity and corruption of governments, ushered in greater economic security, they nevertheless mark an important milestone in the history of the peasant regions, and their psychological effect has been considerable. It may be stated without exaggeration that, in regions where "land hunger" had always been present, these reforms averted peasant revolts such as marked the overthrow of despotism and the eventual triumph of Bolshevism in Russia. In Russia the peasants seized the estates ; outside that country the same procedure was cloaked in legal forms. But the results were largely, though not universally, similar.

The extent of the reforms was greatest in Yugoslavia and Rumania, while in Austria, Hungary, and Poland the results were inconsiderable. The procedure adopted consisted of laying down a maximum holding which the expropriated landowner was permitted to retain ; this amounted nominally to 600 acres in Czechoslovakia and 1,200 acres in Rumania and Yugoslavia.

In both the latter countries, however, the reforms left most estates considerably below the figure mentioned in size.

The average area of the new farms created out of the expropriated lands also varied from country to country. In Poland the size of the new holdings was from 50 to 85 acres, in Czechoslovakia from 14 to 35 acres, in the old Regat of Rumania 12 to 15 acres : in Bessarabia 15 to 25 acres, while in Yugoslavia the new farms were often little more than allotments of from 1 to 4 acres.

Summing up the effects of these reforms, by which the continuance of individual enterprise was made possible in agrarian Europe, the authors of *World Agriculture* state :

In all, in these and the Baltic countries together, 70 million acres have been transferred, equal to 18·47 per cent of the agricultural land. Over two million new farms have been created, and one and a half million tenants have been converted into owners.

It was expected that the distribution of the large estates would be followed by a reduction in the acreage of cereals and a more intensive production of livestock. To a small extent this has happened, but the natural conservatism of the peasants, often the same labourers who formerly worked the land they now own, has prevented any revolutionary changes in the agrarian economy of the nations concerned.

Nor, for reasons already stated, has the transition to small-scale ownership been accompanied by any general improvement in the methods of cultivation. Over wide areas of the peasant regions political or financial conditions, or sometimes both, tend to perpetuate the present poverty of the population and make improvement difficult. Yet these nations contain some of the finest husbandmen in the world, and would yield apt pupils were the means of spreading education in modern agricultural methods, and—equally important—modern implements, forthcoming. That this is so is proved by the example of Czechoslovakia, a democratic state in which not only did the change-over from large to small scale production cause no decline in yield—mainly owing to the fact that the peasants of that country could obtain ample credits on fair terms from the co-operative credit banks—but during the first decade under the new conditions the agricultural population was slowly diminishing in numbers and the total production as definitely rising.

In other nations yields of the basic crops are well below the comparatively high standard of Czechoslovakia. Thus the yield per hectare* of wheat in Yugoslavia is 10·3 quintals, in Bulgaria 12·8 quintals, and in Rumania 11·6 quintals, compared with 17·3 quintals in Czechoslovakia.

In the case of maize, to name another important crop, the yield in Czechoslovakia is 17·1 quintals per hectare, against 8·9 in Poland, 11·3 in Bulgaria, 10·2 in Rumania, and 14 quintals per hectare in Yugoslavia. Lack of agricultural education, of credits and implements, and, in some regions, the absence of land drainage and the poverty of the soil, account for these wide discrepancies rather than lack of industry or skill.

The example of Czechoslovakia, and the figures which I have quoted of yields in other lands, prove conclusively that cereal production could be vastly increased were the standard of farming in Eastern Europe, and the supply of capital available, raised to the level achieved in that country. And, be it added, were world prices raised and consumption increased sufficiently to absorb the larger production.

During recent years special factors have tended to keep down crop yields in Eastern Europe and to intensify the poverty of the peasants. Marketing arrangements are primitive. Railway communications, especially for goods traffic, are poor, and in many regions, such as Croatia and Bessarabia, have deliberately been curtailed as a means of holding back recalcitrant "minorities". Which may be in the interests of governments, but is

---

* One hectare equals 2·4 English acres.

certainly not in the interests of the populations concerned. Roads, never good in the Balkans and Poland, are to-day worse than ever, owing to the financial stringency and the general neglect into which the peasant regions have been permitted to fall. Other factors operating to the same end, and which by affecting the whole agricultural structure of our world have had serious repercussions on the Eastern European countries, have been thus summarized by the authors of *World Agriculture* :

1. The break-up of the Austrian, Russian, and German Empires, and the creation of the separate entities of Austria, Czechoslovakia, Danzig, Estonia, Hungary, Latvia, Lithuania, and Poland, each with its own currency and its own tariff system ; and the consequent creation of some 7,000 miles of new tariff boundaries.

2. The raising of the level of tariff walls in several countries.

3. In the case of Germany, the heavy economic burdens she was called on to bear after the peace treaty.

4. The destruction of the pre-war position of industrial Western Europe as creditors, while the United States of America, previously a debtor nation, has become the world's chief creditor.

5. Lastly, the violent—in some countries unprecedented —disturbance caused by disorganization of currency and exchange, with all the attendant evils which it involved.

To those causes of the agricultural crisis, and others that have been mentioned, there may be added the political difficulties arising out of the treatment of the peasant "minorities"—Croats, Slovenes, Macedonians, Ukrainians, Hungarians, and Bulgarians—created or re-created under the peace settlements. The neglect, and active repression, of these peasant peoples, among whom are numbered some of the most highly developed and enterprising in Eastern Europe, will be discussed in later chapters ; here it will suffice to say that the governments which have attempted to meet demands for justice, and the redemption of pledges given after the war, by police rule and terrorism, cannot escape a special responsibility for the unsatisfactory political and economic

A TYROLESE PEASANT—
member of a picturesque mountain race which has fallen on evil days
since 1918.

MEN WHO FEED VIENNA
Threshing the grain crop on a Lower Austrian farm.

conditions existing to-day in wide regions which were formerly among the most flourishing in all Europe.

That political conflict, conducted largely underground and unseen behind the clouds of police spies, is responsible for many of the troubles which afflict peasant Europe. Viewed from yet another angle, Europe's peasant problem is revealed as an economic conflict between one hundred millions of food producers who form a compact unit on a continent which is the world's greatest market for the crops they grow, and the farmers of the United States, the British Empire, and the Argentine. Those oversea producers, operating generally upon a much larger scale, and with the most modern methods, are intensifying their attack upon the European market. In fact, it has truly been said that the European peasants are, economically, suffering from the effects of the agricultural revolution in the new countries much as the hand-loom weavers suffered by the industrial revolution of a century ago.

How are they faring in that threefold fight against new competitors, world agricultural depression, and, often, repressive governments? What is life like as it is being lived in the Europe of 1934 by that 10 per cent of the world's total agricultural population which inhabits Europe's vast peasant lands outside the frontiers of Russia? Above all, what are these unknown millions, who live beyond the farthest horizon of the tourist routes, thinking about the problems of life and death, freedom and justice, trade and prices, government and work, that weld them into a single political, economic, and social unit? The largest unit, whether viewed from the angle of a single occupation, of production, or of a common heritage of toil, existing in Europe to-day.

Although it would not be possible for anyone to travel through the almost limitless peasant lands, from the Turkish frontier to the Baltic Sea, without being impressed by the essential community of interest which binds together peoples of widely varying race, religion, and language, yet artificial political and economic barriers —and divergences of history—have resulted in widely

varying standards of life and conditions between one
peasant region and the next. Often, as in present-day
Rumania, villages separated by only a few miles are
peopled by peasants of distinct races, who speak differing
languages, cherish in their hearts different ideals, belong
to different churches—and are governed by quite different
methods by a government not over-tender concerning
the treatment of its "minorities". To answer those
questions, therefore, and give a picture of Europe's
peasant peoples to-day, it is necessary to devote some
attention to political frontiers and differing local conditions, both artificial in reality, which have divided this
single immense natural unit—the land of the peasant—
into separate political compartments, and to consider
each nation and its problems separately before once
more viewing them as a whole. Only thus, by studying the
facts underlying their lives and by the results of personal
observation in the nations concerned, does the picture
of Peasant Europe emerge—etched in sharp relief.

CHAPTER II

VIENNA is the "frontier city" separating the industrial West from the agricultural East; the gateway to the limitless farmlands which stretch in almost unbroken succession from its very doors to the Black Sea, the Bosphorus—and the Urals. From the Karntnerstrasse, in the centre of the city, one may reach Bratislava and the farmlands of Czechoslovakia in the course of a morning's travel. Zagreb and the wheatfields of Croatia are an easy day's motor-run away, while, travelling north-east, one may reach the Ukrainian territories in Poland, on the borders of Soviet Russia, in a single night.

Austria's own farmlands are considerably nearer. They surround the city, and splash over the hills which lie to the north and south; prosperous-looking farmhouses built with Germanic thoroughness in days when Austria was Austria, and not the beggar state of Europe. Travel from Vienna to Graz, capital of Styria, and one finds it hard to believe the stories told there of the hardships which the Austrian peasant is suffering; the fault, perhaps, of the memory of certain musical comedies, coupled with the Austrian love of cleanliness and order.

Yet, despite the fact that smallholdings of less than twenty acres predominate, and over 95 per cent of all farmland is owned by the peasants who till it—despite also the important fact that Austria is an importing country so far as food is concerned, and that the Christian-Social régime, depending upon the peasants for its strength, was fully alive to the interests of the rural population—the Austrian government was unable to arrest the advancing tide of agricultural depression when

it lapped at the eastern frontiers. Immutably, that tide
rolled on, until it had submerged the country districts
which form the only hinterland that stricken Vienna can
call her own, to be halted finally on the western frontiers
of that country by barricades of tariffs, quotas, and
"special arrangements" erected by Germany, France, and
Switzerland.

Thus, geographically and economically, Austria forms
the natural frontier of "peasant Europe", and an appreci-
able section of its population has, in recent years, shared
a common fate with the peasant races dwelling to the
east, over some of whom the Habsburgs once ruled.

The coming of peace found the 32 per cent of Austria's
population engaged in farming impoverished, their soil
neglected, and their livestock decimated. They tackled
the task of reconstruction with characteristic energy, and
in the ten years which followed 1919 increased the
volume of wheat grown within the restricted frontiers of
the new Austria by 40 per cent, of rye by 100 per cent, of
barley by over 150 per cent, and of sugar-beet by 800
per cent. That progress has, despite the recent difficult
years, been fully maintained.

For 1932, Austria's production of wheat totalled
345,000 tons, while that country produced 605,000 tons
of rye, 301,000 tons of barley, 454,500 tons of oats,
1,000,000 tons of beetroot, 2,278,600 tons of potatoes,
97,000 hectolitres of wine, and 20,000,000 hectolitres of
milk. Compared with 1919, the value of the agricultural
output had increased by 950,000 Schillinge ; compared
with the prices ruling in 1928, on the other hand, Austrian
farmers had lost 650,000 Schillinge owing to the fall in
prices. Expressed in the all-important terms of self-
sufficiency, Austria is now producing 75 per cent of
the rye, half the wheat, and all the sugar, milk, cheese,
and eggs needed to feed the population of that country.

Her herds of livestock, decimated during the war
and the famine, have been re-created ; to-day Austria
has over 2,000,000 head of cattle, or, as her farmers will
put it, "one cow for every three inhabitants". She has as
many pigs, and 248,000 horses engaged in agriculture

remind the enquirer that the average size of holdings is too small for mechanized agriculture to be introduced.

The greatest triumph of the Austrian peasantry, however, lies in the field of home-produced milk. Between 1920 and 1928 the annual deliveries of home-produced milk to the markets of Vienna rose from 28 to 286 million litres. Trace the effect of that concentrated drive to free the population from dependence upon foreign nations for this essential article of food and it will be discovered that the peasantry did more than improve their own incomes; they actually wiped out their nation's adverse trade balance of 40 million Schillinge a year in a cataract of milk! Between 1924 and 1929, the imports of milk and other dairy products fell from 40 to 9 million Schillinge, while during the same years exports of dairy products rose from 1·1 to 10·5 million Schillinge. Forty million Schillinge to the good during critical years—years when industry could give little aid to the government. To achieve that miracle, it was necessary to establish over 300 new co-operative dairy-farming and cheese-making stations. It was done, and to-day in this respect Austrian farming is a pattern to the rest of Europe.

If the national aim of a self-supporting Austria proves incapable of achievement, it will be the fault not of her farmers but of her frontiers. It is exceedingly doubtful, to say the least, whether the most intensive cultivation of the restricted area of agricultural land left to Austria can provide for the needs of her cities in their entirety. But the margin of imports required is moving steadily downward; apart from corn, meat, and dairy products, Austria now produces all the sugar she needs, all the potatoes, 90 per cent of the wine, and during six months in each year all the vegetables needed. It is by no means certain that, in the interests of Austria as a whole, that country should be in a position to dispense entirely with foreign imports, for her purchases of foodstuffs from Hungary, Rumania, Yugoslavia, and Poland provide the Austrian government with a useful argument when seeking outlets for the products of industrial Vienna.

Since 1919, however, and particularly during the past five years, Austria's position as an importing country on the very doorstep of agrarian Europe has proved a doubtful blessing. Failing to find markets for their agricultural "surpluses" in the western markets, the Succession States have poured their products into little Austria, assisted by the calamitous fall in prices which has enabled them to scale tariff walls with an ease unknown in normal times.

The importance of Austria as a customer to those peasant states whose conditions are discussed in later chapters of this book is strikingly shown by some figures prepared for the League of Nations by Dr. Engelbert Dollfuss, the present Chancellor and leader of the predominantly peasant party within that state.

"Hungary", states Dr. Dollfuss, "markets 50 per cent of her cattle and fat pigs for slaughter in Austria, and 33 to 66 per cent of her grain and flour products, to mention only the most important commodities. Yugoslavia exports 60 per cent of her cattle, 66 per cent of her pigs, 98 per cent of her sheep, 86 per cent of her eggs, 33 per cent of her cereals, and 40 per cent of her fruit crop to Austria. Rumania exports to Austria 59 per cent of her wheatmeal, 73 per cent of her cattle, and 42 per cent of her pigs." *

It is possible to trace, in those figures, the manner in which the economic entity of the old Austro-Hungarian Empire has survived the passing of its political expression, and to sympathize, therefore, with the Viennese argument that under existing conditions Austria is reaping the disadvantages of the old order without its advantages—free entry into surrounding markets for the manufactured goods which Austria formerly sent to Bohemia, Moravia, Hungary, Croatia, Transylvania, and

---

* *The Agricultural Crisis*, vol. i. Geneva, 1931, p. 100. Measured by values, Austria's imports from Poland amounted, in 1932, to 105·8 million Schillinge, from Hungary 136.6 million Schillinge, from Rumania 81·5 millions, and from Yugoslavia 108 million Schillinge. ("Report on the Financial and Economic Position of Austria, 1933", published by H.M. Stationery Office, London.)

the Bukovina in exchange for the food which flowed into her markets from those provinces.

There is, however, one factor in Austria's agricultural situation which has hit her peasants even harder than foreign imports. This is the well-known *Preisschere*, or "scissor phenomenon", which has widened the margin of difference between what the peasant buys and what he sells. Taking pre-war figures as 100, by 1931 the peasants' index number for sales stood at 108, whereas his overhead expenses stood at 163.

Analyse those figures and it will be discovered that the purchasing power of agricultural products in Austria had by 1931 declined 34 per cent as compared with the farmer's expenses, and by 41 per cent as compared with clothing only, 36 per cent as compared with household utensils, and 15 per cent as compared with his food bills! Since 1931 that same tendency has been aggravated; by 1933 the Austrian peasant, despite tariff protection, found his purchasing power had declined by half.

That fact, which is too well documented to admit of doubt, is hard to realize as the traveller journeys through the villages of Austria, or sits among her peasants at some wine-garden watching a game of ninepins (a favourite recreation in rural Austria), or listening to some political argument. The enquirer who is sensitive to the signs of bad times, however, will detect the presence of unanswered economic conundrums in the frequency and violence of the latter; Austria's drift toward dictatorship and the "corporate state" is the visible evidence that life has not been easy in that land during recent years. Nor, in happier days, would one motor from Vienna to the Yugoslav frontier along a Styrian road on which was painted every fifty yards a huge swastika sign—put there not by city agitators, but by peasants who have turned in their extremity from the Christian-Social policies of Dr. Dollfuss to Hitlerism, partly as a protest against economic conditions, partly, before Major Fey's *coup* of February 1934, as their *riposte* to the Social Democrats ruling in Vienna and other cities.

That interest in political developments which has

welled up in the very heart of Austria is the only outward sign of the strain which the traveller will find. Go into the peasants' homes at dinner-time. In nine out of ten you will find them eating soup, potatoes, smoked ham, eggs and butter, washed down with milk or beer. One hundred millions of peasants living to the east would imagine that the millennium had come if they enjoyed such a diet.

Enquire about education, and you will find that schooling is compulsory for every child up to the age of fourteen, and that Austria's percentage of illiterates is so small as to be almost negligible. That nation has not forgotten her great traditions.

True, her peasants are making their own spirits from potatoes—to light their homes. But they *have* lamps. They are still well dressed and, politics apart, apparently light-hearted. Their national health record is good; the infant mortality rate is the lowest in Central or Eastern Europe; and the yield of their crops per hectare is the highest in that region, with the solitary exception of Czechoslovakia.

Which, then, among these conflicting signs gives the clue to the real conditions of agricultural Austria to-day? Let us survey briefly the conditions existing in typical peasant districts, situated in different parts of that country—the first those mountain villages nestling on the slopes of the Tyrolese hillsides, the second those low houses covered with white plaster which are typical of the peasant communities of the Marchfeld, an hour's train ride from Vienna, and the third the wine-growers in the romantic Danube narrows, the Wachau.

The Tyrolese (and with him the Carinthian, Salzburgian, and Upper Styrian) is a mountaineer who looks down with pride but also with envy upon his colleague of the lowlands. The "horn peasant" is full of disdain for the "corn peasant", who cannot rival his traditions, his songs, his dances, his picturesque costumes. But perhaps he would be glad to-day if his few widely distributed patches of rye on the mountainside would yield corn more abundantly. He has to depend upon his "horn crop",

THE RAMPARTS OF OLD SERBIA

Kalemegdan Gardens and fortress at Belgrade, against which the Austrians directed the first shots fired in the world war.

THE CATHEDRAL AT ZAGREB
One of the many historic buildings in the Croatian capital.

upon the few head of cattle which are his own, and on the trees of the mountain forests that belong to him.

The loyal Tyrolese gave the Habsburg Emperors their best soldiers. The *Kaiser Jaeger,* or Emperor's Yeomanry, regiments were the favourites for difficult duties throughout the Austro-Hungarian Empire. The whole Innsbruck army corps was privileged ; its men wore the Tyrolese mountain flower, the edelweiss, in their caps. All this has gone ; the heroic defence of the Tyrolese mountaineers against Italy was in vain. The break-up of the old empire has hit the Tyrolese peasants not only spiritually but economically. To-day there is no army to speak of, no large official class ; therefore there is no place within the state structure for the younger sons of the Tyrolese mountain peasants. The mountaineer must sell more of his milk and timber to keep his larger family.

The export of timber to Hungary, Italy, Germany, and France thus became a question of major importance for the Alpine provinces of Austria. For a time, following the war, it provided a living for many thousands of peasants. Then came a new catastrophe. Soviet Russia, needing ever more foreign credits to finance her Five Year Plan, threw large quantities of timber upon the European markets. Prices slumped. Stalin's great programme of industrialization thus caused the bankruptcy of many timber companies in the Carinthian provincial towns, of saw-mills near Salzburg, and increased the poverty of the peasants in the mountains of the far-away Tyrol.

In 1928, 262,000 wagons of timber were exported ; by 1932 that figure had fallen to 63,000. In the former year 75 million Schillinge worth of timber was sent to Germany alone. Two years later, exports to Germany had dropped to 26·5 million Schillinge, and in 1932 to 2·3 million. To-day the ruling world prices do not cover the cost of production.

A secondary "trade" in these Alpine provinces—and a valuable one until a year or so ago—was the growing tourist traffic. During the summer months the west

C

of Austria, and especially the Tyrol, was transformed into a recreation ground for the Germans of the plains, the families of Hanover and Leipsic, and visitors from Western Europe generally. During the winter, ski-ing on the Arlberg and in other parts of the Tyrol attracted large numbers of visitors. This tourist traffic gave the mountain peasant a chance to sell milk, beef, and cheese; it also gave his younger sons employment as guides and waiters.

This second asset also received its *congé*, or something very like it, owing to unforeseen political events. In 1933 the new Nazi government of Germany instituted a special 500 Reichsmark visa, payable by any of their citizens travelling to Austria on holiday bent—one move in that country's campaign to force a Nazi régime upon Austria. During the warm months of that year the hotels and inns of the Tyrol and Salzburg stood empty, and the mountain peasant cursed the political controversy which had robbed him of a sure income.

Remember, in addition to these special factors, the great agrarian crisis, which has forced down the prices of timber, meat, and milk below profitable levels, and you will know why the Tyrolese mountaineers look dissatisfied as they collect round the church on a Sunday after Mass, smoking their pipes and discussing the situation.

These mountaineers do not lack imagination, however. How otherwise explain the venture which caused a Cabinet Minister to resign in order that he might be free to emigrate, at the head of a group of his countrymen, to a far-off continent and there build a new life? The Minister was Herr Thaler, the Austrian Minister of Agriculture. who. with his long red beard, was a typical and picturesque representative of the Tyrolese peasantry. As Minister of Agriculture in several Cabinets he fought for the "horn peasants". Then he went on a visit to South America. What he saw in Paraguay convinced him that there was a chance there to find homes and employment for the younger sons of the Tyrolese mountaineers. And so upon his return he resigned from the government and began lecturing on the possibilities of founding Austrian colonies in the New World. He was ridiculed at first, but finally he found enough money and support to sail with the first group of peasants—most of them Tyrolese like himself—to their South American home. And more are to follow.

The Tyrolese mountain peasant, as he goes wood-cutting in his short leather breeches, or the dairymaid as she drives the cattle to mountain-meadows where she will spend the summer alone in a wooden hut, is a figure full of the innate conservatism and loyalty to the past. Yet Herr Thaler's energy, his stubbornness in advancing his scheme, show that, once the Tyrolese is convinced that a change is needed, he will travel as far as South America to look for it. And the world agri-cultural crisis has left the peasants desperate. By the beginning of 1934, increasing numbers of them were listening to the voices of Herr Hitler's Nazi propa-gandists, to various "schools" of Fascist thought, or to unorthodox monetary theorists like Herr Unterguggen-berger, the mayor of the Tyrolese town of Woergl, who invented "vanishing money", and actually established this unusual form of currency with some success in his home town before the national authorities intervened. No people are more loyal than the Tyrolese while condi-tions are tolerable; none more dangerous when the times are conducive to desperate measures.

The peasant of the Marchfeld lowlands forms a complete contrast. In that region prosperous villages are clustered together, surrounded by cornfields. Here, also, the traveller notices the smoking chimneys of sugar factories, which now constitute one of the most important rural industries of Austria.

The sugar-beet is grown in a wide radius around each of the factories, and is important to the peasants for several reasons. A sure market is provided for the crop, the produce of each field being assigned to one of the factories as soon as it is planted. After the sugar has been extracted, the grower receives back the surplus for use as cattle-food. Incidentally, this sugar industry has

provided Austrian agriculture with a special problem:
that of the Slovakian seasonal labourers who formerly
migrated to Austria in considerable numbers each harvest
season. This migration, during years when Austria possessed a standing army of unemployed, gave rise to
high feeling. The Austrian government, therefore, under-
took the systematic education of unemployed workers
in beet-harvesting work, and by subsidizing farmers
employing only native workers the amount of foreign
labour has been considerably reduced.*

True, the crisis has not passed unnoticed across the
cornlands, but its incidence differs from the problems
experienced in the mountain regions. The "corn peasant's"
problem is the market at Vienna. That city is by far
the largest food market in Central or Eastern Europe.
Every other province of Austria is agriculturally self-
supporting. Vienna, the city which houses one-third of
the Austrian population, is the one great outlet for the
food products of the Austrian farms, and at the same
time the one great outlet for the agricultural products
of the Eastern European countries.

When the agrarian crisis came, the peasants in the
districts around the city found themselves completely
dependent on the buying power of the capital. Simultaneously, the increasing competition of the Balkan
countries revealed the desperate plight of those predominantly agricultural nations, while rising unemployment in industry reduced the buying power of the urban
population.

The Lower Austrian peasants fought this situation
through that excellent organization the Lower Austrian
Bauern-Bund. No trade union ever defended the interests
of its members with greater energy or skill than this
powerful alliance of independent peasant proprietors.
The Bauern-Bund, indeed, occupied a strategically
powerful position in Austrian political affairs. Dr. Buresch,
one-time Chancellor and Finance Minister, was for

---

* The number of Slovakian seasonal labourers admitted was 13,500 in 1932,
and for 1934 it is not expected to exceed 8,000.

many years its President. Dr. Dollfuss, the celebrated "pocket Dictator", began his political career as secretary of the same organization. From its privileged position as the power behind the Christian-Social Party, the Bauern-Bund was able to fight the oncoming crisis by tariffs, quotas, restrictions, and other means at the disposal of the government. It is, indeed, proof of the extreme gravity of the crisis that not even the privileged position occupied by the peasants of Austria could keep hard times from their doors.

Nevertheless, it remains only natural that the Marchfeld peasants in their well-kept white villages should react to the crisis differently from their compatriots of the mountains. The Lower Austrian smallholders may complain, but they always know that the government is staffed by their executives, and that everything possible will be done to protect their interests. These Lower Austrians, who were responsible for the great parade of peasants held at Vienna only a few days before the violent suppression of the democratically elected Social-Democratic rulers of that city, are the staunchest supporters of Dr. Dollfuss. Against the onslaught of National Socialism, the Bauern-Bund represents Europe's strongest bulwark. In seeking to bully Austria into a Nazi régime, Herr Hitler is fighting the massed forces of the Lower Austrian peasantry. Only when those peasants waver in their allegiance will the Austrian "Patriotic Front" fall.

You do not have to travel far from the strongholds of the Lower Austrian Bauern-Bund (or its smaller brother, the Upper Austrian Bauern-Bund) to find a very different picture, however. Go to the wine districts in the Burgenland province in the east of Austria, ceded from Hungary in 1921. Or go to the centre of Lower Austria itself, to the wine-growing Wachau valley. There the Danube flows through a hill country dotted with medieval castles, the most picturesque of these being Duernstein, the castle from which King Richard the Lionhearted, during his imprisonment, looked longingly for the coming of messengers bearing his ransom and listened to the melodies of Blondel.

Here in the Wachau, Hitlerism is rampant. Duernstein and its neighbouring castles were covered with
swastikas until Chancellor Dollfuss issued orders that
the Nazi notables in each village should be made to wash
all Nazi emblems off the ancient walls.

The wine districts are sharply divided from the
neighbouring cornlands. There holdings are small, the
vast majority of "farms" being of less than two and a
half acres in extent. Wine-culture is conducted on
more intensive lines than any other branch of farming;
the vineyards demand the entire time and labour of the
peasant family to which each belongs. At least a quarter
of a million people are entirely engaged in this work,
cultivating the orderly vineyards that cover the mountain-
sides.

For generations a certain natural antagonism has
existed between wine-growers and corn peasants, born
of the fact that the former have more direct contacts with
the towns, and are more directly dependent upon the
prosperity of the urban dwellers, than any other peasants
in Austria. It is the privilege of every wine-grower to sell
his own wine in his back garden; once a piece of scrub
has been hung at the end of a pole as a sign, another
Heurigen, or wine-garden, has come into being. Round
these *Heurigen* gardens centred a great part of the culture
of old Austria. Schubert and Johann Strauss made them
famous, just as certain film-producers are extending
their popularity by a different medium to-day. And for
many years, during summer days and nights, the people
of the cities have visited the wine-gardens and sampled
the new wines.

This connection with the cities has given the wine-
peasants a mental outlook approximating more closely
to the petty bourgeois class than to the peasants. When
the "corn peasants", through their Bauern-Bund, became
identified with the Christian-Social party, the wine-
growers swung their votes over to the Pangermanist
party, which was anti-Clerical and to a certain degree
Liberal in outlook. And when the world crisis, and
political events within Austria and Germany, killed the

Liberal movement, the wine-growers, like the tradesmen in the cities, went Nazi.

Between these three extremes—represented by the desperation of the Tyrolese, the clericalism of the "corn peasant", and the Nazi cause—the Austrian peasants are searching for a new basis of contentment, mixing loyalty to the old traditions with a widespread and deep desire for a change which will protect their children from the troubles which have afflicted their countryside since 1918.

The solution of those problems, in the political sphere, may be found either in Fascism or a return of the Habsburgs. If so, the more serious economic aspects of the crisis will remain, calling insistently for redress. Hemmed in between the Succession States, and subjected to severe competition from Hungary, Rumania, and Yugoslavia, in which nations agricultural prices have fallen to the lowest levels found in all Europe, the plight of Austria's peasantry is not an enviable one. And the task confronting any government which leans upon them for support must remain correspondingly difficult.

The "black spots" in that countryside are many; against them can, however, be set one big asset. If the economic condition of the Austrian countrymen, taken as a whole, was in 1933 better than the conditions of the peasant populations in most of the neighbouring countries, that fact was due less to her geographical position than to the twin factors that the Austrian government represents the peasantry more directly than any other government in Europe, with the solitary exception of Bulgaria, and that in Vienna the Austrian food-producer has control over a great city which, as industrial activity increases, will absorb more and more of the products of the countryside. Vienna was, indeed, the one asset left to those peasants by the peace treaties—a fact which should cause whatever new or reformed government that controls the capital city to be chary of reducing the standard of living of the industrial workers. For, be it noted, the Social-Democratic rulers of Vienna, in fostering the interests of the Austrian working class, were also, economically speaking, improving the lot of the peasants—whether they grew corn, cattle or wine, or sugar.

The answer to the riddle of the Austrian countryside is—purchasing power. And while nationalistic policies hold the field in Europe, it is the internal purchasing power of a nation which forms its most valuable possession. In this sense, at least, the interests of industrial worker and peasant are identical.

CHAPTER III

THE KINGDOM OF SERBS, CROATS, AND SLOVENES

WHEN a typical peasant proprietor, living outside Osijek, was asked what were the subjects of the greatest interest to peasants living under the Yugoslav dictatorship, he answered, "First, freedom to live our national life; secondly, education for our children; thirdly, debts and taxes. And then the question of the agricultural crisis."

Enquiries made among the peasants in all parts of the political unit known to the world as "Yugoslavia" did not alter the emphasis thus placed upon political dissatisfaction with the autocratic methods by which King Alexander is attempting to solve the problems which surround his government. In this post-war state of 14,000,000 people, over 80 per cent of whom are agriculturists, a life-and-death struggle has been proceeding ever since the day of its birth in 1918: a struggle between the so-called "minorities"—Croats, Slovenes, Montenegrins, and Macedonians—on the one hand, and the Pan-Serb autocracy on the other.

The dictatorship, which racially represents not more than 41 per cent of the population, and politically represents but a fraction converted to King Alexander's dream of a centralized, militaristic state under Serb domination, has denied, by its acts, the whole basis on which the "Kingdom of Serbs, Croats, and Slovenes," was accepted by the Powers in 1919—a basis of autonomy and equal rights for all races within its frontiers.

Under Austro-Hungarian rule, the ancient and highly civilized Croat nation, while politically unwilling and divided provinces of the "ramshackle Empire", enjoyed considerable privileges, at least so far as Croatia was concerned.

Thus the four main departments of government, those of Justice, Agriculture, Education and Home Affairs (including control of the police force), were situated at Zagreb, the Croatian capital, and staffed almost entirely by officials of the Croat race. The Croats had their own Parliament ("Sabor") in Zagreb, and a local government responsible to that parliament.

The police, trained in the Western European tradition, were friends and not persecutors, and no attempt was made to repress the unity, national identity, and consciousness of 5,000,000 Croats who were the inheritors of a once independent and great nation. Under these conditions the Roman Catholic and Westernized Croats attained a level of culture and economic well-being which found no counterpart in any other region of the Balkan Peninsula, and if they were anxious to terminate their association within the Austrian empire, it was in order that, free entirely from alien domination, their progress might be quickened.

In 1919 the Croats, together with other races mentioned above, were incorporated into the new nation of the Southern Slavs. The fifteen years which have passed since that event have brought to the Croats, and all other minorities within "Yugoslavia", the bitterest disappointments with which any people have been confronted in post-war Europe. Not only have all promises of regional autonomy been falsified by the event, but the Croats have seen their country and their people dominated by a race which, despite a great history and undoubted fine qualities, has been reared in the traditions of the police state and lags a century behind them in everything which makes for civilization. Moreover, under the Pan-Serb régime the weapons of repression, assassination, and persecution have been used to the utmost limit in the effort to turn Croats, Slovenes, and other minorities into hybrid creatures called "Yugoslavs", which means, in practice, Serbs.

The Croat Peasant Party, representing 90 per cent

of the Croat nation, was declared illegal and suppressed. Stephan Radich, leader and national idol of Croatia, was shot dead in the Skuptshima in 1928. Doctor Machek, his successor, has been twice placed on trial and sentenced for voicing the grievances of his people, and was, at the beginning of 1934, still incarcerated in a Serbian prison-house. Joseph Predavec, another leader of the Croat Peasant Party, was assassinated at his home at Dugo Selo a few days after he had received the writer. A strong Serbian police post stationed in the village was apparently no protection to a Croat national leader.

The Croat national colours have been banned, despite which fact in nearly 200 peasant households visited by the author in 1933 there was prominently displayed on the walls the inevitable portrait of Radich surrounded by the national colours of the Croat people. The only reason why this flagrant infringement of the law was not in every case visited by stern sentences was that even a royal dictatorship cannot deny the impulses of an entire people.

The Croat conscripts in the army are sent to serve in other parts of the country, and under conditions which, however normal in Serbia, are regarded as an affront to this highly cultured race.

Croat peasants have been arrested and punished for singing their national songs at weddings. Croat newspapers have been suppressed for daring to criticize the countless acts of terrorism and torture which have disgraced the police administration at Zagreb. And on the occasion of the much advertised but rare visits of King Alexander to the Croatian capital, every known leader of the people is first carefully placed in a prison cell.

If the conditions under which the various nationalities in Yugoslavia have been existing, briefly indicated by these few facts, concerned only a section of politically active people, they would have no place in this volume. But those conditions overshadow the lives of entire peasant races at present included in the "Yugoslav" kingdom, and the issues which lie behind the terrorism affect every man, woman, and child in that country. It is for this reason that, despite difficult times and one of the lowest agricultural yields in Europe, the economic question is entirely secondary to the all-important political factor manifest in the struggle for freedom.

The unity of Yugoslavia is a figment of the imagination created for political ends. There is no more affinity between the Roman Catholic and westernized Croat farmer, and the Orthodox easternized Serb smallholder, than there is between the Scottish farmer and the Macedonian. The Montenegrins and other mountain peoples show varying differences in their standards of life. But whereas no common bond is discernible between the Serbs on the one side and the repressed nationalities on the other, persecution and hatred for the present régime have proved a sufficiently powerful unifying force to draw all the oppressed nationalities and minorities, representing two-thirds of the whole population, together in a common determination to throw off the alien rule at the earliest possible moment. The alternative to this, which not only the peoples concerned but Europe generally must face, is for a highly developed people to sink back to a level of impoveiishment and neglect which has been unknown in those regions for a century past.

Travelling southward from Vienna by road, the essential unity of Croatia and Slovenia with Western Europe proclaims itself by a housing standard, and a standard of cultivation, which even to-day bears the hall-mark of Austrian civilization. It is not until Southern Croatia is reached, and the Drina river crossed, that the traveller sees the first settlements of Serbian ex-Service men, and the housing standard sinks to the Balkan level.

The conditions of the Croat peasants naturally vary according to individual prosperity. Forty per cent were definitely well-to-do in pre-war days—a high percentage for a peasant race which tells its own tale. Conditions under which this 40 per cent are living still equal the Swiss or Austrian standards in housing and cleanliness. Their homes, built of wood, or brick and stone, often contain four rooms and cost the equivalent of £200 for materials alone, compared with an average cost of £20 for the

A PEASANT MARTYR

Stephan Radich, leader of the Croat nation and one of the greatest orators of post-war Europe, addressing a meeting at Zagreb shortly before his assassination in the Yugoslav parliament.

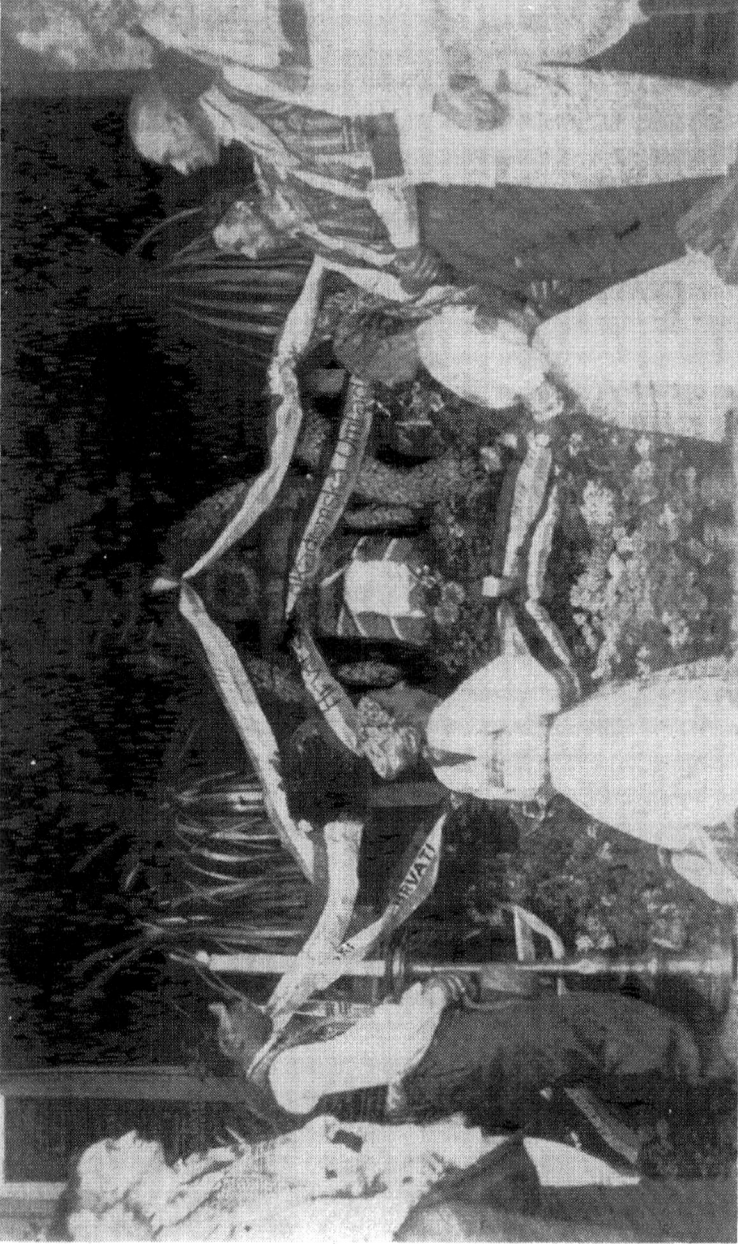

SALUTE TO RADICH !

No grave in Eastern Europe attracts more pilgrims than that of Stephan Radich at Zagreb. Croat peasants mourn their lost leader on August 8th, 1933—the anniversary of his murder.

homes of the Serbs who are to-day the ruling class in Croatia.

Account books which I have seen show that the annual gross income of these prosperous farms was in pre-slump days as high as 30,000 dinars, or 2,000 dinars per acre—this on a farm with four cows, two horses, six pigs, etc. Not only are most of these richer peasants literate, but many of them number a filled bookcase among their family treasures, and the writer has seen German editions of Jack London, Croatian editions of Shakespeare, H. G. Wells, and other famous writers with which remote peasant families interest themselves during winter days—a standard which is again higher than anything found in other parts of South-eastern Europe.

The villages are picturesque settlements, often situated around open common land and always dominated by the two hall-marks of the Croatian peasant community—the church, and the ducks and geese on the village green. The latter may be met at nightfall proceeding home down the village street, where each group sorts itself out and goes unerringly into the right gateway where it belongs.

One other sight in these villages reminds the traveller of the high standard of living—the ubiquitous Bata posters and shops. Before money disappeared from the peasant lands with the oncoming crisis, the Croats were the good customers of the famous Zlin factories, and Bata shops exist in villages too small to possess even a general store. Modern farming machinery was about to make its appearance when prices fell, and such tractors as Yugoslavia possessed were left to rot in the fields. The result is that to-day Yugoslavia, with only 12,000 motor vehicles of all descriptions, still lags behind other peasant nations in the matter of transport, and on the excellent Austrian-built main roads of the northern districts the ox-cart and the single-horse wagon still reign supreme.

By way of contrast one sees in such towns as Osijek the effects of the wide dissemination of factory products. The young women who throng the centre square of that town on summer evenings are dressed very much as their counterparts in Great Britain—with high-heeled Bata shoes, cheap dresses, and, not infrequently, lipstick and platinum blonde hair !

Outside the minority of town-dwellers there exist three categories of agriculturists—the large land-owners, the pre-war peasant class, and the post-war colonists.

The large land-owners now represent only about 5 per cent of the total acreage, and the estates left to them after the sweeping agrarian reform which followed the war are in few cases more than 500 acres in extent. A succession of droughts and bad years leading up to the world depression left this class in 1933, both in "minority" regions and in parts of Serbia, with barely enough seed to sow the ground.

The "middle" or pre-war peasants may be sub-divided into two sections; those owning more than fifteen hectares and belonging to the more progressive races are still maintaining a certain standard of comfort. Others farming less than that area, and particularly in the Serbian districts, were always poor. After a short period of prosperity following the war they increased their standard of living and, following the collapse of prices, attempted to maintain the improved conditions by borrowing money on credit. To-day many tens of thousands of such farms are unable to pay the banks even the five to six per cent which is the most favourable rate of interest charged on agricultural debts.

The third category of post-war colonists are in the worst plight of all. This class is composed of the original beneficiaries of the agrarian reform carried out after the war, mainly at the expense of the Croatian regions. The colonists, 90 per cent of whom were Serbs, originally received from the state a bare ten acres of soil and nothing more. In these circumstances, lacking capital, the proper equipment of the new holdings proved an impossible task. Many of the new settlers borrowed the seed necessary to raise their first crops, and have never since been free from debt.

Their economic plight has now become so bad that there is some danger that the main object of the "reform" —the "planting" of Serb settlers in non-Serb regions—

may not be realized, many of the colonists having sold their indebted lands and retired to the regions from whence they came. While areas of land needed by the native Croats have thus been restored to them, it is only after the peasants have bought out the Serbian settlers, and thus in turn shouldered a burden of debt which will prove an embarrassment to the new cultivators.

Some interesting facts concerning the economic and social structure of typical householders in the Croatian regions were revealed by investigations carried out in the Sava Banat region of that country during 1931, based on questionnaires collected from over one hundred peasant families in that region.

A distinguishing feature of the territory covered by this investigation is that holdings of from three to seventeen English acres were in the majority, the largest single group being composed of farms of twelve acres.

It was found that there is a striking relation between the size of holdings and the size of the families working them. In the majority of cases farms of five hectares were supporting five members of a family. This connection between the amount of land available and the size of the family applies only in those regions with a comparatively high standard of living; elsewhere the pressure upon available food and available land becomes steadily more intense.

The investigation yielded some interesting information concerning the high rate of capital investments in the agricultural industry in Croatia.

The average amount of capital invested was shown to be from 7,000 to 9,000 dinars per hectare for all sizes of farm property. The average investment in buildings alone amount to more than 2,500 dinars per hectare, which is a considerably higher figure than that found in any other part of Europe south of Hungary. Investments in machinery and tools accounted for a further 800 dinars, with the exception of smallholdings under two hectares. Investments in live stock were heavier on the smaller farms than on more extensive properties, amounting to 1,700 dinars per hectare on holdings of over fifteen hectares and double that amount on holdings of from two to five hectares. Only the holdings of the larger class (i.e. of over fifteen hectares) employed any hired labour.

Turning to income, this investigation showed that in normal years the average crop income of peasant households farming above two hectares amounts to about 2,600 dinars per hectare of arable land. Some of the intensely cultivated small-holdings earned as much as 4,000 dinars per hectare. In the region selected for this investigation the farms under fifteen hectares produced mainly live stock for market, whereas the larger farms were mainly devoted to corn. A Croatian peasant holding of from two to five hectares, intensively cultivated by the entire family, enjoyed a cash income prior to 1929 which often amounted to 1,000 dinars per hectare. This income fell in the case of the larger farms, producing mainly corn, to 500 dinars per hectare.

The low earnings, in terms of cash, which are general throughout Yugoslavia, and especially affect the Serbian countryside, may in part be traced to the lack of agricultural education. The majority of the peasants in Croatia are skilled agriculturists hampered by lack of capital and government neglect, but in other parts the prevailing ignorance of modern agricultural methods is profound. Thousands of the peasants have no knowledge of rotation of crops and cultivate only maize or wheat. If these crops fail, or disease attacks them, as happened in 1926, 1927, and again in 1932, the luckless peasant proprietors are left without enough food to keep their families, quite apart from the task of satisfying the demand of the tax-collector.

With a wider variety of crops—sugar-beet, fruit, vegetables—pigs, poultry, etc., conditions would improve, but the Yugoslav peasants remain in a primitive state of development, and their marketing arrangements suffer accordingly.

The Yugoslav government essayed an attempt to assist its stricken agriculturists through the formation of a chartered company for the export of agricultural products. This company was established in 1930 to centralize and co-ordinate the activities of exporters and agricultural co-operative organizations, its capital of thirty million dinars being mostly subscribed by the state. Shortly after its formation the authorities claimed that it was handling more than 70 per cent of the total export trade in cereals, but the organization collapsed completely in August 1933—one more victim of world conditions and the innate deficiencies of the Serbs called upon to assume the rôle of administrators.

Government agricultural schools and a system of agricultural inspection also exist. Unfortunately, although these facilities look imposing on paper, it is impossible to trace any benefits from them when talking at the fireside of Serbian peasants who toil all day in bare feet on the stony hillsides of that land. Observation suggests that the agricultural inspectors whose task it is to instruct the peasants could themselves undergo a course of instruction with advantage. Many of them know nothing of crops, have never worked on the land, and confine their activities to collecting statistics.

Other reforms introduced by the government have had more beneficial results. In order to reduce the cost of agricultural production and increase the return secured by the peasants during critical years, the tax on revenue from land was reduced from 12 to 10 per cent, thereby relieving peasants of more than 100,000,000 dinars of taxation per year at one stroke of the pen. The import duties on certain agricultural implements were removed, export duties on oil, seed, and wool were cancelled, and transport rates for the export of cereals by rail and water were reduced by from 20 to 45 per cent. Further, a provisional moratorium on peasant and private debts was enforced by decree, as related in a later chapter.

These concessions, while they show that the intentions of the government are more beneficial in the economic than the political sphere, have not gone very far to mitigate the severity of the crisis in a country noteworthy for the low yield of crops. In no way are the primitive conditions still existing over the greater part of Yugoslavia, outside Croatia, Baranja, Backa and Banat, so clearly evident as in the fact that the average yield of

D

crops per hectare is less even than in Rumania. Thus in
the case of wheat the yield for the year 1931 was 10·3
quintals per hectare compared with 11·6 for Rumania
and 15·9 for Austria ; in the case of rye the average yield
was 8 quintals per hectare compared with 11·9 for
Rumania and 14 quintals for Austria; the yield in
oats was 7 quintals per hectare compared with 10·6 for
Rumania and 12·8 for Austria.

Only in the case of maize was the position reversed,
the average yield of that crop being 14 quintals per
hectare compared with 10·2 for Rumania. That this
standard is still low is revealed by the further fact that the
corresponding yield for Czechoslovakia was 17·1 quintals
and for Austria as high as 20·9.

The poverty resulting from these low yields has been
intensified by the familiar "scissors" process in prices.
Expressed in terms of gold, the return to the peasant on the
crops he grows was, in 1933, 30 per cent below the 1913
figure, whereas the prices of manufactured products purchased by the peasant remain considerably higher than the
pre-war figure. Taking 1913 as 100, M. Pochtitch, a
Croatian economist, has estimated that the price of horse-
shoes in June 1929 was 172, coffee 186, ploughs 134,
scythes 193, carts 162, clothing 331, woollen cloth 293,
woollen stockings 264, hats 288, and shoes 327. The gap
represented between these high prices and the low
prices for everything which the peasant has for sale more
than accounts for the critical position of the mass of
cultivators.

Since 1929 agricultural prices have nose-dived to new
record low levels—a fact which makes it hardly surprising that when the writer took a census of the actual
cash possessed by 300 peasant families in different
parts of Yugoslavia, the result revealed a figure fraction-
ally less than one shilling per family. Nor is it surprising
if large numbers, especially of the "middle" and smaller
peasants, are to-day well content if at the end of a year's
toil they have produced enough food to keep their own
families in health, without any thought of marketing anything except perhaps a few eggs.

In the absence of a sweeping transformation of her agriculture, Yugoslavia will remain a predominantly cereal-producing country and the fortunes of her people linked with the price level of wheat and maize. Half the cultivated area of the country is devoted to the production of these and other cereal crops. The precise area under any crop fluctuates from year to year, but it remains true that grain exports, in normal years, represent at least one-third of the country's total exports, while vegetable and animal products together account for nearly two-thirds of the annual export trade. In these circumstances the decline in the value of agricultural products proved as serious judged from the national viewpoint as it did from the point of view of the individual peasant.

The figures are eloquent! Wheat prices, in dinars per quintal, on the Novi Sad grain exchange (the main market of the country) fell from 500 dinars in January 1924 to 155 in December 1930 and 93 at the end of 1933. Maize fell from 240 dinars in January 1925 to 85 in December 1930 and 70 at the end of 1933. The market value of the corn crop as a whole fell from 15,100 million dinars in 1928 to 9,800 million dinars in 1931 and 7,100 millions in 1932—a reduction of over 50 per cent in four years. And 1933 prices were even lower! Those figures provide abundant explanation for the fact that a foreign trade surplus of 327,000,000 dinars in 1929 became a deficit of 180,000,000 dinars in 1930.

In the years which have since passed the peasant has almost ceased to be a consumer of anything but his own foodstuffs. Production of Yugoslav industry has declined by over 30 per cent; the sugar-factories are faced with unsold stocks totalling more than 50,000 tons, consumption of soap in 1933 was only half the 1928 figure, and the sale of matches and oil had fallen by 25 per cent.

As has been the case with other nations similarly affected, Yugoslavia has sought to improve matters by the use of fiscal restrictions, by preferential arrangements with other countries, and by exploring any and every scheme proposed for common action by the agrarian governments in Eastern Europe, or for re-orientations of interests either in the Balkans or the Danube Basin. Numerous international conferences have been held, but the expectations thus raised have not been fulfilled, and the experiences of recent years have only gone to show that in the vital matter of prices no agricultural nation is strong enough to anticipate world recovery. It is, indeed, highly improbable that Yugoslavia, with a state budget in which 50 per cent of the total revenue is absorbed for military purposes, would find her position any better than that of her disarmed neighbours.

Sitting round the common table in peasant homesteads in Croatia and other "minority" regions, however, the main topic of conversation is not economic difficulties, but political problems which lie nearer the hearts of 60 per cent of the people of "Yugoslavia"—the problems created by the words in the Preamble to the Treaty of Saint Germain—"Whereas the Serb, Croat, and Slovene peoples of the former Austro-Hungarian monarchy have of their own free will determined to unite with Serbia in a permanent union . . ."

That opening statement of the Treaty which was responsible for the political fiction known as "Yugoslavia" did not then, and has not since, represented the true feelings of the peoples thereby condemned to place themselves at the mercy of Serb rule. As to that, it is sufficient to say that the decision to place Croats, Slovenes, and Macedonians inside an enlarged Serb nation was never ratified, or even submitted for ratification, to any gathering of competent representatives of Croatia, or of the other peoples concerned. From that day to this the accredited leaders of the Croat people, who were originally prepared to co-operate with the Serbs in the dual government of their different peoples on terms of mutual equality, have never ceased to protest and agitate, by every means at their disposal, against the attempt to sink the identity of their country and its people, and place both under the heel of a police-ridden Pan-Serbian state. And five million Croat peasants have supported those leaders in their protest with a singleness of purpose and unity which contrast strangely, in the eyes of the unbiased observer, with the inspired statements of government apologists at Belgrade that "there is no Croatian question".

The baneful influence of Serb domination on both the political conditions in that country, and the present standards and future prospects of the various nationalities and minority peoples in Yugoslavia, are of such vital importance to these peasant races, to say nothing of the peace of the Balkans, that further consideration may well be given to the subject.

CHAPTER IV

CROATIA'S FIGHT FOR JUSTICE

THE political differences which to-day separate the militarist Pan-Serbian dictatorship on the one hand and the democratic Croat nation (with which is associated the Slovenes and other minorities within the Yugoslav state) on the other, arise from, and are the consequence of, a deep moral and cultural gulf which separates the Serbian state from the peasant nations brought within the new frontiers of "Yugoslavia" in 1919. Those frontiers, it has been said, were created by bad faith and broken pledges, and have ever since been maintained by violence directed against defenceless populations.

For the genesis of the present bitter controversy—a controversy which, unless a solution can be found, can end only in the disintegration of Yugoslavia—one must go back to November 9, 1918. On that day M. Pashich, the veteran Prime Minister of Serbia, and other representatives of all political parties in that country, met the representatives of the National Council of Zagreb, and with them signed an agreement at Geneva setting forth the temporary constitution of the new partnership of races in which Serbs and Croats were the largest national units.

Under the constitution thus ratified, and which, it was provided, should remain in force until a contrary decision had been registered by the peoples concerned, two governments were to be formed—one at Belgrade for Serbia, and one at Zagreb, charged with the government of Croatia and the former Austro-Hungarian provinces. There were to be, in addition, a few joint ministries representative of the whole of the new kingdom concerned with such matters as foreign affairs, the army, and external matters. A similar measure of autonomy was foreseen for Montenegro, incorporated within the same frontiers after a chequered pre-war history.

Before the ink was dry on the paper recording this agreement the Serbian government had withdrawn its negotiators from the joint Cabinet of twelve members which thus came into being, and had formulated secret plans for placing Croatia and the other new provinces under the heel of Belgrade.

On December 1, 1918, the "union" of the separate nation of Croatia into the new kingdom of "Serbs, Croats, and Slovenes" (since rechristened "Yugoslavia") was announced. The dawn of new liberty for Croatia was merged into the twilight of a people's hopes as it became clear that Serbia was bent not upon co-operation but conquest; that the "perfect partnership" of all Southern Slavs, fostered for years by romantics, meant, in practice, *Serbia über alles.*

From that day to this the Croatian leaders have refused to recognize the illegal annexation of their country, and the Croat people have solidly supported them in their protest. At no time since 1918 would the suppression by the Serbs of the separate government at Zagreb, expressly provided for by the agreement between the two peoples signed in November of that year, have stood any chance of acceptance by a free vote of the people thus deprived of their pledged rights.

Ignoring such considerations, and intoxicated with dreams of power, the Serbian militarists proceeded to occupy Croatia and the former Austro-Hungarian provinces with their armed forces, and ushered in the era of exploitation and oppression which continues to this day. Promises concerning the composition and powers of the Constituent Assembly went unheeded. The political system was first distorted so thoroughly that the Serbs, representing 41 per cent of the population, were always securely in possession of 67 per cent of the seats, and, finally, all pretence of democratic government was swept away by the proclamation of a royal dictatorship in 1929.

The constitution thus overthrown had been little better

than the dictatorship which replaced it, and was originally voted in 1921 only by means of the votes of Turkish and Albanian deputies from Macedonia and Kossovo—votes given under the threat of murder. Which did not, however, prevent the Serbian authorities from claiming that this vote established the legality of Serb domination throughout the country.

Faced with this denial, not only of elementary liberties but of the very fact of their existence as a separate nation, the Croatian people, ably led by Stephan Radich, struggled to find a *modus vivendi* which would bridge the moral chasm dividing the two Southern Slav nations, and it was not until Radich had been murdered, Dr. Machek imprisoned, and hundreds of Croats deprived of their liberty and tortured for the "crime" of voicing the opinions of their people that, regretfully, Croatia decided that the days of compromise had passed and that the problem had become not one of federal government versus centralism but a much more significant and deeper issue—nothing less than the struggle of a whole people for complete independence and the severing of all bonds linking them with a race which has elevated bad faith, violence, and the non-observance of solemn obligations into the accepted canons of political conduct. "With such people", declared Doctor Krnyevitch, one of the Croatian leaders now living in exile, "there is no place for understanding and even less for a durable human partnership."

The conditions of persecution which the Croats have endured find their counterpart in the territories of the Slovenes and national minorities who now look to Zagreb for leadership against the common foe. Spurred on by a determination to secure justice and freedom, these completely peasant peoples, lacking arms, money, and any means of attracting powerful allies elsewhere, have nevertheless managed not only to preserve their political associations for years after those same bodies were suppressed by the Serbian dictatorship, but have actually achieved a closer and more genuine unity in the hour of tribulation than ever before. Those portraits of the murdered Radich, enshrined in the forbidden Croat

THE VOICE OF CROATIA

The greatest mass-meeting ever seen in the Balkans, and evidence of the strength of the Croat Peasant Party; a demonstration held at Zagreb in September 1927 to protest against the military occupation and "annexation" of Croatia by the Serbs.

A CROAT FARMHOUSE

This photograph taken by the author typifies the high housing standard attained by this virile peasant race under the Austrian Empire.

national colours, hanging on the farmhouse walls of that land, are symbolic of one of the most gallant fights ever put up by a defenceless peasant people against oppressive government. There is something particularly heroic in the way in which, as each Croat national leader is murdered or imprisoned, another leader is ready and waiting to step into his place so that this struggle of a whole people for justice and freedom may be carried on to what every Croat believes is its only end—the liberation of his country from the thraldom of an alien and politically inferior race.

There is no parallel in all Europe, outside the Ukrainian regions, to this spectacle of a whole nation which has had its own national government and national legislative body being kept, against its will, under alien domination. Kept, moreover, under this domination despite the fact that in the election of 1927—the last held before the proclamation of the Royal dictatorship—out of 67 successful candidates in the Croat regions, 63 were representatives of the Croat Peasant Party, a record in solidarity for any democratically elected political party in Europe. It is not difficult to see the irony of the fact that the Croats, after having preserved in large measure their national and political freedom right down to 1918, should have had all liberties wrested from them, and a Balkan police régime imposed upon their country, as the result of a peace settlement based, or supposedly based, on the principle of self-determination.

The Croat case against the "Yugoslav" régime was outlined to the writer by Joseph Predavec, vice-president of the Croat Peasant Party and the third most prominent leader of the Croat people, in the course of a discussion with the writer which took place a few days after M. Predavec had been released from a Serbian prison and, as it transpired, only one week before this gifted Croat peasant-patriot was to share the fate of Stephan Radich, and in his turn fall to an assassin's bullet.

"Croatia is not content to remain the prisoner of a backward Serbian state," declared Joseph Predavec, "and the reasons which lie behind that refusal to subordinate our nationhood to the requirements of a Pan-Serb régime may conveniently be summarized into a five-point charter.

"The first point concerns the national aspirations of our people. This, the psychological question, is the most important. As Croats, we are proud of our race, of its history and its standards of cultural life to-day. We know that those standards are the highest found in any part of Yugoslavia; yet we are allowed no voice in the government which rules over us, and even our national flag is forbidden.

"Secondly, we demand freedom—for our homes, our private lives, and our thoughts; in a word, that freedom of press, pulpit, platform, and conscience which is part of the birthright of the British people and which we formerly enjoyed in the Austro-Hungarian Empire.

"We neither understand nor appreciate the methods or the rule of Serbia, under which there is no security in private life, and imprisonment without trial, and for expressing private opinions, is an everyday occurrence. Here in Croatia peasants have been arrested for singing the Croatian songs which were heard in every home until 1919, and which are part of the heritage of our race. And while the Serbian police, in a recent case brought to my notice, refused to arrest two men who had stolen a peasant woman's geese until the poor woman had paid a sum of 200 dinars, any suspicion of political 'disloyalty' will cause those same police to turn houses upside down. No restrictions are imposed on the police treatment of political prisoners, and torture and persecution are the everyday companions of our people.

"Thirdly, we demand the right which belongs to every independent people, to pay no taxes except those levied by our own elected representatives. The Croats, as a progressive peasant race, know quite well the value of government assistance to a farming community. Under Serbian rule, Croatia is enduring most oppressive taxation for the benefit of the governing race. No attempt is made to maintain in repair the roads on which our farmers depend for transport. The money gathered up by the tax-collectors is spent either in improving Serbian cities or in paying the army and police who now occupy Croatia and deny us freedom.

"The fourth point in our programme concerns Croatia's demand for government 'of Croats, for Croats, by Croats'. Right up to 1918 we lived under the guidance of native Croatian officials. The four main internal departments of government for this province were housed at Zagreb, and in all internal matters, even under the Habsburgs, the Croat people were their own masters. Now, if you want to find those government departments, you must search for them at Belgrade, the capital of an alien race, while in their place at Zagreb you will find a garrison of 8,000 Serb and Albanian troops. You will further find that all the police, civil service, and even the railwaymen on the state system, are Serbs. Every post is reserved for the members of the predominant race, despite the fact that the Croatian people are by common consent a century ahead of the Serbs in civilization. For evidence on that point you have only to refer to the Croat conscripts serving in the Yugoslav army—boys from homes where the Austrian standards of cleanliness are maintained, who, having donned the 'Yugoslav' uniform, find that it is customary in Serbia for troops to clean out stables with their hands, and then eat food without any opportunity of cleansing themselves! The bitterness in our hearts over this sort of degradation should be understood by any Western European.

"The Croatian people, in other words, have been reduced to a slave status, fulfilling the three prime functions of all serfs —to provide taxes for the government, troops for the military aggrandizement of the state, and lucrative employment for the ruling race.

"Which brings me to the fifth and last point—a point which, together with the second, goes to the very root of Croatia's opposition to the existing régime and all its works. There are two different methods of ruling any country: the Balkan method of rule by force, and the Western European method of rule by consent. Under the first the police are tyrants. Under the second they are

friends; recruited from the population they serve.
Between these two conceptions of government, aptly
represented by Serbia on the one side, and Croatia, with
her western traditions, Catholic faith, and high standards
of culture, on the other, there is no room for compromise.
The Croatian people are determined not to cease the one-
sided struggle until their nation has been freed from the
police rule which has cursed this peasant land since 1919."

The police rule of which Joseph Predavec spoke is
there for any independent traveller to sample for himself. It was perhaps natural that the writer should be
required to produce his papers to an armed Serbian guard
before entering the village where the Croat peasant leader
lived, for the Belgrade authorities exhibit a curious interest in any foreign visitor who has facilities for talking
directly with the people of that country. But this precaution against the true facts concerning the plight of the
"minorities" becoming known to the outside world does
not fully explain the constant police examinations, at the
rate of about four a day, to which the traveller by road in
Yugoslavia has so often to submit. Certainly no country in
Europe, with the solitary exceptions of Soviet Russia and
Poland, so completely qualify for the description of
politzia staat as does this peasant land of Yugoslavia.

Travelling through the villages of Croatia in the
company of Joseph Predavec, on the occasion of his first
appearance there since his release from prison, the writer
saw a glimpse of that nation as it might be, freed from alien
control. At village after village the whole population turned
out to greet this dynamic leader of a peasant people upon
his unheralded arrival. By methods akin to the "bush
telephone", the news spread to the peasants in the fields,
and they, too, dropped their tools and came running up
to catch a glimpse of one of the men who were fighting
their battle for justice. There was no doubt during that
journey of over one hundred miles regarding that 90
per cent membership which the Croat Peasant Party
claims to have among the people. That fact is noteworthy,
for every one of those peasants who thus directly risked
the displeasure of the local officials by openly cheering

an "enemy" of the "Yugoslav" government was a poor peasant, living on the borderline of want, and often indebted to the authorities for unpaid taxes. To such people a fine of a few dinars would have been serious, and the loss of their liberty catastrophic. Yet they came— men and women and children gathering round the car in which we travelled and cheering the man who, together with the imprisoned Dr. Machek, was carrying out the policy of the beloved Stephan Radich.

An official of the Yugoslav Foreign Office, referring recently to an extremely well-informed newspaper corre- spondent stationed in the Balkans, informed that corre- spondent's editor that "your man is so ignorant that he still thinks there is a Croatian question". Had that Yugoslav official been present with M. Predavec during that journey he would have discovered where a charge of ignorance might most fairly lie.

Reference has been made to the systematic use of torture and terrorism by Yugoslav authorities in their efforts to turn Croats into "Yugoslavs". Detailed par- ticulars of such cases have no place in this book, but not a little of the anger felt by the Croat people may be traced to the petty persecution and ill-treatment meted out to countless humble peasants under the present dictatorship.

Such excesses are inherent in a régime which seeks to suppress the political opinions of the population by force. In Croatia, the police are to-day the representatives not of the people they rule, but of the police department at Belgrade, a very different thing. The village "elders" who formerly were elected by the peasants, exist no longer, and their powers are vested in the Serbian gendarmerie, whose one concern is the violent suppression of every sign of national consciousness on the part of Croats or Slovenes.

The position thus created was summed up by Stephan Radich in a speech delivered in the parliament at Belgrade in 1927, when he declared : "Formerly, when a peasant saw a gendarme, he felt that his life and property were fully secure ; now, when the gendarmes appear in a village, it is known that illegality and persecution may be expected."

The Croat Peasant Party, being synonymous with the Croat nation, has borne the brunt of this repression by which the Serbs have sought to stifle the demand of the minorities for autonomy and equal partnership within the new "Yugoslav" state.

It may be recorded, therefore, that this peasant political movement, while deeply conscious of the cultural and national ideals of the Croat race, stands aloof from any form either of chauvinism or revolution. Croat nationalism is entirely free alike from hatred, intolerance or extremism. The first principle of that political creed to which the whole Croat people subscribe is that the peasants *ARE* the people, and, that being so, any form of class struggle within Croatia is unthinkable. The peasants forming 80 per cent of the nation and being the main producers of wealth, the remaining 20 per cent were required to co-ordinate their interests with those of the peasantry to whose toil they owe their well-being.

Three principles have animated the Croat Peasant Party since its inception in 1899. They are (a) the essential unity of the whole Croat people; (b) a sincere and active religious faith as the moral basis of society; and (c) the sacred principle of nationality. The Croats regard respect for nationality, and self-determination in regard to all internal affairs, as essential to any democratic conception of government, or to a natural cultural and social development.

Ever since the first general meeting of the party, held in December, 1904, peasants have formed a majority on the executive committee which directs its activities. And so strong was the appeal of the party's programme that in every election held during the post-war years, up to the suppression of democracy in Yugoslavia, the representatives of the Croat Peasant Party gained an overwhelming majority of the total votes polled throughout Croatia.

The Serbs having seized Croatia by force of arms, and later suppressed all democratic institutions throughout the boundaries of the Yugoslav state, this great peasant movement was declared illegal in 1929. Croatia, in common with the Serb and Slovene territories, found itself the unwilling victim of a Royal dictatorship. From that fatal decision to override the deepest convictions of the entire Croat and Slovene peoples have come dire results and continued unrest. The "minorities" within the Yugoslav state have been drawn together in a common defence of common interests. The economic conditions in this divided nation have gone from bad to worse. Reforms badly needed have been held up, or amended, owing to political considerations.

Alone among all the political forces within Yugoslavia, the Croat Peasant Party has been strengthened by adversity—even as the cultural activities of Croats and Slovenes alike have been curtailed and thwarted, to the detriment of the whole of Eastern Europe. On the other hand, the dictatorship, learning by bitter experience that one cannot wipe out national aspirations by suppressing political parties, and imprisoning and murdering national leaders, has floundered ever deeper into that régime of persecution which is in reality a policy of despair and an admission both of fear and failure. In Croatia to-day the strength of the national patriotism for the Croat cause rises in direct ratio with the numbers of Croats arrested, ill-treated and imprisoned by the ruling party.

At the very root of the struggle thus symbolized by the repressive policy of the dictatorship is the one all-important fact—that the representatives of Croatia have never signified their assent either to the absorption of their country within a Balkan nation ruled from a common parliament house at Belgrade or to the oppression of their people and the denial of their separate nationality implied by King Alexander's dream of one "Yugoslav" state. Behind the desire of the Croats to leave the Habsburg Empire was the determination that the Croatian peasants should rule themselves through their National Assembly established at Zagreb. And neither Serbian bayonets, French influence, nor the murder and torture of their people have caused them to swerve by a hair's-breadth from that aim.

This simple peasant people demands to-day, as Stephan Radich and the Croat deputies demanded in 1918, freedom to live their own lives, to rule themselves, and to pursue their national development along those lines of westernized progress which they have followed in the past.

If many Croats have decided that the day has passed when they are content to remain inside the frontiers of "Yugoslavia" on any terms, the responsibility lies not with the long-suffering Croat peoples but with the government which has broken every promise made to them, and cast the shadow of the trooper and the armed gendarme over those smiling, peaceful farmsteads where dwell the members of this virile and industrious western race.

"Who would say", recently asked August Koshutich, former Cabinet Minister, and foreign representative of the Croat people, "that the Croatian nation is to-day living in a state which is a 'natural creation', when within its boundaries there is for the Croats neither a natural life, nor even a natural death?"

Five million people echo that question. It is for Europe to answer.

CHAPTER V

BOUNDED on the north by Rumania and on the south by Greece and Turkey, confined within a territory which became suddenly smaller under the terms of the peace settlements of 1919, live the Bulgarians, a hardy independent peasant people that have won for themselves the nickname of "the Scotsmen of the Balkans".

Like the Croats and Ukrainians, the Bulgarians are an exclusively peasant people, with a peasant psychology and the love of the soil in their very bones. Countless generations of peasant ancestors, right back to the Thracians who occupied the territory that is the modern Bulgaria at the time of Christ, have shaped their habits, customs, and thoughts; to-day every Bulgarian is a peasant, and everything in that country conforms to the peasant mould.

The very soil of Bulgaria and of those regions inhabited by men and women of Bulgarian race outside the existing frontiers has shaped the destiny of this most romantic of European peoples. On those plains, and among the Balkan hills, bygone generations of peasants saw the eagles of Imperial Rome sweep across the land, the hosts of Crusaders streaming through their fields, Barbarians looting and killing, and the land submerged by the Turkish tide. There followed five centuries of subjugation before the Russians appeared in the rôle of deliverers, rolled back the forces of Islam, and in the red dawn of that first day of freedom witnessed the birth of Bulgarian freedom which had been the dream and aim of countless brave spirits all down the ages of servitude.

Those who fashioned the new nation were peasants

E

to the last man ; statesmen, soldiers, doctors, writers, lawyers, teachers—all had to be called forth from the ranks of the toiling cultivators who lived in a thousand scattered villages, tucked away in the hills and plains. And being peasants, who understood the problems of the peasant state, they understood that the future prosperity of their country depended not upon palatial government departments, military adventures, or diplomatic intrigues, but upon the broad backs of the peasant smallholders who formed so large a proportion of the total population that in a very real sense those little peasant communities *were* Bulgaria.

To-day, seventy years later, the nation is still a peasant land. Eighty per cent of Bulgaria's total population of 5,478,471 inhabitants earn their daily bread by tilling the soil and live in villages, while most of the remaining 20 per cent dwell in small towns, or are primarily engaged in activities connected with agriculture. Only ten cities in the whole country can boast of a population of 25,000 persons. Ninety-five per cent of the total exports consist of agricultural products, including tobacco and other industrial plants, livestock and animal products, and—until recently—cereals.*

These figures show that both the internal economy and the financial resources of the country are dependent upon the prosperity of the Bulgarian countryside. If crops fail, or the prices of agricultural produce fall below the range of normal fluctuations, the standard of living of the Bulgarian peasantry falls in sympathy, while the credit of both nation and individuals is dangerously strained.

How sensitive is this all-peasant land to world conditions was revealed by the agricultural crisis which developed in 1928. Not even defeats in two major wars within one generation had such disastrous repercussions upon the Bulgarian people, both materially and psychologically, as had the catastrophic fall in the prices of, and restrictions in the markets for, agricultural products during the years which have followed. Especially was this

---

* Prior to 1914 cereals accounted for from 60 to 70 per cent of total exports. This group has now fallen to only abo ut 12 per cent.

true of the trade in cereals, notably wheat, which formerly represented the largest single item in Bulgaria's trade budget.

Faced with the effects of the world agricultural crisis and the uneconomic price obtainable for wheat, the principal item of export, in the markets of Europe, the government remembered the old saying that "every Bulgarian is a gardener at heart" and came to a dramatic decision. Bulgaria should cease to be a farm, except for the purpose of growing enough bread and meat for its own inhabitants, and should be transformed into a garden.

Travelling through the countryside with Professor Atanasoff, of the Faculty of Agriculture at Sofia, and other experts, I witnessed the first-fruits of that plan designed to restore the fortunes of the country, and, by broadening the basis of her greatest industry, render her "slump-proof" in future.

On the outskirts of one village a peasant family was cutting a tiny strip of wheat with hand sickles. The soil in which that wheat, and other strips of corn alongside, was growing had been ploughed with primitive wooden ploughs which merely scratched the surface of the ground, and it would be threshed on the threshing-floor by drawing a board, to which flints had been attached, over the ears of corn. With such rudimentary implements it was not surprising to learn that the yield per acre is almost the lowest in Europe. Moreover, when that wheat was taken to market, its value would hardly pay the cost of cultivation.

Those strips of corn, which in the past covered 70 per cent of the area of arable land in the country, are ceasing to be as important as once they were. They belong to the old Bulgaria which is passing. The war, which handed over the rich corn lands of the Dobruja to Rumania, and the prices of wheat in world markets during recent years, forced Bulgaria to face facts. Wheat and oats might still give a golden gleam to the fields ripe for harvest, but these crops no longer put money into the pockets of the peasantry. So in future grain-production, so recently the nation's biggest export, will be concentrated on those areas where soil and other conditions are most favourable, while the government agricultural stations are providing the peasants with improved varieties of seed yielding twenty per cent more to the acre than before.

Not far away from those strips of golden corn I came upon a different scene—a land of orchards heavy with fruit, and fields of strawberries and vegetables. This was the new Bulgaria which is dawning, the beginnings of the garden-land of to-morrow which the experts have glimpsed from afar.

All over Eastern Europe—in Rumania, Bukovina, Hungary—I came across little "pockets" of Bulgarians who settled in foreign parts long ago. They were easy to recognize, for always they were growing fruit and vegetables. In the near future a large slice of the population of the homeland will be doing the same thing, for the word has gone forth that there is money in strawberries, peas, and wine, whereas the world has too much wheat.

I saw some of the vineyards at Stara Zagora, and sampled the wines made there—wines that you can buy to-day at one penny per kilo owing to the dearth of customers. More will be heard about Bulgaria's wines, for already the area of the vineyards has doubled since the war, while Bulgaria's exports of this one item have risen from 200,000 kilogrammes in 1928 to 6,500,000 in 1932. And the potential export figure, based upon the present area of production, is at least three times the latter figure !

In the task of transforming the country from a farm into a garden the peasants are assisted at every turn by a government thoroughly awake to the vital issues at stake. Since her old markets have largely disappeared, Bulgaria must win new markets for her new crops. Therefore every precaution is being taken to ensure that each chicken, egg, crate of fruit, and bottle of wine exported will be of a quality calculated to assist, and not retard, the progress of the country. To this end a system of inspection, based upon the Danish model, has been instituted, and strict methods of grading adopted.

Not all the crops which formerly featured prominently

THE TOBACCO HARVEST OF MACEDONIA

Peasant women of Peruschitza tending the crop which represented nearly half Bulgaria's export trade in 1930.

TENDING THE FAMILY WEALTH

Peasant women of Southern Bulgaria drying tobacco outside their home.

in the internal economy of the country have been super-seded. Wheat will still be grown in sufficient quantities to satisfy internal needs. The cultivation of cotton, in Southern Bulgaria, is being rapidly extended so that the nation can produce a higher percentage of the raw cotton needed for her textile mills. Similar efforts are being made to increase the production of other "industrial plants", including flax, hemp, olive oil, and sunflower seeds.

It is safe to say that the two crops which have in the past lent an air of romance to Bulgarian agriculture will retain their former important place in the national scheme of things. These are the production of the rare rose-oil, which perfumes lovely women the world over, and the cultivation of the aromatic oriental tobacco which delights the connoisseur.

Concerning the famous "Rose Valley", situated be-tween the Balkan Mountains and the *Sredno Goro,* or Middle Mountains, more will be said in a later chapter. In that valley, from 25,000 acres of rose-gardens which scent the very air, comes the world-famous attar of roses which is exported to all parts of the world. And although the all-pervading depression has reduced the value of this export to one-tenth of the 1929 figure, it is safe to say that rose-culture will retain in the new Bulgaria the prominent place which it occupied in the old.

The tobacco harvest is destined to assume an even greater importance when the transformation is com-plete, for in regard to this crop the territorial changes wrought by the world war favoured Bulgaria, some of the best tobacco being grown in the mountain regions of the south incorporated in Bulgaria under the peace settle-ment.

The annual production of tobacco rose from 5,772 tons in 1912 to 52,216 tons in 1923, while the relative importance of this branch of agriculture is revealed by the fact that tobacco formed over 42 per cent of Bulgaria's total exports in 1930 and 32 per cent in 1932—the latter figure reflecting the effects of the world depression.

Changes are coming more gradually in those regions devoted to raising cattle and livestock. Bulgaria possesses

1,816,000 head of cattle and more buffaloes, sheep, and goats than any other nation in Europe. While the total numbers of livestock have scarcely changed since 1910—proof of the innate conservatism of the peasants—efforts are being made to improve the herds, some eighty-five societies existing with that aim in view, while every village possesses its cattle-raising committee.

Steps are now being taken to increase the number of poultry and ducks raised annually, and to extend the production of butter and eggs for export. But changes come slowly in the Bulgarian countryside, where farming methods have evolved during centuries. It is mainly on this account that nearly 9,000,000 sheep still roam over lands which might, and eventually will, be put to more productive uses ; the sheep-owners have their "rights", sanctioned by age-long custom, and public support has to be gained for changes before they can safely be put into operation.

This natural conservatism of the peasants is a factor which must be taken into account throughout the peasant regions, and has undoubtedly retarded and hampered efforts made by the Bulgarian government to improve the standard of life in the villages during the past decade. Nevertheless, the call to create a new land—a garden-land —has gone forth, and the experts are speaking hopefully of the day when Bulgaria will be exporting poultry, eggs, fruit, vegetables, and wine to all parts of Europe. Already the results obtained are impressive enough to encourage the hope that greater benefits will accrue as the transformation proceeds during the years immediately ahead.

The knowledge and skill needed to carry out this planned transformation from a predominantly corn-growing nation to a variety of distinct, and more lucrative, forms of cultivation have been supplied by an agricultural educational system which is equal to that existing in any other European country.

This system has as its apex the Faculty of Agriculture, which is a department of the University of Sofia, and includes four agricultural high schools, fifteen practical agricultural schools, seven or eight of which are reserved for women, thirty winter schools for adult peasants, and a network of agricultural continuation schools, of which in June 1933 110 had already been opened out of 800 projected. These continuation schools will, when the present programme is completed, cover every large village and town throughout the country.

Every child who has completed the seven-year course in a primary school is obliged to attend an agricultural continuation school for two terms of four months each. During these terms, held in the winter months when work in the fields is at a standstill, the boys are given instruction in modern methods of farming, with special reference to the type of cultivation predominating in the region where the school is situated, while the girls are taught home-making, cooking, sewing, care of children, and the rudiments of hygiene.

The existence of these schools is gradually changing conditions even in the most primitive villages. In this respect the influence of the girls is proving especially important. In districts where no continuation school has yet been opened pails of drinking-water stand all day un-covered and open to any contamination. The girl who has completed the course at a school learns that all water should be covered. Similarly, boys and girls are taught to wash their hands before eating : previously few peasants ever washed between daybreak and dark. Again, the scholars are taught to make the best use of the abundance of vegetables and food grown on the farms, and to preserve fruits and vegetables. The aim of these village continuation schools, if achieved, will revolutionize the sanitation and hygiene of the villages, and make the Bulgarian peasant and his wife the best educated agriculturists in the Balkans.

The same aim is to be found in the organization of the fifteen practical agricultural schools, where, during a course lasting two years, the girls live in dormitories and supply their own needs, learning cooking, mothercraft, the care of poultry, and fruit and vegetable growing.

Thus, slowly, there is emerging a new generation, composed of the young men and women who have had the benefit of a modern education in practical farming designed to fit them to take their places in the new Bulgaria which is being created out of the turmoil and stress of military defeat, and the lessons of the agricultural crisis which followed.

Progress must be slow. The girl-student who, while studying at an agricultural school, or high school, has learnt to wear a hat, must still be careful to take it off when approaching the village where she lives, lest she be ostracized—the penalty for departing from the accepted standards of village life. The boys, returning with a knowledge of new methods of tilling the soil, or new crops which promise greater financial rewards, must introduce the subject to their old-fashioned parents with tact and discretion if an insurmountable barrier of parental opposition is not to arise between them and the putting into practice of their newly gained knowledge. But the time will come when the younger generation will own the soil of Bulgaria, and be the masters of their own destiny, and on that day Bulgaria will reap a rich dividend for the thoroughness with which she seeks to till the human soil to-day.

Bulgaria has discovered the vital truth that the key to future prosperity of the agrarian nations is to be found in education and then more education. And she is applying that truth to her national life with an energy, and upon a scale, despite her present poverty, which is a shining example to agricultural Europe.

One factor has materially contributed to the smoothness of the changes now in process. Bulgaria was fortunate in not having to institute any sweeping agrarian reforms after the war; her agrarian "revolution" occurred when the large estates owned by the Turks were parcelled out among the peasants over sixty years ago. To-day the 76,700 square kilometres of arable land in Bulgaria is divided into 800,000 peasant holdings, the average area of which is thirteen acres. Only 11 per cent of the cultivated land is contained in holdings of over sixty acres. These number only 4,766 for the whole country, and in that total is included a number of estates owned or controlled by government institutions, such as livestock breeding farms, experimental stations, agricultural schools, and fruit nurseries. More than half the landowners, tilling one-quarter of the total arable land, possess farms of less than thirteen acres each, while another quarter of the total land available is included in holdings of from twenty-five to thirty-five acres.

The fact which emerges from these dry statistics is that Bulgaria is a land of peasant proprietors, and that the land is owned almost entirely by the people who work it; in no other country in Europe does the small farmer, employing no labour outside the circle of his family, reign so securely. In this connection one further fact may be quoted : the total number of landless families is only about 100,000, while there are only 211,000 agricultural labourers employed for wages in the whole country.*

Two factors are continually at work making for the even distribution of landed property in that country—the inheritance laws, which provide for the distribution of land among all the children of a family, and the acquisition of fresh land through marriage and inheritance. These factors explain the fact that "strip farming" is still almost universal, the average peasant-holding comprising from five to twenty separate strips of land often distributed over the entire territory of the commune.

While no radical reform in the system of land ownership was necessary after the world war, since 1914, however, a number of minor changes have occurred, due to political and economic causes, and also arising out of the effects of the peace settlement upon the fortunes of the Bulgarian people.

As a result of the terms of the Neuilly Peace Treaty of 1919, which severed from Bulgaria some of the most fertile regions populated by the Bulgarian race, there has since been a ceaseless influx of refugees from Macedonia, Thrace, Dobruja, and from the Western Borderlands annexed by Yugoslavia. The Bulgarian government was therefore faced, at the moment when the national fortunes were at their lowest ebb and when their nation was being

* Census of 1926.

cold-shouldered by the rest of Europe, with the problem of settling thousands of families, and providing them with the means of life, within the reduced limits of the nation.

This problem, and the co-related question of providing land for the landless within Bulgaria, was handed over to the Department for Agricultural Labour Estates, specially created for the purpose, and up to 1933 some 66,000 families of refugees and landless peasants had been settled and provided with land totalling 350,000 acres. At the beginning of that year the department was faced with the problem of settling a further 64,000 families. Independently of this work, the Refugees Settlement Department had been able, by means of a special loan issued externally in 1926 under the auspices of the League of Nations, to settle a further 30,102 refugee families which had migrated back to their homeland from sections of that country lost under the peace treaties. The families settled by means of this loan were, further, supplied with homesteads, agricultural implements, farm animals, and seeds.

Equally important in the post-war history of this peasant state is another reform instituted since the war, the so-called "Co-massation", or grouping into one complete section of the various separate and distinct parcels of ground constituting, almost universally, the holding of one owner.

While the Soviet authorities have been seeking to extend the size of the average holding in Russia, and eliminate the wasteful system of strip farming, by collectivization, Bulgaria has been quietly grappling with the same problem by different methods and without any such element of compulsion as has caused widespread unrest and resistance within Soviet Russia.

Not even in that country was the land parcelled out in such small strips as are to be seen when driving through any part of the Bulgarian countryside. And the waste and inefficiency of this small-scale system was increasing rather than diminishing. Thus, whereas in 1908 the number of "strips" constituting a typical peasant holding in Bulgaria was eleven, by 1926 the *average* had grown to seventeen. And those seventeen "fields"—often in quarter-acre lots—would be distributed at all points of the compass, some of them often being five miles apart. With the object of eliminating the waste and delay involved in this method of farming small areas, a start has been made in the task of "grouping" village farms so that each peasant has his area of land gathered together in one plot.

Owing to financial difficulties facing the country, this reform has up to date been carried out in only a limited number of villages, but early in the task of combining holdings a certain antagonism was met with from the peasants it was intended to benefit. One of the greatest enemies of the Bulgarian peasant is hail, and the peasants affected by measures of grouping complained that, whereas with their land distributed in twelve or more different plots, one section of their crops might be destroyed by hail and the rest escape, after grouping had been achieved one hailstorm, if passing over their land, would spell ruin to the entire harvest. The government recognized the objection as reasonable, and forthwith arranged for government hail insurance to be made at low rates. In Bulgarian villages to-day, therefore, the visitor sees prominently displayed two pictorial posters, on the "before and after" type not unknown in this country. The first depicts a peasant bemoaning the loss of his crop through hail; the second shows a smiling peasant watching his harvest being damaged by the same agency, with a government hail insurance policy sticking out of his pocket !

A further reform put into operation during recent years has for its object the same aim of increasing the efficiency of Bulgaria's peasant farms by the introduction of more up-to-date methods of cultivation. This is the elimination of community-land within the confines of the villages by its division among the inhabitants. Before such land is sub-divided, a referendum of the whole population affected is taken, and the decision of the majority is accepted in every case. That the division of the former common land is in accordance with the wishes of the population is made clear by the fact that the area of community-land is now only one-third of the 1928 figure.

The small area of the majority of farm-holdings has in the past gone far to hamper any general improvement in the methods of cultivation. So long as the "strip" system of cultivation endured, and corn formed the main crop, it was impossible to mechanize cultivation, or to increase substantially the low yield of the crops. An even greater obstacle to effecting improvements, however, was the lack of agricultural credit and the extreme poverty, measured by money standards, of the Bulgarian peasantry. That obstacle remains—a formidable barrier blocking the road to progress. Neither peasants nor state to-day possess the resources necessary to carry out the modernization and re-equipment of the farms on the scale necessary to bring them up to the standards existing in Western Europe.

The Bulgarian peasant is, in most cases, too poor even to renew his implements without the aid of a loan, while the small area of his holding, and the paucity of his livestock, make it difficult, if not impossible, for him individually to provide security for any loan without state aid. One effect of this shortage of capital resources is to be seen in the fact that the estimated shortage of agricultural implements, based upon the requirements of a reasonably efficient standard of cultivation, in 1929 amounted to 280,000 ploughs, 472,000 harrows, and 31,000 sowing machines.

To enable the peasants to secure credits without getting into the hands of moneylenders—the unseen plague of peasant Europe—an Agricultural Bank was founded in 1903, and this organization, working in conjunction with the 2,449 agricultural co-operative societies now existing in Bulgaria, provide about 80 per cent of the agricultural credits available, the remaining 20 per cent coming from private banks and moneylenders.*

In other ways, the co-operative societies secure many advantages for the peasants, enabling them to improve their methods of cultivation, to market their products more advantageously, and to secure, in normal times,

---

* During 1930 the Agricultural Bank advanced loans to private individuals, co-operative societies, and other bodies, amounting to nearly £10,000,000.

THE MOST ROMANTIC HARVEST IN THE WORLD

Gathering rose-buds at Karlovo, Bulgaria's "capital of roses". From these blooms comes the famous attar of roses.

HOME OF A WORLD-FAMOUS PERFUME
The interior of a rose distillery at Karlovo.

greater stability of prices. The small area of individual holdings, on the other hand, and the fact that they are mostly farmed by owners, provides a fertile field for the spread of co-operative methods.

The thrifty streak which exists in every Bulgarian peasant, and which reveals itself in a distaste for, and condemnation of, anything savouring of ostentation in life, finds little scope in the hard poverty which has been the lot of most Bulgarian peasants since the world war. No definite statistics showing the savings of the peasant population are available, the Post Office Savings Bank alone publishing separate figures for general and peasant investors. These accounts show that in 1931, out of a total of 42,887 active accounts, only 5,214 were registered in the names of peasants, representing 12·16 per cent of the whole. Many Bulgarian peasants, like their French counterparts, have a certain distrust of placing their money in banks, or allowing the authorities to know what they possess, and prefer to conceal their savings in their homes. It is more probable, however, that the paucity of savings is due to the dearth of actual cash in the villages owing to the effects of the agricultural crisis, and also to a certain fear, existing early in 1933, concerning the future stability of the Bulgarian lev, which caused the minority of peasants who possessed any funds to prefer to invest them in land or buildings rather than to retain them in the form of cash.

If progressive government alone could circumvent the effects of the shortage of cash in the villages, then Bulgaria would be one of the wealthiest countries rather than one of the poorest. The Bulgarian smallholder in these days often has no cash income at all, but he has at his disposal a network of agronomic authorities ready to assist him with advice to make his contribution to the realization of the new Bulgaria which is dawning.

In the American Agricultural Mission, called "The People's Village University", founded at Pordim in 1929 by Mr. Edward B. Haskell, Bulgaria possesses the first "folk school" on the Danish model to be established in the Balkans—a school where peasant girls are taught mother-

craft, domestic science, history, arithmetic, gardening, bee-
keeping, and other practical subjects, such as mending
clothes and the care of furniture, and youths are instructed in practical farming. The course at this school
lasts for ten months and those who pass through its class-
rooms are destined to become, together with the pupils
trained in the government agricultural schools, the
pioneers of new ways of life in the villages.

Co-operative associations receive government subsidies for encouraging the production of new crops in place
of old and for improving stock-breeding. A complete
system of sanitary stations has been established to safeguard the health of the peasant regions. As a result, although the death-rate remains high, some diseases, such
as malaria, are rapidly disappearing. Further, a system
of premiums exists to reward individual agriculturists who
effect improvements and developments in livestock, fruits
and fruit trees, milk yields, and in other branches of
agriculture.

Unfortunately, governments, however progressive, cannot shield a peasant people from the effects of an agricultural crisis which has dislocated the national finances of
agrarian nations the world over, and any improvement
in material conditions of the Bulgarian peasantry—even a
return to the low standard obtaining until 1928—must
wait for an increase in the prices of agricultural products.
This is, for Bulgaria and other agrarian nations, the
crucial problem of the day. The prices of certain types of
tobacco had in 1933 fallen to from one penny to two-
pence-halfpenny per kilogramme, a low record which
Bulgaria hopes will never be equalled again. The price of
rose-oil had dropped from £240 per kilogramme, to as low as
£60. Raw silk, an ancillary industry of the countryside,
had fallen to 25 per cent of its former value, while the
world price of cereals in that year made their cultivation, except for internal consumption, unprofitable.

On the other hand, the existing indebtedness of the
peasants, contracted at a higher price level, was constantly growing owing to unpaid interest being added to the
principal outstanding. This was, perhaps, the most

tragic factor of all, and one which demanded swift solution; hence the steps taken by a sympathetic government to extend the period over which repayments were spread, and attempts to arrange for long-term credits at reduced rates of interest.

Until these and other problems are solved, the progress which Bulgaria makes in the transformation of her agriculture must appear disappointing to many who realize the vital importance of the proposed transformation upon her future prosperity. But the plans are there; the expert advisers are waiting; and the aim and nature of the new Bulgaria has been decided. Step by step, in the face of accumulated difficulties which might well deter a less courageous and persevering people, the Bulgarian nation is moving towards the day when her countryside, dependent no longer upon her exports of grain, will have ceased to be a farm, and will have adopted a new rôle as the garden-state of Eastern Europe, sending across her frontiers the products of her orchards, gardens, and dairies in exchange for those factory products from the west which she will need in increasing abundance when the purchasing power of her people is restored.

To-day Bulgaria's equipment is worn out. Her peasants are too poor to buy even new scythes with which to gather their harvests. But her people are inured to hardship, and because they cannot sell their crops they are feeding better than before hard times came. To-day Bulgaria is poverty-stricken, but she is also patient. She can wait. She can afford to wait longer than the factories of the west can wait. And when the waiting period is over, the effects of her planning, and her great effort to improve the education of her people, will be seen in a new Bulgaria. A new market will be available for the world's factories. And a new era in Bulgarian history will have dawned.

CHAPTER VI

BULGARIA TO-DAY

I FIRST met the Bulgarian peasants in the main hall of the
Central Police Headquarters at Sofia : a crowd of two
hundred or more dark-skinned men clad in muddy peasant
homespuns, sheepskin caps, and home-made shoes, carrying bundles. Some of them may have been young, but
every face in that gathering was a weatherbeaten and
lined replica of Methuselah. They were the younger sons,
and some of the landless, who each year, as the harvest
season approaches, migrate to other lands in search of
harvest work. Each summer two hundred thousand of
them go to Yugoslavia, Hungary, and Rumania, to return
when the breath of winter calls a halt to work in the
fields.

Most of that crowd had tramped miles to reach Sofia,
seeking passports which would enable them to leave
Bulgaria. There, in the Police Headquarters, they were
shepherded by tall members of the Bulgarian "Ogpu".
Indeed, the scene was reminiscent of any official department in Soviet Russia. The same evidence of grinding
poverty. The same patient eyes. The same alert soldiers
with revolvers in their belts. Only in one respect was the
Russian atmosphere missing. At Sofia the officials are not
only efficient, but speedy ; one may complete one's
business in that large building in half a day, and graft is
absent from the proceedings. For which Bulgaria may be
thankful ; that country is unique among the Balkan
nations. Elsewhere graft, bribery, and corruption is the
order of the day.

I talked with some of the crowd. One bearded giant
was going to Yugoslavia. He intended to tramp two

hundred miles on the chance of getting a month's harvest work at one shilling a day. "I have land," he said, "but it is only three acres, and my wife and family can look after it. If I am lucky I shall bring back enough cash to provide us with matches and salt for a whole year."

Another man unrolled his bundle and proudly displayed six loaves of bread baked by his wife. "It will last me for three weeks," he told me, "and if I am lucky I shall pick up some vegetables along the road. My family has land, but there are too many of us, and one can be spared."

"If there is no work to be found we can always come back," remarked a third. "And food waits for us at home."

"Food waits for us at home!" Would any other people set out on a trek of two or three hundred miles on a diet of bread as light-heartedly as do these hardy representatives of the peasantry who grow each season, on their scattered half-acre strips of soil, over thirty million quintals of wheat and corn, not to mention other crops? When it is remembered that almost every grain of that mountain of corn is sown, tended, and garnered with hand labour by peasants whose tools not infrequently date from Adam, and whose plots are often five miles from the homestead, the willingness of those migrant labourers to live on bread alone is less surprising. Life on tramp can hold few horrors for young men brought up in the stern, hard school which is village life in Bulgaria.

If the true definition of a peasant is one who tills the soil, not in order to live, but because he loves it, then the men who inhabit those villages are true sons of the earth. Not for nothing have their ancestors been farmers since the dawn of time. Nor was it any accident of fate that the dream of a "Green International", banding together all the peasant-states of Eastern Europe—a dream which fluttered the diplomatic dovecotes during the early years after the war—originated in the brain of the murdered Bulgarian agrarian leader, Stambuliski, probably the greatest peasant leader of his generation. If that dream ever comes true—and stranger things have happened—its strongest supporters will be found in Bulgaria.

F

The Bulgarian peasant has a love for the land he tills in his very bones. To him the soil is sacred, and to sell one inch of it a cardinal sin. Times may change. Wars may interrupt the even rhythm of life. Governments come and go. National boundaries expand and contract. But the land is changeless, and it absorbs its children from the cradle until, in the fullness of time, they return to its safe keeping.

The land and the village form the peasant's universe. In Bulgaria the two are usually separate; there are few farms, in the English sense of the word. The homes are grouped in villages and small townships, often some miles from the soil which the inhabitants cultivate. They prefer it that way; it once made for security, it now makes for sociability. By living in a village all may share the common things. And the absence of modern roads helps to confine life to the bounds of the settlements; no one dashes off on Saturday nights to a cinema show in the nearest town.

Not so long ago the villagers shared a common home with their animals. Mr. R. H. Markham, a writer who is an authority on Bulgaria and the Balkans, thus describes the long, low gloomy huts which sheltered the peasantry in the not far distant past:

This simple dwelling was built in the ground like a shallow cellar, was largely without windows, utterly without ventilation, and was covered with a thatched roof. In one end was an open fireplace where the soups and stews were cooked in kettles hanging over the fire and in which bread was baked under large inverted copper pans covered with hot ashes or coals. In the middle of the hut stood the cattle and buffalo, while in the further end was a slightly raised platform which at night was covered with mats and served as a family bed. There was no stove, and its absence was not felt because the farm animals in a small, hermetically closed hut served as a central heating plant. There was practically no furniture. Men and women, children and adults, sick and well, lived very closely together.*

That type of dwelling may still exist, but it has become

* *Meet Bulgaria.*   By R. H. Markham.   Published by the author at Sofia.

rare. Measuring the present standard of living in the Bulgarian villages by the furniture in the homes—as good a "yard-stick" as any—the Bulgarian standard compares favourably with the conditions found in any of the definitely Eastern European lands. The peasantry live in modern two-roomed dwellings, often built of brick from designs supplied by the state, and their animals are housed separately. The earth floors have been replaced by brick and wood. There are windows that open. And furniture has come to the villages. Many, though not all, of the inhabitants now sleep on beds, and eat sitting at tables. Separate plates for each person have replaced the old communal bowl. Electric light, even, has come to some of the villages, although most still depend for illumination upon the oil lamp. And if sanitation lags behind, the population does not ask for miracles.

This transformation of the villages has had two beneficial results. The Bulgarian people have been "lifted off the floor"; they have been raised from the conditions of penury to the status of citizenship, with a stake, however small, in their country. Poverty remains in a more extreme form than in most European countries, but it is no longer as degrading as once it was; the poorest Bulgarian peasant to-day generally has his land, his house, some pieces of furniture, and his self-respect. Those things no man can take from him. And with this psychological transformation the health of the people has improved. The death-rate, though still high, is falling, and the sickness rate with it,* and as material conditions improve with the changes in agriculture, the health chart of Bulgaria should register further improvement.

Diet has changed less than the homes themselves. The Bulgarians eat more bread, and less meat, than any of their neighbours. Bread, potatoes, tomatoes, onions, and cheese are the staple items on the national menu, with meat, eggs, milk, and butter at rarer intervals. An

* The annual number of deaths among the Bulgarian peasantry averaged 86,219 during the period 1921–1925; 81,193 during 1926–30; and 75,539 during 1931. These figures would have been considerably lower but for the fact that Bulgaria has the highest tuberculosis mortality rate in Europe—a relic of bad conditions in the past.

average peasant family will consume at least one and a half pounds of bread per person every day, and next to bread in popularity come onions and tomatoes.

It has been estimated that every family in Bulgaria consumes, on an average, 120 lb. of onions each year, and, in addition, quantities of garlic. The reputed health-preserving properties of these two items of diet finds confirmation in the fact that there are living in Bulgaria to-day 15,000 persons aged ninety and older !

During the winter season the staple foods are sauerkraut, pickled peppers, gherkins, and, for meat, home-cured bacon and ham. In general only water and coffee is drunk—the capacity to make perfect Turkish coffee being one of the few things the retreating Turks left behind them.

With the exception of coffee and salt, every item consumed in a peasant household is home-grown. It is possible to live for years in a Bulgarian village household without eating anything purchased for money.

Money, indeed, is less important than labour in the village social economy. When one can erect a house of sound peasant workmanship at a total cost of £20, and one's needs for cash are confined to paying the tax-collector and buying one or two articles that even Bulgaria's fertile soil cannot produce, money does not occupy the prominent place in the daily lives of the people that it does in industrial nations.

There are few capitalists in Bulgaria, but the means of production are, as has been shown, more widely spread than in almost any other land. Like food, all the clothing necessary for the family, including boots, is home-made. Repairs to the house, and the making of new furniture, are jobs for the menfolk during winter days. In fact, it has truly been said that if the Bulgarian peasants could discover a method of making only four more things— salt, matches, soap, and kerosene—their villages could withstand a siege lasting a century ! And even that short list can be reduced, for from pig-fat it is possible to make a perfectly serviceable brand of soap.

When civilization came to these scattered communities,

THE BUFFALO AS "MAID OF ALL WORK"
Bulgarian peasants resting on the road to Sofia.

THE NEW GENERATION

A Rumanian peasant-child begins a life of toil by minding the family cattle on the Bucarest-Czernowitz road.

it arrived not as a grocer's shop, or cinema, but typified by the church and schoolhouse. And to-day those two institutions, represented by the largest buildings in each village and reinforced by the co-operative society store, form the main link between the outside world and those peasant homes with their whitewashed walls and thatched roofs.

The homes are small, according to western standards, but it must be remembered that families spend little time in them during the greater part of the year. Only in the winter does the dwelling become the focus of family activity.

In spring, summer, and early autumn the land is the centre of life and the only thing that matters. During those months the whole family rises each morning at daybreak. Blankets and mats are folded up, men and women make a hasty toilet in the yard adjoining the house, and working clothes are donned—a heavy dress in the case of the women and wide, deep-seated pants and blouses in the case of the men. Oxen are yoked, babies tied to the mothers' backs, and off the entire family goes to the particular piece of their domain which their *chorbadjia* has ordained shall be the scene of their labours on that day.

Although the field may be five miles or more away, they set out breakfastless, and not until ten o'clock, or thereabouts, is there a pause for food—black bread and perhaps a little cheese or sour milk. Then work again, the whole family hoeing, reaping, carrying, indifferent alike to sun and rain, until one or two o'clock, when, if the land is not too far from the dwelling, a member of the family acting as cook for the day will bring to the field a pot of vegetable soup or stew. The midday meal over, work is resumed until the light fails, when the whole family rides or trudges homewards.

Back in the village, there are cows and buffaloes to be milked, eggs to be gathered, and animals to be settled for the night. Not until these tasks are finished does the family assemble for the evening meal. And, finally, the family discard their moccasins and outer garments, and retire to bed.

Such is a typical day in a Bulgarian village family's life during seven months of the year. Only in winter, when frost makes it impossible to till the soil, and during the urgent rush of harvest days, is the routine varied.

During the harvest season, when every minute is of value if the crops are to be gathered to the last blade of grass and the last ear of corn, the whole family sleeps in the fields. It is during those hectic days that one may see babies and young children lying under hedges during the day, oblivious alike of scorching heat and pelting rain. Verily these peasants are a hardy race.

Watch the bands of peasants departing for the fields at daybreak, or returning at night, singing their national songs. It all seems very casual. And yet few industrial concerns are run with such flawless precision as the human personnel which gathers the fruit of the earth in Bulgaria.

That machine is presided over by the *chorbadjia*, or village "boss". Assisting him in carrying out his orders are other *chorbadjias*, for there is one presiding over the destinies of each family. These men, the grandfathers of the village community, control finance, and the buying and selling of crops. They allocate the daily tasks between each member of the household so that there is no overlapping, and nothing is forgotten. They know all there is to know about the soil, the seasons and the weather. Their control extends to such matters as education, marriage, and dress. And from their decisions there is, among the most conservative class in the world, no appeal. So complete is their power that before the new Bulgaria can arise, and more lucrative crops replace old ones, it is the *chorbadjias* that the government experts must convert to new ways. For in deciding which crop shall be grown on each piece of land, all the village *chorbadjias* act together; and few question their judgment. They, and their kind in other lands, are the real dictators of the peasant nations. It is the village leaders, and not governments or garrisons, who have preserved customs and habits through the centuries and maintained the traditions of their race undefiled. In very truth they "walk in the ways of their fathers and make everybody walk in theirs", as Mr. Markham has written. They are the living embodiment of the law concerning the survival of the fittest, for they have been raised in a hard school; by their skill and their physical strength they have won their place in the community, and every *chorbadjia* has a lifetime of bitter experience behind him.

It is they who preserved the Bulgarian nation [states Mr. Markham]. Although illiterate and persecuted by Turks and Greeks, they were too obdurate and stubborn to adopt foreign vogues. They were too set in their ways to resent being ridiculed by more cultured peoples. They were too obstinate in their devotion to rustic habits and a peasant "jargon" to accept modern customs and speech, and by that they preserved Bulgarianism for centuries against overwhelming foreign encroachment. You may picture the Bulgarians as a faithful flock being led through long, hard ages, by stern, thin-faced, beardless, long-moustached *chorbadjias*, with black "kalpaks" on their heads, with tiny bands of wool along the collars of their coats to denote authority, with unspeakably ugly pants, huge-seated and tight-legged, and with low coarse shoes on their feet. These grandpas are silent, and the only sound they make is the clicking of the beads in their hands, yet with their grim visages they eloquently say, "Let the world do as it pleases, but as for us and our families, we'll follow the gods of Bulgaria." And they have.*

Largely owing to these "wise old men", life in the 5,000 villages of Bulgaria, if hard and narrow, presents few complexities to the inhabitants. Every decision of importance is taken by the village elders, who direct both the economic and spiritual life of the community— and direct it unerringly along the accustomed roads, without worrying about the crossroads which life presents in other lands.

If you refer to a modern text-book on local government in Bulgaria you will discover that the councils which rule the local communities are elected by the obligatory votes of the entire literate population of adult age. These councils consist of from eight to twelve members, who

---

* *Meet Bulgaria*, p. 113.

from among their number appoint a *kmet,* or mayor, and a deputy-mayor. Bulgaria is nothing if not democratic, and the law provides for every emergency. Thus it is laid down that "in cases where the council disapproves of the actions of its mayor, or where for any reason the council has been dismissed, the community shall be governed by a commission of three persons appointed by the district governor for a period not exceeding three months, during which time a new council must be elected by the population".

These village councils are frequently only the assembly of the *chorbadjias* called by a more modern name, for no voter would gainsay the right of the wise men to sit in the place appointed by the state for those who rule the destinies of the community. Not even the county sheriff (*okoliisky nachalnik*), who is the direct representative of the government and of the police, wields more power. True, the fact that such an office exists proves that the machinery of civilized government functions in remote Bulgarian villages as it does in Balham or Birmingham. But no county sheriff ever appointed held the same unquestioned power that every *chorbadjia* enjoys by virtue of his place in the community or the household. His power does not rest upon governments or police, but upon something more lasting and more powerful : tradition and custom—the two things least susceptible to change in peasant life.

Stern as is life in these remote villages, it would be wrong to suggest that their inhabitants know no pleasures, or that life is all work. If the peasants toil for hours which to-day find no counterpart in Western Europe, and for financial rewards which would appear extremely meagre to the citizen of a Western European state, they also have their holidays, feast days, and gala occasions, when whole villages are given over to pleasure. Indeed, the recreations and entertainments among the peasants may be described as abundant and various.

One of the best known of these village entertainments is the so-called *sedenka,* the etymological meaning of which is sitting, or staying. A *sedenka* is usually held during the dead season, after the products of the earth have been fully collected and stored. They are usually organized by the village girls and young men, and the family in whose house the *sedenka* is held reap some profit from the entertainment, it being the custom for the guests, while watching the efforts of the villagers to amuse the company, to perform some sitting task, such as shelling maize, to an accompaniment of national songs, wit, and humour. On holidays, dances are held in the village square, while other entertainments, accompanied by much eating and drinking, take place on the occasions of baptisms and marriages, and during the Christmas and Easter festivals, which last for three days.

The peasants have a great respect for the traditional holidays of their race, and a deep religious feeling. Many of these holidays are associated with the most important dates in the year's work on the land, such as sowing and harvest. The various native customs observed on these occasions are innumerable, and vary in different districts.*

One of the most curious of all is *Eniovden* (the day of Enio), falling on July 7, when the length of the day begins to decrease and the nights to lengthen. On that day the peasants believe and say that "Enio has thrown his fur on his shoulders and started to go for snow". The belief is current among them that on the morning of *Eniovden* the sun is "trembling and turning" towards the winter, and they assemble in the early morning on the higher pieces of ground in an effort to observe this change. In all parts the custom prevails, on the night of *Eniovden*, to gather medicinal herbs, which, because they have been gathered on that night, are believed to possess highly curative properties. In some districts it is customary to light fires in the squares and streets on the same evening, and jump over the flames, as a protection against disease.

The fact that there is practically no migration from

---

* The various native customs existing in Bulgaria are described in *Narodni Umotvorenia* (National Folklore), issued by the Bulgarian Academy of Science at Sofia.

the villages to the cities, or back again, has made easy the task of preserving these and countless other customs. Bulgarian village life is changing—to-day, more younger sons, when they marry, build separate homes for their brides than formerly—but the changes arise from village psychology and are not dictated by the cities. Educational standards are improving. Sixty per cent of all the peasants can read and write, and increasing numbers of peasant girls and boys are going to the agricultural schools, or even to the university at Sofia. But most of them regard these facilities in the light of opportunities to become better farmers rather than as an avenue of escape from the land, and when they return to the village they conform, in matters of custom and social habits, to the rigid village standard.

In addition to those continuing their studies after leaving the primary schools, many peasant girls upon leaving school migrate to the cities to work as domestic servants. It is the custom to engage them for definite periods—from St. George's Day in May until November, and from November until May. Many, upon their arrival in a city, have never previously seen the inside of a modern house, but they are quick to learn their duties, and, being thrifty, they soon save enough to return to the village and get married. Few remain permanently in "service", for the Bulgarian peasant women, like the men, prefer the country life and the hard toil of the farm. In taking this decision, they are following in the footsteps of their mothers, who during the recent wars, when the greater part of the men were away on military service, managed the farms and maintained the food output of the country at its pre-war level.

It has truly been said, indeed, that the peasant lands could manage to survive without their men, but not without the women, and observation in many lands suggests that it is the women who shoulder the heaviest burdens. They work beside their menfolk in the fields, cook the meals, rear the children, attend to pigs and poultry, weave the wool and cotton materials from which all the clothes for the family are made, and make the exquisite embroideries and linens for which the peasant regions are famous. Most young girls make their entire trousseaux during the winter days, complete with all household linen and such furnishings as the peasant home needs. Into their dresses and skirts they embroider the hopes and joys and sorrows of their people. Their songs of freedom are sung with needles as well as with lips.

Those embroideries are, indeed, the supreme miracle of the peasant lands. The girls who work them—often devoting the leisure of years to a single garment—have no quiet rooms in which to work apart from the family confusion, no light other than the flickering oil lamp. The cloth is woven in the loom in a corner. The colours grew on the roadside, and were gathered by the hands that later worked the design. Many a two-roomed cottage on a Bulgarian hillside, which never knew enough chairs for all the family to sit down together, can boast chests filled with a profusion of exquisitely worked linen and clothing which would grace the dowry of a princess. The embroideries differ in small details, but in their general colour schemes and patterns nearly every region has its distinctive traditional styles. And it would be easier to change the frontiers of Bulgaria than to alter the style of embroideries on a peasant's sleeve—so strong is the conservatism of the countryside.

Those peasants follow the Biblical injunction which bids them "render unto Cæsar the things that are Cæsar's". They will listen to the agricultural missionaries who move among them, preaching the doctrine of the new Bulgaria which is coming. They may even be persuaded to change the habits of a lifetime in the matter of crops and cultivation, for these are matters, they realize, dictated by conditions in the wider world outside their valleys and hills. But their own world—the village —belongs to them, to the *chorbadjias*, and it takes longer to alter traditional habits and customs there.

Yet the forces of change are already knocking at the door in the shape of the ubiquitous omnibus, which, braving the peasant roads, is slowly pushing out further from the cities and linking up outlying parts. The wireless, gramophone, and the hire-purchase system may still belong to the future. The travelling cinema is a rarity. But these things will follow in the wake of those lumbering ramshackle vehicles which amble and lurch through the pot-holes of the Balkan roads. Only improved highways are necessary to bring the forces of change swooping down on those peasant hamlets. And improved roads are coming. The new Bulgaria is not overlooking the fact that good roads mean quick communication between buyer and seller in the peasant regions. And with roads and education, village life, as it has been lived in those communities through twenty turbulent centuries, will slowly be transformed. The village girl who, fresh from an agricultural training school, covers up a pail of drinking-water which her mother always left uncovered is, for those who know Bulgaria, the herald of a new day.

CHAPTER VII

BULGARIAN INTERLUDE

To travel by bus from Sofia to Karlovo, in the centre of Bulgaria's famous Rose Valley on the sunny side of the Balkan mountains, would yesterday have seemed as fantastic as to find omnibuses running "from the Bank to Mandalay". But that was yesterday. To-day you may step in a motor-coach in Sofia at 9 a.m., travel for eight hours through remotest Bulgaria, crossing two mountain ranges on the way, and by five o'clock in the evening be deposited, shaken but triumphant, in Karlovo, the capital of the kingdom of roses, where the very air is scented with the all-pervading essence which is Bulgaria's most famous crop.

I was informed in Sofia that "no one travels to Karlovo by bus because the train is more comfortable". To do so, I gathered, was still considered an adventure. But I had come to see the new Bulgaria dawning—and surely nothing was more typical of the transformation coming to that land than the Sofia-Karlovo daily bus. So the warnings of friends went unheeded, and I purchased the ticket which was a passport entitling me to make the most romantic bus ride in Europe.

The bus, I was informed, left at precisely 9 a.m., and in deference to the order I took a taxi from my hotel to the starting-point. I need not have worried; the Bulgarian conception of time is almost as liberal as the Russian. It was 9.15 when the passengers were allotted their seats, the doors firmly closed, and the task of stowing the luggage begun—this latter ranging from the conventional suitcase to sacks, bags, baskets, and boxes.

For another twenty minutes the driver and his

assistant struggled with canvas wrappings, string, and rope until every nook and cranny of the car—a lightweight charabanc seating twelve—was full and overflowing with bundles. Before they had finished the running-board was piled high on both sides, rendering both ingress and exit impossible. No one complained; it was obviously the usual thing to be fenced in, and since everyone had contributed generously to the mountain of baggage, all were content that nothing was to be left behind.

The last sack tied into place, the lanky assistant named Sam climbed into a far-back corner, and the owner-driver, a fat, jovial, unshaven Bulgarian known to all his passengers, apparently, as "Uncle", entered by the one open door, and at 9.35 precisely we were off on the road to romance.

By that hour in the morning Sofia has been busy for some time, and the cobbled streets were jammed with a multitude of slow-moving little wooden carts pulled by horses little larger than Dartmoor ponies. The manner in which these carts ambled from right to left in sudden jerks, or sometimes refused to move at all, despite much hooting, would have destroyed the nerves of many a British motorist. But "Uncle" placidly remained undisturbed, and he threaded his way through the maze in a manner befitting the first bus to brave that traffic. Fortunately, Sofia is far from large, and another five minutes should have enabled us to escape. And so we should have done had it not been for the level crossing.

Of all the banes which await the motorist in the Balkans level-crossings are the most noticeable. A special word of warning concerning them is printed in *Europa*, the international motoring guide, reading thus: "When the poles are lowered, the motorist must not, of course, proceed," and then adding: "If the poles are not lowered, however, the traveller must not take it as evidence that the railway is clear."

We were not allowed out of Sofia without our level-crossing. Even as our driver strove to out-manœuvre a peasant-cart containing a man, his wife, and a load of vegetables, the two poles ahead sank into place, and the traffic stream came to a halt.

By now, although only ten minutes away from the centre of the city, the stone-paved streets had changed into something that might have been originally sand, gravel, or just plain earth. Whatever the origin of that road, weeks of rain had converted it into a lake of liquid mud a foot deep. Into this Plutonic sea we plunged, followed by a chain of carts and vehicles stretching back as far as the eye could see. And there we stuck for thirty-five minutes, while a light engine, with a handful of goods wagons hitched behind, shunted backwards and forwards in front of our very noses.

Those thirty-five minutes were not without their diversions, however. Before ten minutes had elapsed, the horses were pulling at their bridles, the mules were kicking, the donkeys neighing in their usual macabre fashion, and in another five minutes the chain had become a plunging medley of animals, carts, and men. Throwing off footgear, and rolling up their trousers, the drivers waded into the mud in an endeavour to quieten the frightened animals. And then, just when the drivers had almost exhausted their vocabulary, the engine disappeared, the poles lifted, and we jerked forward in the wake of a lorry laden with soda siphons which our driver had cunningly adopted as leader.

But our traffic problem had not begun yet. For a few hundred yards we proceeded at a fair pace along a road three-quarters filled with struggling animals—oxen, horses, donkeys, water-buffaloes, mules, with a few cows and goats as makeweight. Half of that cavalcade was driven by peasants bringing their produce to town, sometimes a man, sometimes a sturdy, brown-faced woman, here and there a roguish lad of nine or ten years. The other half were coming from a brick and tile factory in the neighbourhood, and their carts, heavily laden, were proving difficult burdens for the lean beasts which strained through the clinging mud.

At this point we met what might have been, but for "Uncle's" ingenuity, another half-hour halt. The road,

I had noticed, was piled high on both sides with heaps of flints and stones, but I knew too much of Balkan habits to imagine that these signified anything except that those stones had probably stood there for seven years, and would remain undisturbed for seven years more. Not so, however. The Bulgarian government—out of sheer cussedness, it seemed—had decided to do something about it, and they were now doing it, with the result that three-quarters of the main road into Sofia was "up", while through the remaining quarter enfiladed a long, slow stream of shouting, cursing drivers.

It was at this point that our driver showed his mettle. "Uncle" took one look at that stream of traffic, in the middle of which a cart laden with pantiles had become bogged to its axles, followed by another look at a front garden adjoining the roadside, by crossing which we could accomplish a detour which would land us on a side road and enable us to leap ahead of the obstruction. We swerved, and took that garden in our stride, immorally and inconsiderately sweeping over box-edging and a bed of marguerites, and so reached a road which was clear of anything but bumps and hollows.

I write "anything but". I am not sure whether the line of peasant-carts would not have been preferable. Looking back on the moments which followed, I realize that "Uncle" must have known the surface of that road by heart . . . and we had more than an hour's delay to make up! Pressing his foot on the accelerator, he drove the bus madly forward, north, east, or west as the road permitted. We seemed to be climbing banks, falling down hollows, and fording river-beds. Now we were on flint road, now sand, now grass, now soft muddy ground. The trees swept past our dizzy vision like a green ribbon, leaving only their perfume of the soft, sweet acacia flowers in our minds.

At last we pulled up in the first village on our route —a quiet, charming place with a wide street and two or three old inns outside which peasants were sitting and drinking. Here we stopped to distribute parcels and letters, and to take aboard more. For "Uncle" was an

A PEASANT HOME IN RUMANIA

The photograph shows the farmstead of a "rich" family in the Old Kingdom.

THE WORST ROAD IN EUROPE!

The main highway between Bucarest and Jassy, in Rumania, photographed by the author at midsummer.

unofficial postman whose speed was Mercury's compared with the official post.

A drink or two, a few minutes' gossip, and some water for the car, and we were off again. From now onwards the road mounted steadily and steeply, until we were travelling on a continuous spiral, beneath which plains and valleys lay in a complicated and variegated patchwork of scenery and colour. The eternal peasant lands which stretch like a green barrier between east and west—waving fields of rye intermingled with strips of maize, wheat, and beans, presenting from above a symphony of greens which would later turn to gold.

On we climbed, the ground becoming thickly sown with pieces of grey granite rock and low bushes of evergreens and scrub. Children darted from the thickets, laughingly to hurl tight little bunches of cornflowers and lilac into the car. And while we journeyed, "Uncle", relieved from the stress of competing with four-legged traffic, took it upon himself to act as guide and interpreter, for, as he repeated with pride : "United States —fine country ; England—very rich country. I have been there. And to Switzerland, France, and Germany. But Bulgaria best and loveliest of all countries."

Back in his slim, ardent, exploring youth, "Uncle" had migrated to the United States, I learnt, and there spent eight profitable years, sending home much money and making more, until he was a rich man, as Bulgaria counts riches. But, swallowed up in the mechanized West, his heart had ached for the hills and valleys of his homeland. He missed the scent of the lilac, the acacia, and the roses. Above all the roses, pride of all Bulgaria ! He missed the friendly gossip over coffee and *bozo* and *sladko*, the vines heavy with grapes, and the nuts, and the snows that linger on the mountain tops through the blue skies of June. He missed the songs and shrewd proverbs which express the soul of Bulgaria, and the strain of melancholy dourness and tenacity which hardens and straightens life. Above all, he missed the land—his own land— even though its people are the poorest in Europe, its capital small and shabby, its towns rare and its villages

and primitive little settlements perched in distant cracks
in the mountains, far from such places as Coney Island
or cinemas. And so "Uncle" came home, to ease the ache
in his heart by driving every day through the country
that for eight long years had formed the centre of his
dreams.

Every half hour or so we came upon one of those
remote little villages, clusters of whitewashed houses,
huddling together in a leafy valley with streams running
across the main street, or hanging on the precipitous
slopes of a mountain, whose steep sides had formed the
streets into strange shapes and directions. Each time as
we entered, hooting violently to announce our arrival,
the quietness would vanish. First would appear all the
village children, followed swiftly by their mothers.
Flowers would be pelted at us, rings of baked bread,
sprinkled with salt, offered for sale. Gipsies, arrayed in
every conceivable rag imaginable, would trail by the
car incuriously, their piercing black eyes looking out of
a mass of matted curls without a trace of shyness, their
bronze bodies glinting in the sunshine.

Sometimes Turkish girls—not so shy as the boys,
I observed, in spite of the harem tradition behind them
—clad in blouse and faded cotton trousers, would come
and stare out of liquid brown eyes. Bulgarian girls surrounded the car, laughing cheerfully when I produced my
camera to photograph their brown heads, swathed in
full white kerchiefs. These fulfil a very necessary function,
for even the tough skin of the country peasant would
be blistered and burnt under the grilling sun when
working in the open fields did they not wrap those kerchiefs round their chins, leaving only the mouth, tip of
the nose, and eyes exposed.

The dress of these Bulgarian peasant women is a
very nondescript affair on working days—a skirt, a jumper
or blouse, an apron and the kerchief, with a string of
beads as a concession to femininity. Most of the girls and
women have bare legs and feet—wonderful feet, straight
and firm and well shaped, like those of Greek statues.
They have shoes, but these are reserved for visits to the

nearest town. And at the point the girl considers that town to have come to an end, off come the shoes, to be slung round the neck with string, and she walks happily home with bare feet.

These mountain villages breathe an air of happiness and jollity and comfort, despite the stern conditions of life there. Looking at the friendliness of the scene— women washing in the stream, or waiting outside the communal ovens for bread, and men sitting outside the cafés—it was strange to remember that in those very spots the most bloody conflicts in the final revolution against the Turkish yoke had taken place. But the Bulgarians seem to bear no malice against the considerable Turkish population still living in their midst. And, to complete the population of the villages, there are the animals always in evidence—ducks and geese, goats, curly-haired pigs, or the ubiquitous Balkan sheep, white, brown, and black.

A foreigner may be excused for feeling that one can have too much of sheep. He meets them not only in every other piece of pasture, and away up the hillsides with their lone shepherds, looking like a picture out of the Old Testament, but at every turn in Bulgarian life. When we halted for lunch, at a village basking in the sunlight on a little plateau with the peaks of the Balkan range behind us, the most plutocratic of the passengers went into the local eating-house for lunch. Out of the six variations of lamb the menu offered, I chose *kebab*, fresh minced lamb rissoles, with which was served a salad of cucumber and a dish of rice—at a cost of five-pence—followed by *yoghourt* and stewed cherries; after which the proprietor offered me sheep's milk cheese, freshly made, and I kept the bus waiting while I rounded off the repast with Turkish coffee made over a charcoal fire by the lad who waited upon customers.

Delicious coffee—at a penny a cup; but the lad, despite the intense heat of the day, wore a sheepskin coat and a tall hat of the same material, and the smell rose to high heaven. Across the street was the shop that made those hats, testified to by a row of wooden blocks along the pavement with shaped caps on them drying in the sun.

Every little house we passed on that ride had sheep-skins hanging out to dry in various stages of curing. The old women sitting on the doorsteps carded the sheepwool; and the young shepherd girls did the same as they minded their flocks. Inside the houses the fat was being melted down for tallow candles. There is no escaping the sheep in that region, and the stranger who is sensitive either to smells or associations had better shun the mountain valleys and villages of Bulgaria.

Once more we set off—a flying start over a good road which, as the hands crawled round the clock, descended towards the Valley of Roses.

Nowhere else in the world could the traveller see so many roses at once—fields and fields of them filling the valley, with rows upon rows, ranging from little bushes on the ground to larger ones which reached as high as a man—the blossoms all deep bright pink with a trace of yellow in their hearts, small and sweetly perfumed. The flower which yields the richest and most enduring scent in the world !

The air was heavy with it as we approached; every breeze that blew carried its softness, a lingering sweetness intensely feminine and reminiscent of the harem and women in courtyards where fountains played in the sunlight. There was hardly any relation between that perfume and the sharp subtlety of the modern products of Paris, and yet there is not one of them, probably, that has not a small portion of that costly liquid—attar of roses—in its foundation. Liquid more precious than gold.

The season of the rose harvest lasts only three weeks—for from twenty to thirty days from the end of May. During that short time, the peasant who has grown these lovely blooms must be up, and all his family with him, at dawn, picking furiously before the sun has come to open the blossoms and draw some of their sweetness from them. A ton of the flowers produces less than a pound of pure rose-oil, yet such is its value that the peasant who grows roses can earn from one decare of land (1,000 square metres) one-third more than can be obtained from the same area of wheat. Every 70 kilogrammes of blooms that enter a rose distillery produce just 20 grammes of the precious essence. Very little for so much labour, yet the fact that a small flagon of the oil will sell for £1,000 in Paris makes this one of the most flourishing valleys in Bulgaria.

A fortunate accident to our bus—a choked carburettor—delayed us for half an hour in a large village not far from Karlovo, our destination. The car stopped outside tall whitewashed walls. Fascinating walls, and more fascinating still what they concealed—for this was a rose distillery. Even as I looked and wondered, two of the passengers pulled at the bell. A young man answered their summons, and the three disappeared inside. Five minutes later, as I stood leaning by the car, the young man reappeared and approached me. Was I a stranger? Had I seen the rose factory? Would it interest me to see inside, even though, regrettably, it was not working? The demand for attar of roses was not what it used to be.

And so I passed through the door in the wall, into a tall, cool building in which great copper cauldrons stood in a row, each with its little baby cauldron beside it, in which the roses are boiled with water, hundreds of pounds at a time. The copper cauldrons were empty, the great storehouse, once filled with sacks of roses, was empty too. Yet around that building hung the ineradicable scent of roses—the roses from the harvest of twelve months before. The young man explained that this year the government had commandeered all rose supplies for the co-operative distilleries.

"We must take tea," declared the lady passenger who had first entered, and whom I discovered was the aunt of the young man, come to housekeep for him for a time. By now, I had been long enough in Bulgaria if not to expect kindness, at least not to be surprised by it, and a few minutes later we were sitting round a table in a room which faced a ridge of dark hills covered with bushes, while our hostess poured out delicious pale gold tea and pressed on us rose jam, or *sladko,* sweet bread, butter (a rarity in poor Bulgaria), and other delicacies. It was an idyllic scene and an idyllic meal, and time passed without our knowledge. When I at last bade farewell to them, and once more made my way to the street, I found that "Uncle", the car, and all his passengers had been waiting a good half hour for me. But there was no word of complaint, only happy smiles that the stranger had been entertained and "shown the sights" of their beloved country. Bulgarians, I felt, made our English "railway compartment" manners appear rather churlish.

We reached Karlovo at six o'clock that evening, clasping balls, wreaths, and staffs of roses, tightly bound together, which had been thrown to us on the way. A long straight road stretched for the last part of the journey, with Karlovo rising up from it on a hill, with its minarets, its domes, its trees silhouetted against the sky.

The capital of the "Kingdom of Roses" is an important town, as Bulgarian towns go. It possesses an "hotel". But I carried with me an introduction to a family living in a little country house somewhere in that maze of streets. It lay, when found, behind a high wall, and was built on a foundation of cellars, some of which held wood and charcoal for the winter, some the garden tools, and another the inevitable weaving machine on which Bulgarian housewives make everything from rugs to bed-coverings and sheets.

Over the cellars ran a long wooden verandah, off which opened all the rooms in the house—all bed-sitting rooms, for Bulgarian housing notions are very economical of space.

Members of the family filtered through various doors to welcome me. "What would I like to do?" "What had I come to see?" When I replied that, having paid my respects, I proposed to make my way to the hotel, the suggestion was indignantly vetoed. How could I imagine that they would allow a visitor who had travelled so far to sleep at the hotel? I found it more difficult to imagine where they could possibly find space to stow a visitor away, even for one night, but while some of the family strolled round the streets of Karlovo with me in the delicious coolness of the evening the accommodation had been so adjusted that I found a room swept and garnished as if it was kept exclusively for the use of stray callers from London or New York.

Every visitor who seeks the real Bulgaria should see Karlovo in the evening. The town itself, set in the very heart of the Rose Valley, preserves in its character many traces of the long Turkish occupation. Little streams, crystal clear as they ripple over pebbles, flow down the sides of the streets, so that one has to step over them to walk into the shops, which have open fronts reminiscent of North African cities. Within sat the craftsmen, busily engaged in their various occupations. There were, of course, the butchers, as old as the Arabian Nights, and the open bakeries with their antique ovens; there were numerous saddlers and shoemakers. There was the local photographer, his shop filled with photographs of an American film star who had included Karlovo in a world itinerary. Most fascinating of all, there were the coppersmiths, hammering away in dark corners, while their wares hung in rows or were stacked in piles—beautiful hand-beaten shapes in very red-looking copper.

"You must see our waterfall; it is famous," said my friends. And because I knew it would please them, I reluctantly left the shops and began to climb upwards, along a road fringed with trees—chestnuts, walnuts, cherry. High up on the mountainside we reached the "sight" which the town loves to show the visitor. Waterfalls are often overrated. When you have seen one, the rest is repetition. But Karlovo's waterfall is interesting because civilization has reached out to that rugged mountainside and caught it up, and harnessed it for the use of man. Standing beside it was a tall cement building—a power plant. And down in the town every little Turkish-built cottage and farm had electric light installed!

Back in the little house the evening meal was waiting

—black bread, a rather salty fish in oil, minced lamb mixed with rice and cooked in vine leaves, pumpkin and pimento in tomato sauce, and a sort of meat rissole. Good, if unfamiliar, food, followed by sound sleep, a breakfast of bread, sugar, and milk, and a dash for the market-place, where my bus waited for passengers.

A short delay and the return journey had begun. The luggage had changed in quality without diminishing in quantity. Agricultural produce was now very much in evidence. Bundles of strong-smelling onions competed cheek-by-jowl with a mountain of roses picked that very morning. In another corner was a box of cherries, while, lashed to the sides, the rapidly spreading red stain on a canvas bag denoted the presence of a newly slaughtered lamb. Just before we started, a woman handed into "Uncle's" care a decidedly lively hen, and another confided to his safe keeping three hefty peasant girls, going to take a "place" at Sofia. Each girl had her string of beads, her stiff clean cotton dress, squeaky new shoes, and Dick Whittington bundle. Each wore upon her face the same solemn, half-terrified, half-obstinate and utterly immovable expression. Each was utterly dumb from the beginning of that journey to the end.

On sped Europe's most romantic bus, through the same hills, the same valleys, the same villages. Everywhere we stopped to take letters or deliver them, to spread the latest news, to buy or sell. "Would I not buy a little pig—only three shillings?" urged a peasant youth, as he did his best to land the animal in my lap. I looked for "Uncle" to explain, in Bulgarian, that I had no use for a pig, however small and well-mannered, but our driver had disappeared.

Fifteen minutes later he was still missing. I had noticed, during my altercation with the pig-seller, an even fiercer argument between "Uncle" and a woman who owed him the fare for a past journey. "But my husband won't give me the money," she said in despair. There was only one thing to do if the bad debt was to be recovered, and "Uncle", in no way inferior to the average London bus-driver in resource, had done it—

OFF THE BEATEN TRACK IN BESSARABIA

The entrance to a village on the Bessarabian plains. Formerly a Russian province, this land of vast horizons escaped "Red" rule only to stagnate under Rumanian neglect.

PEASANT HOME OUTSIDE KISHINEV

The photograph reveals a housing standard which is a relic of Czarist days, when the large estate flourished.

he had gone in search of the missing husband. When he returned, he was hot, but he had got his money. Flushed but triumphant, he refused to drive on until he had bought strawberry fizzes for all his passengers.

Hotter and hotter burned the sun, the green boughs we had gathered from a walnut tree at the last stop proving no protection from its rays. Suddenly there was a smell of roses, as sudden and violent as if Hans Andersen's little mouse had stirred the pot with her tail. Someone at the back of the car had taken the cork out of a flask of rosewater and was inviting the company to partake. In due course it came round to me, and passed on to a young Turk, who, smiling upon us all, filled his mouth full and squirted it out again like a fountain over the passengers. For one minute I imagined that another Bulgarian revolution might result, and feared for the Turk, but I need not have worried, for the company shrieked with mirth, all except the three maidens at the back, who, mindful of their important mission, preserved their immobile expressions.

At last, tired, dirty, and hot, we neared Sofia once more. Was there such a place? We were brought back to stern realities even before we entered its streets. A picket of soldiers held up the bus while a non-commissioned officer searched the entire party for firearms. Bulgaria is in the Balkans—among these friendly people I had almost overlooked that fact. There being no Macedonian conspirators concealed amongst us, no bombs and no rifles under the onions or roses, we reached the city without further delay.

"Had I enjoyed myself?" "Uncle" demanded. "And did I not agree with him that Bulgaria was the best, the most beautiful country in the world?" "Surely after all I had seen I would write a book to tell the world to come and see the Rose Valley?"—and he held out a grimy paw, a paw that delighted in generous giving and geniality, and helping the poor and the stranger along the road. I took it and shook it warmly, expressing a hope that we would meet again.

And standing there, with the busy traffic of Sofia

passing by, I watched the most romantic bus-driver in Europe back the most romantic bus into its garage for the night, before, at 9 a.m. next morning, setting out to brave once more the pot-holes on the road that links Karlovo with the world. May the legion of other bus-drivers who will presently travel along the roads of Bulgaria be as kind and as gracious as the man who exchanged "good money" driving in the streets of New York for the jokes and bumps of the Rose Valley route —because his heart hungered for his Bulgarian hills.

CHAPTER VIII

WILL "GREATER RUMANIA" ACHIEVE GREATNESS?

UNDER the peace settlement, Rumania secured "all and more than all" she deserved, and the area of the territory over which flies the Rumanian flag was increased by exactly 209 per cent. Ever since that date "Greater Rumania" has been suffering from chronic national indigestion.

A nation in which corruption has been exalted into a flourishing industry was called upon to absorb whole provinces formerly governed by Austria, Hungary, and Russia, many of the inhabitants of which had been accustomed to a standard of culture and life unknown under the old Regat. More recently, a nation which still puts its faith in cereals has seen the value of its main crops fall by as much as 70 per cent—and the total value of its exports cut in half. The result has been an intensification of poverty among the peasants of the "old lands", a state of acute tension among the diverse millions of new subjects of the Rumanian state, and a complete bankruptcy of statesmanship at Bucarest. Or, as it was picturesquely expressed by a foreign diplomat in that city : "Queen Marie gave Rumania its chance, and King Carol muffed it."

Between considerations of high politics and the Rumanian peasant there is a wide gulf spanned only by the tax-collector and the corruption which he feeds. The mental horizon of the typical peasant in the Old Kingdom is, like his physical horizon, bounded by the limits of his little estate, and the thousand similar parcels of Mother Earth which surround his patch and constitute, with the village, his world. That gulf, and its inner meaning, is aptly expressed in the common saying that "you can trust a Rumanian as long as his shirt hangs out"—only when the countryman becomes someone of importance and begins to wear his shirt *inside* his trousers, town-fashion, does the innate honesty which is the characteristic of peasants the world over wilt under the influence of bad example.

The most striking fact concerning this peasant nation is that, despite a peace settlement more generous than the wildest dreams of her statesmen; despite the absorption, on paper, if not in spirit, of millions of Hungarians, Ukrainians, and Bulgarians—all skilled in husbandry— within her frontiers; and despite a measure of land reform which redistributed no less than 30 per cent of the total area of arable land in the whole country among peasant proprietors, Rumania has, in the past twenty years, made no progress whatever from the agrarian point of view. There has, indeed, been a slight proportional decline in production at a time when every factor was favourable, given wise and benign rule, to a marked increase and a rise in the standard of living.

That this is so is shown by official statistics. "To be proportional to the increase in the area of the country, and in the area under cultivation in all the provinces now included in Rumania, the area sown with cereals should have represented 208 per cent as compared with the area sown in pre-war Rumania, and the production should have been 233 per cent," Professor Jon Raducanu has stated.

In 1929 (an exceptionally favourable year) the area under cultivation increased only by 196 per cent and production amounted only to 226 per cent, while the average for the years 1924-28 was 150 per cent.*

The same authority goes on to suggest that this decrease in agricultural production is due to two causes : (a) the disorganization and dislocation caused by the war and (b) the agrarian reform, which transferred land from large landowners into the hands of peasants whose resources and knowledge were inferior. To which I would add a third factor, which, from personal observation, must

---

* *The Agricultural Crisis.* League of Nations, Geneva, p. 255.

severely limit the possibilities of any considerable improvement in the low standard of cultivation existing in the Old Kingdom—the absence of the means to buy fertilizers and the equally general absence of any concerted attempt to introduce any system of land drainage. The writer has seen whole areas of cornland in the Old Kingdom under water at the height of the summer, when in other regions —including Rumania's new provinces—crops were almost ready for harvesting.

Those waterlogged acres illuminate much. In a nation where the soil is wealth, disregard for the condition of farmers is an ominous sign. It implies neglect of fundamental things—and thereby reveals one of the main reasons for the backward condition of the Rumanian peasantry.

Travel north from Bucarest through Ploesti, along the main road which stretches to Cernauti, capital of the Bukovina. For the first hundred miles the villages suggest a certain prosperity. The houses, built of wood with roofs of tiles or ugly tin-sheeting, are surrounded by stockades, and often contain three rooms. The land is devoted to cereals, and some big estates survive.

Beyond the first hundred miles, the influence of Bucarest evaporates, and one crosses a frontier that does not appear on the maps—the frontier of poverty. The wooden villas are seen no more ; in their place are more modest huts built of wattle and mud, with roofs of dirty thatch and dried manure. One room and one window becomes the standard allowance ; the wooden floors give place to bare ground on which sleep the peasant, his family, and very often pigs, poultry, and ducks also. In the larger villages there are schools, but not in all ; the Bulgarian passion for education is unknown here.

Poverty of land and home is equalled by poverty of resources. In the Old Kingdom, the peasant who owns a horse comes definitely within the *kulak* class of richer families. There are few ploughs ; the crops are raised by hand labour, the peasants often sleeping in the fields and not returning to their homes for days during the sowing and harvest seasons. Every town in Rumania has its garrison, and, labour being cheaper than machinery, the soldiers are hired out to work on the estates during the summer. But it is the peasant millions, cultivating their handful of acres foot by foot, with long-handled hoes, who carry the Rumanian nation—and the swollen ranks of the army and police—upon their shoulders.

It would, however, be incorrect to imply that the government has done nothing for the peasant. Rumania has lived in uncomfortable juxtaposition to Communist Russia for nearly twenty years, and the rulers of the state wisely decided to inoculate their nation against the revolutionary virus which infiltrated through Eastern Europe after the war by introducing a sweeping land reform.

This redistribution of land formed the most important measure ever carried out in Rumania, and resulted in 1,368,000 peasant families being provided with that measure of security implied by ownership of the soil they cultivate. A few figures showing its effects upon the nation may therefore be given here.

According to statistics quoted by Dr. David Mitrany in his monumental work *The Land and Peasant in Rumania*, published on behalf of the Carnegie Endowment, in all six million hectares were distributed under four separate agrarian laws, of which four million hectares were arable land. "Not all of that area has been handed over to individual smallholders," states Dr. Mitrany. "A considerable portion of it has been used for the establishment of communal grazings and woodlands, as well as for the creation of a land reserve from which public needs—such as the building of roads, town extensions, model farms, etc.—might be satisfied."

Four million hectares were, however, handed over to peasants in Greater Rumania, the number of families provided with holdings being 630,000 in the Old Kingdom, 310,583 in Transylvania, 71,000 in Bukovina, and 357,000 in Bessarabia.

Taking the arable area of the country as a whole, before the reforms, 40 per cent represented large estates, and 60 per cent small properties. To-day, 90 per cent represents smallholdings, and the total area of the surviving estates constitutes only 10 per cent of the area.*

It would, perhaps, have been too much to hope that even the most sweeping measure of reform would satisfy everyone, or obliterate completely a "land hunger" which had existed for centuries. Out of nearly two million names placed on the "resettlement lists", over 600,000 received no land whatever, and were left outside the reform. The fact that, in apportioning the land, preference was given to the landless peasant makes it probable that many of those thus overlooked possessed some land, though perhaps not enough to satisfy the needs of their families.

Further, it was found impossible, in administering the reform, to provide the fortunate two-thirds of the applicants with the amount of land originally decided upon as the minimum holding. "The official summaries show that an average of 2·65 hectares of arable land was distributed per head," states Dr. Mitrany, "to which would have to be added an individual average of 0·61 hectares in the shape of communal grazings, and 0·35 hectares as communal woodlands."

In the past, Rumania's greatest problem has been a compound of two evils—excessively large estates on the one hand, and excessively small peasant holdings on the other. The reform, important as it undoubtedly was, has remedied the first without abolishing the second of these evils.

"It is clear", states Dr. Mitrany, "that the reform has increased the number of families owning land, but not, in the same proportion, the number of those who could derive an existence from their holdings alone. Many landless labourers have been made poor owners, but not independent cultivators."

It is impossible that it should be otherwise; not even the increased area of Greater Rumania would permit the government to provide the 80 per cent of its total population represented by the peasantry with enough land to make them independent *so long as the*

* *The Land and Peasant in Rumania.* By David Mitrany, pp. 220–222. Oxford University Press, London.

standard of cultivation remains as low as it is at present.
Even were the remaining 10 per cent of the total area
of arable land represented by large estates distributed,
the present ratios would remain substantially unaltered.
Hence the importance which her peasant leaders place
upon the intensification of agriculture, the development
of co-operative buying and selling, and the development
of industries which would provide a market for agricultural products and an outlet for surplus labour.

That there is ample scope for raising the standard
of cultivation, and thereby the conditions of the peasantry,
is shown by the fact that the yield of wheat per hectare
(in quintals) in Rumania is only 11·6, compared with
17·3 quintals in Czechoslovakia, and of oats, 10·6 quintals,
compared with 15·9 quintals in Czechoslovakia. The
same proportion holds good for maize and other cereal
crops.*

Before the standard of cultivation can be improved,
however, two further reforms will be needed, of which
there are, at present, no sign. Taxation, at present excessive, must be reduced in order to provide the cultivator
with a greater incentive to raise larger crops, and the
means of communication and transport must be improved.

Taxation is one of the "burning questions" among
the peasantry of Greater Rumania. Too poor to own a
plough or even a horse, they are nevertheless not too
poor to work for six months of the year for the benefit
of the most corrupt bureaucracy in all Europe. The
peasant who is allowed to sit around in a government
or police office at Bucarest for days without any official
even asking him his business—because his rags proclaim
the fact that he has no *baksheesh* to offer for prompt
attention—must nevertheless pay out more than 40
per cent of the total value of his production, *even before
the world agricultural crisis,* in taxes used to maintain
officialdom and army.† Moreover, these taxes are levied,
not upon profits, as in the case of manufacturers, but

---

* The average yield per hectare over the whole country was 12 quintals in
1913 and 12·2 quintals in 1929.

† Bucarest *Argus*, October 17, 1924.

THE PRISON AT KISHINEV
A building with a grim history.

MEET THE UKRAINIANS

A young Ukrainian peasant woman and her children pose before the author's camera in the Northern Bukovina.

upon land, houses, and the means of production. In Rumania, the peasant takes all the risks of production, and the state none ; whatever the yield of the harvest, the government demands its full pound of flesh. It is, therefore, scarcely surprising that every peasant with whom I have talked, in both the old and new regions, has declared that "the tax-collectors take everything and give nothing". That sentiment is universal in rural Rumania.

Next to the iniquities of the tax-gatherers, and the price of corn and cattle, the main topic of conversation in the villages is transport—and the lack of it.

"What is the use of trying to grow more when we cannot get what we already produce carried to the markets?" an old Rumanian peasant asked me in the summer of 1933—and the facts bear out his complaint.

Rumania's roads and railways have never been adequate to the requirements of her population. They are, in Dr. Mitrany's words, "much below the requirements of an industry whose trading chances depend on the possibility of transporting great bulk safely and cheaply within a short space of time".

To say that most of the country roads are mere tracks is to give the reader little conception of conditions in a nation in which even the main roads are so bad that ten miles an hour is an adventurous speed for a heavy car. Those who wish to test the truth of this statement have only to journey over the forty kilometres which separate Targo-Fromash from Jassy in order to discover for themselves the urgency of the problem. I had often been told that passengers in the long-distance motor-omnibuses in Rumania suffer from sea-sickness, but I never believed it until I watched one of these vehicles lurching from pot-hole to pot-hole along that main highway which is the only means of approach to Rumania's ancient capital !

At the end of 1928, Rumania possessed 87,500 kilometres of classified roads, of which only 16,500 kilometres were claimed as "good" by the Rumanians themselves. Of the balance, 28,000 kilometres were

H

classified as "fit for traffic in dry seasons", and the balance were mere cart-tracks, mostly impassable for any vehicle except the peasant-cart.

"Since the war," declares Dr. Mitrany, "almost nothing has been done to improve the quantity or quality of the roads; in fact, even the few principal arterial roads, like that which runs in the highly industrialized Prahova valley, have been allowed to fall into disrepair. The new provinces have received even less attention. Only now, ten years after the war, has the construction of a road been undertaken to link up Jassy with Bessarabia."*

What happened to that project I know not. Probably, like the new steel and concrete bridges which have been built with "reparation" money but not linked with the roads they were intended to serve, so that no vehicle has ever run over them, the first fine enthusiasm died before the project got beyond the planning stage; at all events, having personally ignored the advice of friends, and penetrated to Chisinau (Kishinev) in a large Packard —at the expense of three broken springs—I was not surprised to learn there that when the Rumanian "Minister for Bessarabia" set out on a tour of the roads in that province, during the summer of 1928, he was obliged to turn back after only three days' travelling. Roads spell comfort for the tourist; they mean life, and the means of life, to the peasant who depends upon swift transport to get his crops, and especially dairy products, to market. The fact that the amount set aside for the repair of existing roads in the Rumanian budget is only one-tenth of the amount which the government admits is necessary to maintain the road system (without in any way extending it), and that it was possible for a visitor to travel from end to end of Rumania during 1933 without seeing more than a dozen labourers at work on the highways of that country, affords ample support for the complaints of the peasants.

Nor does the Rumanian railway system make amends

---

* *The Land and Peasant in Rumania*, p. 442.

for the appalling nature of the roads. That system was shaped by industrial and military, rather than agricultural, considerations, and never, at any time in history, has it proved adequate to the demands made upon it by those who produce the national wealth. In pre-war days, mountains of sacks of corn stacked in the open round railway stations were a common sight, while, since the war, enquiries conducted by Rumanian newspapers have revealed the amazing fact that the retail prices of agricultural products often vary by as much as 300 per cent in towns which are only thirty or forty miles apart—perhaps the most damning evidence of neglect of even the first needs of the peasantry ever recorded against a European government.

The truth is that the Rumanian railway system is too inadequate and inefficient even to distribute the food needed by the population within that country, without taking into account the imperative necessity of exporting the maximum quantity of agricultural produce, if the nation, and the individual, is to attain any degree of prosperity. In pre-war days it was the ubiquitous ox-cart which kept the channels of agriculture flowing, at *two miles an hour*—and at two miles per hour it floweth still. Imagine a farmer in Wiltshire possessing an abundance of milk, cheese, butter, poultry, eggs, and corn, but with no means of getting any of these things to London and turning them into money except by carrying them on an ox-cart and taking three days over the journey, and three days back again, and one of the reasons for the poverty of the Rumanian peasantry becomes obvious. In no other country in Eastern Europe is transport so backward. As recently as 1924 it was estimated by experts that it was utterly impossible for the railway system to handle the annual surplus of corn available for export—amounting to about seven million tons. Even by borrowing thousands of railway wagons from other nations it has been proved impossible to shift all the available corn to the ports before Christmas—and it must be borne in mind that swiftness of delivery is a vital factor in the prices obtained for agrarian products.

It will be seen, therefore, that while the land reforms
have placed the means of production in the hands of a
large section of the landless peasantry, the means of
transport is inadequate to handle the existing scale of
production, without taking into account the increase in
yield which must be both grown *and sold* if the standard
of the peasantry is to be raised above the wretchedly low
level prevailing in 1933. Ownership of the land has
enabled the Rumanian peasant (and the peasants of
minority races in Bessarabia, Bukovina, and Transylvania)
to feed his family and escape from actual hunger ; it
has not done anything to mitigate his poverty of cash
resources or to raise the taxable capacity of the nation
as a whole.

The impossibility of improving conditions until the
transport system has been revolutionized may account
for the apparent indifference of the government to agriculture. One might imagine that the administration of a
state which draws almost its entire wealth from the land,
and 80 per cent of the population of which are peasants,
would be constant in its efforts to improve and foster
production. Actually the budget of the Ministry of
Agriculture represents only about 3 per cent of the
total national budget, and of this modest appropriation
less than half is devoted annually to agricultural training
and research, state experimental farms, and breeding
stations. Well may Dr. Mitrany remark that "the size
of this budget hardly corresponds to the importance of
the agricultural industry, or to the magnitude of the
problems which the land reform has raised".

The author has taken considerable pains to discover
what the Rumanian government has done, apart from
the land reform made necessary by political conditions,
for the peasantry of that country, but without much
success. An Institute of Agronomical Research was
founded a few years ago, but nothing has been done to
improve roads ; indeed, in the new territories, the
standard of highways has gone down as the good roads
inherited from Austria and Hungary fell into disrepair
through neglect. Nothing has been done to provide

either credits or equipment for the poorer peasants, or fertilizers for the soil. Above all, there is nothing in the actions of successive governments to suggest that the serious plight of the producers, owing to deficiencies in the national transport services, is even now recognized at Bucarest. Having provided Greater Rumania with an outsize in armies, maintained at the expense of the peasantry, the rulers of that land apparently considered that no further efforts were called for, until, with the advancing world crisis, steps had to be taken to deal with agricultural debts, and certain sums were made available for funding private indebtedness, which often carried interest at as high as 30 per cent, by the issue of state loans at 6 to 8 per cent.*

In Rumania the peasants have been left to get along as best they may, without either help or any further hindrance than is indicated by periodic visits from the tax-gatherers. The result has been complete stagnation of agriculture generally, and even a retrogression in conditions, at a time when other nations, no better circumstanced, but possessing more enlightened governments, were making strenuous efforts to raise the standard of production within their borders. Even Bulgaria, the poorest nation in Eastern Europe, found it possible to invest state money, amounting to fifty million leva, in farm machinery, which was sold to the peasants at less than the original cost, repayments being spread over several years.

In view of this neglect, and the small area of the average holding, the wonder is not that Rumania should have been obliged to suspend the service on her debts owing to other nations, but that the total production of the country has been maintained at figures relatively near to the pre-war level.

Those peasant families, inured to hardships, live on an average five to a room, in wattle-and-mud huts, in a country which, in pre-war days, had a death-rate (25·3) exceeded only by Russia. Farming their tiny holdings

---

* *International Labour Office Year Book*, 1931, p. 408.

with totally inadequate tools, they produced in 1930 over 11,000,000 tons of cereals—wheat, rye, barley, oats, and maize, those crops representing over 40 per cent of the entire national income.*

The effects of the world agricultural crisis upon the families which produced this mountain of corn is strikingly shown by some figures issued by the League of Nations, which recorded that the net value of that 1930 harvest to Rumanian producers amounted to £25,588,000, compared with the sum of £65,160,000 which the same quantity of cereals would have realized had prices been maintained at the level ruling in July 1929 !† The fall in values, moreover, continued right down to the end of 1933, exports for the first ten months of that year representing an increase, over the same period of 1932, of 2½ per cent, but realizing 8¼ per cent less.‡

By the end of 1930—that is, while the precipitous decline in agricultural prices still continued—every smallholder in Rumania, in so far as he grew crops for export, was working at a loss.

Wheat, costing £5 18s. 4½d. per hectare to produce, was selling at £4 7s. for the same quantity. A hectare of barley cost £5 14s. in labour, seed, and taxation, and fetched only £1 15s. 3d., while maize cost £4 14s. 1d. and brought in £2 12s. 9d. per hectare.

Rumania's yield of grain per hectare, it may be added, has remained one of the lowest in all Europe, despite the fact that the black earth of the Baragan, the Burnas, the Budjac, and north-eastern Moldavia and Bessarabia is almost as rich as the world-famous Ukrainian soil, enabling the peasants in those parts to dispense with artificial fertilizer. Wheat, oats, barley, and rye have been grown in these regions since the dawn of time, and the fact that *mamaliga*, or maize porridge, is a national dish, eaten by rich and poor alike, bears witness to the part which maize has played in Rumanian history.

Four-fifths of all the arable land in the country is

---

* The total production of corn fell, in 1932, to 9,881,278 metric tons.
† *The Agricultural Crisis.* Vol. i. League of Nations, p. 260.
‡ *Economist*, December 23, 1933.

devoted to cereals, and in summer the cornfields, golden in the sunshine, give an appearance of prosperity belied by the statistics and the wretched living conditions of those who grow it. In this land there is no question of forsaking corn as the basis of national wealth—every year six million acres of wheat and twelve million acres of maize proclaim to the world that, for Rumania and its people, grain provides the means of life.* If the sight of those oceans of cornlands is not evidence enough, it may be recorded that, in the year 1930, over 300,000 wagon-loads of corn were exported.

Compared with the corn harvest, stock-raising is not of any great importance. The war stripped Rumania of half her cattle, and the number of head has declined further since—from 5,745,000 head in 1922 to 4,552,166 in 1928. The fall in the cost of fodder encouraged breeding during the last four years, and in 1931-32 some increase in the number of cattle was registered. Hopes of increased cattle exports were not fulfilled, however. Exports to Austria fell from 1,000 a week in 1930 to 100 a week in 1932, and trade with other countries similarly declined.

There are some thirteen million sheep in Greater Rumania, yielding 25,000 tons of wool a year, most of which is turned into home-spun garments by the peasants. Three million pigs, some thirty-two million poultry, ten million geese and ducks, and two million turkeys complete the inhabitants of the farmyards of the nation, 82 per cent of these smaller denizens in the villages being the property of peasant families, and feeding on the communal lands found near every settlement.

Such mass-figures appear impressive at first sight, but it unfortunately remains true that in 1933 the average peasant did not own enough poultry, geese, and ducks, if the whole were bartered for oil, to light his cottage for more than a month or two. The conditions of

---

* The total area sown in 1932 with cereals was 10,663,557 hectares, representing 84·22 per cent of the total arable land of the country. Of this area, 2,869,632 hectares were devoted to wheat, and 4,776,258 to maize ; the balance represented the national production of barley, oats and rye.—*Report on Financial and Economic Conditions in Rumania in* 1932. His Majesty's Stationery Office, London. 2s. 6d.

the peasantry have, indeed, sunk so low, owing to neglect and the world crisis, that many years of progressive government must pass before any great change for the better, either in material conditions or the standard of production, can be achieved. Short of the state commandeering food needed to feed their families, as has happened in Soviet Russia, it is difficult to see how the misery of the great mass of the peasants could further be intensified.

Statistics show that fully 30 per cent of all rural dwellings in this peasant state consist of single-roomed homes, built either of wattle-matting covered with clay or clay only. Possessing tiny windows, which are rarely made to open, such houses can be erected for a total expenditure, including stoves, of about £10. Yet, despite this low standard, the task of providing the peasantry with homes equal to the average existing in the former Austro-Hungarian territories of Bukovina and Transylvania has hardly been begun, and it will be many years before the people are provided with that twenty-five metres of air space per person which is laid down by hygienic standards.

Reform is made more difficult by the fact that the average income of the bulk of the peasantry, measured in terms of gold, has actually fallen since 1914.* Similarly, the diet of the peasantry leaves much to be desired, as evidenced by the fact, recorded by Dr. A. Urbeanu, that a single bad harvest suffices to cause pellagra to reappear in the countryside, for in Rumania, even more than in Italy, maize is the national food of the people in hard times.

Faced with conditions which would try the tempers of the townsmen, and enduring an actual deterioration in material possessions compared with the "bad old

---

* M. Garoflid, in the Bucarest *Argus* (July 26, 1923), produced figures showing that, before the war, the income of a middle peasant family, farming five hectares, was 685 lei ; in 1922-23 the average income of this type of family was 15,000 lei, whereas to equal the purchasing power of their pre-war income the amount should have been 22,600 lei.   Other figures pointed to the same conclusion—that the average purchasing power of the Rumanian peasantry, as a whole, had at that date depreciated by 25 per cent despite the land reform.

PEASANT BEAUTY

Ukrainian peasants "snapped" in the Bukovina. The child in the centre of the picture would qualify for a prize in any "beautiful baby" competition.

THE PEASANT SPEAKS

The author talking with his host on the farm at which he stayed outside Czernowitz.

days" before 1914, the Rumanian peasantry have retained their traditional conservatism. It is noteworthy evidence of the peasant's distaste for violent methods that, during every attempt made before 1914 to secure some measure of land reform, their spokesmen always voluntarily offered compensation, under the terms of their demands, to those whom they sought to dispossess.

It is significant that conditions in this respect have changed more during the past ten years than in the previous hundred. Possibly the discovery that "land and liberty" are not always interchangeable terms may have encouraged the peasantry to think; the failure to remedy the most elementary social abuses may have given an impetus to discontent. Whatever the reason, a new distrust may be detected in village debates in Rumania to-day—distrust of parliamentary action as a means of alleviating the conditions of their lives, and distrust of a régime which relies on an enlarged police force, with its hosts of spies, to smother public opinion. In this new stirring of political thought there is nothing of revolution, but rather a wonderment that those who produce 60 per cent of the total national wealth should be always poor.

The dreams and hopes that lie behind those peasant discussions were ably outlined by M. Mihalache in a speech debating the land reform delivered in the Rumanian Chamber in 1921, in which he declared that, from the point of view of the countryside, all worth-while reforms had but one aim and object—to lift the Rumanian peasants out of the morass of physical misery in which they now dwell. That aim forms the main plank in the Peasant Party founded immediately after the war, and which has since grown rapidly in power and influence among the people, if not among those who stand around the throne.

Listening to the party's speakers addressing the peasants at village gatherings, I have marvelled at the enthusiasm with which they cling to their dreams in a nation where the average standard of peasant well-being is, without exception, lower than in any other European nation except Serbia or Russia. There is, indeed, a close superficial affinity between the poverty of the average Rumanian smallholder and the apparently eternal poverty of those Slav cultivators whose lands stretch down to the northern bank of the Dniester River, on the frontier of Bessarabia. The same disregard of the needs and interests of the peasantry as exists in Rumania to-day was seen in Czarist Russia. The same hovels, the same grinding taxation, the same lack of modern equipment or knowledge. Will history have to record that Rumania endured a convulsion as all-shattering in order to burst her bureaucratic bonds; or has a wise, if not completely successful, measure of land reform, and a measure of parliamentary government, averted that danger? As to that, one can only record that the spirit of resignation is passing, and that the Rumanian peasants criticize the omissions and mistakes of their rulers to-day more freely than at any time in the past—a fact not confined to that country, however, but to be observed through the slowly awakening peasant lands. For the peasants of Eastern Europe are stirring in their thought-processes, and the beginnings of a unity transcending national frontiers is, for the first time, discernible.

If the emergence of a definitely peasant opinion has been slow in the Old Kingdom, it has progressed more quickly in the new territories, inhabited by Hungarians, Ukrainians, and other minority peoples who, brought within the frontiers of Greater Rumania without consultation, and against their will, are neither as patient over its corruption and neglect, nor as servile under police rule, as is the native Rumanian. With the possible exception of the mixed population of Bessarabia, the inhabitants of these new territories over which the Rumanian flag was hoisted in 1918 enjoyed, before the war, a standard of culture and well-being unknown amid the Oriental squalor of the village communities of the Regat. Both the Hungarians of Transylvania and the Ukrainians of the Bukovina previously enjoyed a high standard of economic and social welfare, expressed in housing conditions, cultural activities and family income. To-day they find themselves condemned to form part of a nation which is deliberately dragging them down to the low Rumanian level; a nation, moreover, which has no high traditions of culture, art, literature, science, or well-being to offer its new subjects in place of the traditions from which they have been cut off by the new frontiers. How are these minorities who dwell on Bessarabian plains, and in the fertile valleys of Bukovina and Transylvania, faring to-day under the Rumanian *opinshe*?

The answer to that question is important. Upon it depends not only the permanence of the present frontiers of Greater Rumania, or the exaggerated strut cultivated by the Rumanian police in Czernowitz and Kishinev during recent years, but the future peace of Europe. For it must never be forgotten that peace might be shattered as easily, in certain circumstances, by an infuriated peasant host armed with scythes as by an ambitious Power.

Let us glance, first, at conditions to-day in Bessarabia, which has for fifteen years been occupied by a Rumanian army, and governed from Bucarest.

CHAPTER IX

BESSARABIA : A STUDY IN DECAY

IMAGINE the South Downs magnified twenty times, and there rises to the mind a picture of the rolling, treeless plains and gentle hillsides of Bessarabia, former "garden province" of Imperial Russia, and one of the loveliest of all Europe's peasant lands.

Apart from Kishinev, capital city of the province, with its 120,000 population, the largest city in Bessarabia cannot muster more than 30,000 inhabitants. In Kishinev and the smaller towns alike, 50 per cent of the total population are Jews—and at least 75 per cent depend upon the ubiquitous peasant for their daily bread. The remaining 25 per cent is made up of the Rumanian garrison and the horde of officials which descended, like a plague of locusts, upon this rich prize when the lonely plight of the province, bordering on Soviet Russia and in danger of being swallowed up by the Red tide, provided the Rumanian government with an excuse for the annexation of Bessarabia.

It may be argued that, with the collapse of the independent government of Greater Ukraine, just across the Dniester River, and the southward surge of the Bolshevists, any other conceivable fate would have brought worse tribulations for the helpless peasant population than the present era of martial law, neglect, and over-taxation. But it is hard work convincing any Bessarabian of the truth of that assertion. For Bessarabia has not only failed to make any progress in the economic and social sense, but has gone back half a century during fifteen years of Bucarest rule.

Not for nothing do the droshky-drivers of Kishinev spit before they refer to the Rumanian gendarmerie by a Ukrainian name meaning "chicken-stealers". Not for nothing do the traders of Kishinev market mutter contemptuously that "the ladies of Paris taught them to ride" as some much-beribboned Rumanian army officer passes on horseback. Two words, and two words only, can describe the universal opinion in Bessarabia concerning the régime, semi-Oriental in its corruption and oppression, set up by the Rumanian authorities—utter contempt.

True, the Rumanians have accomplished certain things during their occupation, designed to show the world that they take their rule seriously. They have, for example, eliminated the Greek alphabet in the cities as far as is possible. Street names, shop signs, public notices—all now appear in Roman characters, thus ensuring that only a minority of the mixed Ukrainian, Russian, Jewish, and Moldavian population will be able to understand them. Having driven over the so-called main road which runs from Jassy to Kishinev, and sampled the subsidiary dirt-tracks which form the only link between the Bessarabian peasant village and the outside world, I can testify to the fact that the highways of the province are just fifteen years nearer disappearing altogether in a welter of liquid mud. But if the Rumanians have no time for such mundane matters as roads, they revealed their enterprise by erasing the Cyrillic inscription over the massive front of Kishinev cathedral, and replacing it in the Rumanian language. Even enterprise has its limits, however, and so the double Russian cross still rises to the skies over the belfry of the cathedral, looking down on the Roman cross which crowns the dome of that building—a fact which causes the population of the city to hope that one day "civilization will come back to Bessarabia".

It is difficult for those who have not travelled through those picturesque villages, situated among groves of acacia trees, to appreciate the neglect which Bessarabia is suffering to-day. Isolated from direct contact with the world, with the "forbidden frontier" separating the province from the Ukraine under Soviet Russia to the north, and only a totally inadequate railway service to transport the crops which it grows, Bessarabia is at once the poorest and least fortunate region of that backward country. Kishinev was almost a "tradeless city" long before the world depression hit peasant Europe, for of what use is it for buyers to travel so far when the means of transporting their purchases is lacking?

In Czarist days, Bessarabia was a wine-growing country, with the markets of Russia and the Ukraine just across the Dniester. And in summer it was a southern holiday-ground for the wealthy folk from the north. To-day most of the vineyards are dying from neglect (one wine-grower told me that it would take ten years to raise his vineyards to their former prosperous state), while only the hardiest of holiday-makers would brave the sort of police surveillance which attaches to any "foreigner" who ventures into the province.

The Rumanian authorities declare that both their large garrison and the strict police rule are necessary in a country which is an outpost of "Europe" against Bolshevism, and it is true that, standing on the hills above the city from which the villages of the Ukraine under Soviet Russia are clearly discernible across the river, the "Red" domain is very near. But few people, even at Bucarest, really believe that Moscow would contemplate such a perilous adventure as aggressive action to recover Bessarabia, and if the "bogy" lives on, it is partly due to a certain pride at having "dished the Reds" and partly because it provides a ready-made explanation for everything that happens in Bessarabia.

If that land is taxed to the bone to finance the army which occupies its cities, are not those troops a necessary guard to protect the people against Russian attack? If a member of the Ukrainian or Russian minorities is charged the impossible sum, in these days of vanished trade, of 10,000 lei a year to send a child to a primary school, again it is unfortunate, but, after all, the Rumanians saved the country from the Reds.

If the palatial hospital north of Kishinev—one of the most modern in all Russia—is taken over by the military to provide additional barrack accommodation, while the good folks of "green Kishinev" are left to die in their homes, well, it is regrettable, but the gallant Rumanian army must be housed somewhere !

In no part of Europe to-day, save only in the Ukrainian territories now under Polish rule, does one find the lives of the civilian population governed so completely by "military necessity". Is it so very strange if even the Jews, despite memories of nights when the streets of Kishinev ran with the blood of their race, sometimes wish for a return of the "good days" before 1914? Or that the inhabitants of that part of the Ukrainian lands which lie inside the Bessarabian borders, amounting to 12,000 square kilometres, should think longingly of the days when hope of union with Kiev in a nation of their own seemed tantalizingly near, only to fade when the "gipsies" from Bucarest decided that here, on their doorstep, was a plum waiting to be picked?

It would be unjust, however, to imply that there were no inhabitants of Rumanian extraction in Bessarabia before Bucarest decided upon annexation; or that there existed no historic justification for that act. Rumanian historians claim that, prior to the original Russian annexation in 1812, Bessarabia was, as a section of Moldavia, solidly Rumanian in population, the foreign elements being confined to a handful of Bulgarians living in the south-east. And on that fact they based their right to "restore" this fair land to the mother-country to which it rightly belonged.

The claim that Bessarabia was predominantly Rumanian in population could, indeed, have been admitted—in 1812. But not in 1920. In that year Bessarabia had been for more than a century under Russian rule, and evidence that the mass of the peasantry felt no affinity to their neighbours to the south is shown by the spontaneous demand for autonomy which followed the break-up of the Russian Empire, and also by the fact that, according to a Rumanian official estimate, only 20 per cent of the men, and less than 5 per cent of the women, could read or write the Rumanian language.

The history of Bessarabia during the century of Russian rule sheds an interesting light on how the "colonizing" tendencies of great Powers store up trouble for the future, even as the policy of "Rumanizing" Bessarabia and the Bukovina is ensuring the presence of new and troublesome "minorities" in formerly homogeneous regions when, as is inevitable sooner or later, the frontiers of that state are revised in accordance with the desires of the inhabitants.

By 1824 the policy of Russification of Bessarabia was in full swing ; the use of the Russian language had become compulsory in all schools, and the original Rumanian inhabitants were allowed to learn their own language only when they could both read and write in Russian. Later, all church services were conducted in the Russian language, while emigration was encouraged from Russia and from the Russian Ukraine.

Most of the Ukrainians who entered Bessarabia settled in the territories adjoining Odessa, which had formed part of the Ukrainian lands from time immemorial, and to make room for other settlers tens of thousands of inhabitants of Rumanian extraction were encouraged to migrate to other parts of the Russian Empire, where to-day their descendants form communities under Soviet rule. Thus, during the decades of Russian rule, while Bessarabia remained an all-peasant province, the composition of its population was radically changed.

By 1908, a census showed that in this originally homogeneous province, populated entirely by Moldavians, 30 per cent of the people were either Russian or Ukrainian and only 54 per cent Moldavian or Rumanian.

The break-up of the Russian Empire, and the occupation of Bessarabia by the Rumanians, naturally changed once more the composition of its population—more especially in view of the redistribution of large estates

BUILDING.—PEASANT STYLE

Making the mud-bricks used to construct the outer walls of peasant homes in all parts of Eastern Europe.

A VILLAGE MARKET IN HUNGARY

Peasant women buying factory-made textiles on market day—before the agricultural crisis made such luxuries unattainable.

among landless peasants from the south—and there is no reason to question a recent Rumanian estimate that to-day Bessarabia's 2,848,000 population is composed of 60 per cent Rumanian (that is, of original Moldavian race), 12½ per cent Ukrainian and Russian, 10 per cent Jewish, 5½ per cent Bulgarian, and 4¼ per cent German.

Some authorities have quoted these and similar figures to prove that Bessarabia never ceased, throughout the long night of Russification, to remain a Rumanian region in culture, sentiment, and language.

It had a hard life under the Czars; but because these princes would not let any ray of light penetrate to the masses, either by way of self-government or of education, a whole century of alien discipline has left the life of the peasants untouched [states Dr. David Mitrany]. They now return to Rumania as after a long winter sleep, with all the ways which their ancestors took with them in 1812—with, as they still call it, their "Moldavian" language and customs and traditions.*

With all due respect to a great authority on that country, and while it is true that a great number of the original Moldavian peasant families continued to use that tongue in their daily lives, it is debatable whether any considerable proportion of the population of Rumanian race would to-day vote, in a freely conducted plebiscite, for continued co-operation within the kingdom of Rumania.

The peasants of Bessarabia, as in other lands, are apt to think that "the proof of the pudding is in the eating"—and the "pudding" offered them by their Rumanian rulers is very little to their liking. It may further be added that the percentage of conscious Rumanian patriots in Bessarabia in 1917 was certainly no higher than the percentage of Germans in that province—that is, less than 5 per cent. Ex-Kaiser Wilhelm, had he won the Great War, would therefore have had as much

---

* *The Land and Peasant in Rumania*, p. 4.

I

justification for forcibly annexing Bessarabia to the
German Empire as the Bucarest government had when
they took advantage of a struggling autonomous government at Kishinev and submerged Bessarabian freedom
in a flood of bayonets.

Since that date, as stated in the previous chapter,
357,000 hectares of land have been distributed among
landless peasants in Bessarabia, some of which resulted
in the introduction of new settlers from Rumania into
the plains of that province. Officials have multiplied
under a régime which staffs even the minor posts on the
state railways with Rumanian subjects. Thus the policy
of Russification has been suddenly and drastically reversed.
Rumanian is now the official language in all schools.
Any improvement in the conditions of the peasantry
would be followed by fresh hordes of "middle men"
and settlers seeking to escape from the wretched conditions of Rumania proper. The result, in the future, must
be a soufflé of nationalities which will defy the wisdom
of statesmen to disentangle. The outline of the problem
is, indeed, already emerging in the clannish feeling
which exists among the original inhabitants, causing
them to draw together in all matters of trade, amusement,
and social life, leaving the "usurpers" from Rumania
to their own resources.

This problem of nationality is uppermost in Bessarabian life. Its most conspicuous result has been to
keep the old Russia in being long after it had disappeared
everywhere else, except along the Baltic coast. Arriving
at Kishinev, the traveller finds the droshky, with its
bearded driver in the old-style Russian pleated coat,
still the favourite means of transport. At the largest hotel
at Kishinev he will see the furniture redolent of the
Czarist régime, and the rooms precisely as they were
when the last of the Russian troops moved northward—
save only for the inevitable photograph, in many and
crude colours, of King Carol which all wise traders display
prominently on their premises. He will find the building
itself significant testimony to the craftsmanship of those
old Russian builders, who knew well how to shut out

the biting winds of the Bessarabian winter with double windows and huge stoves. He will, if his taste runs to vodka, be privileged to purchase it at a price equivalent to twopence a glass—the cheapest vodka in Europe. And he will be regaled with Russian food on so lavish a scale that it will remind him that even the horse-thieves of Kishinev were the most prosperous horse-thieves in all Russia in the old days. That food, and the vodka, are the only two things in all Bessarabia which bear no taint of the Rumanian influence—and even so you will be fortunate if you do not have to share a table with a corseted Rumanian army officer ! (Not for nothing are corset shops for men, the photographers' studios, and the brothels the only businesses at Kishinev which are flourishing under Rumanian rule.)

Kishinev, however, is no more Bessarabia than Paris is France, or New York typical of the United States. To see the real Bessarabia one must travel to the villages tucked away under the fold of the majestic hills, to plains where the horizon lies thirty miles away in any direction, and where, so naturally have the peasant homes congregated in spots sheltered from the icy winter winds which bring the wolves sweeping across the plains in search of food, one may journey for half a day along some cart-track without sighting a human habitation. In this sea of peasant lands it is wise to travel in sunshine ; the natives, who know best what passes for roads, have a saying that if it rains you may reach the nearest town in one day on horseback, two days by ox-cart, and three days by motor. The traveller who has been caught in a thunderstorm on those plains will sympathize with, if not excuse, the despair of the "Minister for Bessarabia", who, having seen those roads for himself in bad weather, thought better of his grandiose plans for making Bessarabia habitable for travellers.

And yet, without better roads and improved railway facilities, it is hard to conceive better times dawning for the province. For, at the risk of wearying the reader, it must be reiterated that communications are the life-blood of a peasant community—and this province, nearly

100 per cent peasant, has only 530 miles of railway track
and 60 miles scheduled as "passable" roads in its 17,000
square miles!

Bessarabia is also nearly 100 per cent in debt.
Neglect and droughts began the impoverishment of the
community which the sudden drop in the price of grain,
due to the world agricultural crisis, completed. The
Jews, here as elsewhere forming the bulk of the trader-
class, were ready enough to lend money at rates of interest
which often rose to 40 per cent, and thus Bessarabia has
reached a degree of poverty when "only the sunshine is
shared by all".

Apart from a fall in the total head of livestock (horses,
cattle, sheep, and pigs) in the province from 4,000,000 in
1922 to 2,680,000 in 1930, this state of universal bankruptcy does not greatly affect the internal economy
of Rumania, for that nation already produces more grain
than its railways can export; and as for the impoverished
peasants, they eat vegetables during the summer months,
and *mamaliga* during the remainder of the year.

The burden of interest and taxation has, however,
prevented the peasants from reducing the area under
cultivation as prices became unremunerative. Thus the
production of barley, which stood at about 440,000
metric tons per annum in Czarist days, amounted to
609,630 tons in 1930, while the production of maize
rose from 663,000 metric tons to 1,295,021 in 1932.
In the same year the wheat crop, at 346,317 tons,
ranked third in importance among Bessarabian crops.

These figures, comparing favourably with Russian
days, have been attained at the expense of cattle-raising
and other activities formerly favoured by the large estate
owners who are no more. Wheat, barley, maize, and
potatoes are crops suited to a province where large-
scale farming machinery is unknown and the peasant
homestead, averaging on those vast plains about 12
hectares per family, reigns supreme. Such crops have the
additional advantage that they satisfy both the tax-
collector and the stomach—decided advantages in days
when the writer purchased maize in Kishinev market

at 7d. per 34 pounds weight, and new laid eggs, often brought thirty miles to find a purchaser, at 3d. a dozen ! Or when, according to official figures, the price of barley fell 30 per cent, wheat and maize by the same amount, and rye by 50 per cent during a single year— 1930. That slump in prices, general to the whole agricultural world, cost the Bessarabian smallholders over £7,000,000 in vanished wealth in a single twelve-month. And 1930 was *not* the worst year of the depression ! To-day Bessarabia still smiles on the visitor—in summer—for its countryside remains the loveliest in Rumania and its people retain the genius of hospitality which characterize those raised in the Ukrainian and Russian moulds. But it is a superficial smile—with grim need behind it. In the farmhouses the visitor is still offered wine, for it is plentiful and cheap. Any peasant will feel honoured if the traveller will tarry long enough to grow hilarious on vodka. But save only during the months of harvest, the visitor will find little apart from bread and *mamaliga* in any farmhouse at which he may call. He will notice a complete absence of factory products —often an absence even of boots, in a country where the winter climate is as severe as in any part of Europe. And if the traveller is of a sceptical turn of mind, he may contrast the poverty of those peasant homes, from which even the sacred ikons have gone to provide the where-withal for some special dish on a feast-day, with the well-fed opulence of the officials and troops who are "protecting" the population from being swallowed up by Soviet Russia.

Would their fate be any worse if the writ of Moscow ran at Kishinev ? The question is prompted by the proximity of that arbitrary frontier of the Dniester River. A boundary between two philosophies of government, two creeds, two worlds across which runs no road, and which has been bridged by no train since the coming of Communism cut off Russia from the Balkan Slavs.

I put that question to a peasant living in almost 'the last farm in Europe", as he called his holding.

Less than a mile away to the north was the river—and across the river paraded the frontier guards of the Red Army. The peasant had a mother and a brother living behind that impassable screen, whom he has not seen or heard of since 1917, and is unlikely to see again, for there are no motor-coaches or excursion trains running from Bessarabia into the lands of the Ukrainians under the Red flag. Part of his family happened to be ten miles north of the other part on the day when the new frontier appeared. That was all. But it divided that family in half more surely than putting the width of the world between them could have done.

Gazing across his fields towards the river, this son of the Great Ukraine thought over my question before replying.

"We still have something to eat here," he answered, after deliberation. "They had nothing for half of 1933, according to what we hear across the river. So we are better off than they. And I have my land, with no one to dragoon or coerce me into giving it up again. But food and land are not the whole of life, and here in Bessarabia we have nothing else now. We used to be the granary of Europe; now the grain rots in the railway sidings for want of wagons to carry it away. We used to attract many visitors, and be considered a rich land. Now only the hungry wolf makes the mistake of thinking a peasant worth pillaging. Like my brother across the river, I am working for the tax-collector, and praying for better days; so it comes to the same thing in the end."

That peasant spoke with understandable bitterness, for driving poverty, coupled with a life o. hard toil, and continued down the years, will sap the morale of all but the hardiest.

It is, indeed, surprising that, despite the undoubted bad times and the stranglehold of debts which will take not one but several good years to liquidate, there is little or no pro-Communist feeling among the peasantry. That is a significant fact in a region which, despite the "impassable" frontier, is better informed concerning what is happening in Soviet Russia than most parts of

Europe. And where, in the first general election held after the annexation of the province, the Peasants' Party secured an overwhelming victory, winning 72 out of less than 90 seats for the whole of Bessarabia.

What little Communist feeling there was originally has declined rather than increased with the passing years, for at heart the true peasant is ever an individualist, with no liking for any "share-and-share-alike" schemes, however soundly based upon economic needs these may be.

That same fact, however, only makes more baffling the ultimate solution of Bessarabia's future. Given wise government following the war, and a policy aiming at the economic betterment of the peasants whose lives are lived, from cradle to grave, among those majestic Bessarabian hills, the province might have become one of the fairest and most prosperous agricultural regions in all Europe, for it lies within the famous "Black Earth" region, and its soil is abundantly fertile.

Instead, Bessarabia has been allowed to sink back into a state of neglect which justifies the baffled contempt with which the bulk of the population view their inept and indolent "rulers".

What is the solution? Is there no alternative for Bessarabia except Communism—or Rumanian corruption and neglect? Does the key to the puzzle lie in that wide belt of marshes north of Jassy, against which the Rumanian hills break on the southward fringe like a petrified sea; marshes a mile wide forming a natural barrier which heavy transport could not pass except by the solitary railway bridge which links Bessarabia with Bucarest? Gazing on those marshes, and the hills which mark their limits, the traveller feels that if frontiers were ever more than lines on a map, then here, surely, is a frontier intended by na'ure to mark the dividing line between two cultures. And so it used to be, for this valley formed the southernmost limit of the old Russian Empire, and the first railway station at which the train stops to the northward is indubitably of Russian building; as solidly erected and strong as many thought to be the empire which raised it.

Now the frontier has been moved to the north of Kishinev, and a million Ukrainians and Russians, with another million peasants of Rumanian extraction, have changed their nationality to provide the world with one of the enigmas of the peace.

CHAPTER X

BUKOVINA—AND ITS PEOPLES

A PEASANT at whose homestead I stayed in Northern Bukovina in 1933 had two calves ready for market and invited me to accompany him during the negotiations which must precede such a weighty stroke of business in that province to-day.

The peasant had first to apply to the burgomaster of the village in which he dwelt for a card authorizing him to remove the calves from his farm and transport them to Czernowitz for sale. On these cards is detailed the description, age, sex, etc., of the beasts concerned. Nominally they are issued free on request, but the Bukovina being now Rumanian territory, the necessary permit was not forthcoming until *baksheesh,* according to a recognized scale (amounting to from 10d. to 1s. 8d. for a cow or horse) was forthcoming.

Having secured our permit, we set out for market the following dawn. It was a long tramp to Czernowitz; the physical effort involved in reaching the city was only the beginning, however. When we arrived at the market, an "admission tax" had to be paid before the calves could be offered for sale. This tax amounted to 1s. 8d. for a pig and 2s. 6d. for larger animals; in the case of pigs, sheep, hens, and geese it is so high that if the peasant does not find a purchaser at the second attempt he will have paid in tax alone more than the total value of the goods he wants to sell. The value of a sheep in the autumn of 1933, for instance, was 2s. 6d., while the amount charged before a peasant could take a sheep into the market for sale was 1s. 8d.

We were lucky. Both calves were sold on their first

appearance at the market, being bought for export at 600 lei (about 25s.) each. The amount to be deducted from that sum for taxes and graft amounted to 8s. 9d., for each calf, leaving the peasant with 32s. 6d. in cash after feeding the animals for eight months, and devoting one day of his time to their disposal.

That incident illustrates as well as any the difficulties which confront the peasant-farmers of the Bukovina to-day, and explains why many of them no longer care to take their animals to market, but instead sell direct to the small middlemen who call at the farms and, trading on the fear of a fruitless journey to the city, buy livestock and agricultural produce on the spot for prices such as not even Rumania has known before.

The issue—or refusal—of permits, and the levying of fees for this service, is in these days a necessary concomitant of life in the Bukovina. It is exceedingly doubtful whether any minor state in the American Union ever devised so many rules and regulations as the Rumanians enforce to harass the lives of the unfortunate peasants, and especially those of non-Rumanian race.

The methods by which the censorship of theatrical productions is carried out are an excellent example of the high political flavour with which the Rumanian civic dignitaries manage to invest the simplest form of communal activity.

Among the Ukrainian population of the Northern Bukovina dramatic productions, and especially the historical plays of the Ukrainian race, are very popular. In the absence of cinemas in the villages, the travelling dramatic companies and amateur groups still hold sway, and the all-peasant productions, staged in the village institute by local talent, are often of a high standard.

I was anxious to see a performance to be presented by a "company" which had achieved more than local fame, and upon hearing that they intended to produce a famous Ukrainian play dealing with the early history of that race in a village not far from Czernowitz, I travelled there in order to witness the rehearsals and to be present at the performance a few nights later. Thus it came about that I had the privilege of seeing, not the play itself, but the wondrous ways of the Rumanian administration.

Before any play can be performed in the province, permission must be secured from the Prefect of Police at Czernowitz. If those promoting the performance are members of the Rumanian government party, permission is at once given, and all is well. But Rumanians are in a minority in Bukovina, and in the case of those of non-Rumanian race—and this applies especially to Ukrainians and Ukrainian plays—permission is withheld until the book of the play has been submitted for censorship and report to the Rumanian National Theatre at Czernowitz.

The players whom I had journeyed to see were Ukrainians, and the play to be produced had accordingly been submitted to the local theatre authorities—together with the fee of 4s. 2d. charged for "reading". The Czernowitz censor raised no objection to the play, but that was only the first round, as it were, in an epic struggle. Having passed the eagle-eyed gentlemen of the Rumanian National Theatre at Czernowitz, it was necessary to forward the play to the General Direction of Theatres at Bucarest in order to secure the necessary permit, duly filled in and endorsed with one of the innumerable rubber stamps which Rumanian officials keep for all occasions.

This permit is issued free in the case of all plays which have passed the local censor (the only occasion on which I heard of any government transaction in that country which cost nothing), but actually, as the producer himself explained to me, that fact did not mean that it could be secured without cost. For if the play had been submitted to Bucarest by post nothing more would ever have been heard of it ; it was necessary for a member of the company to take it personally if the permit was to be secured by the night fixed for the production. And the third-class return railway fare from Czernowitz to Bucarest is approximately 800 lei (about 35s. at the present rate of exchange).

The money being forthcoming, and the journey made,

the permit was back in the village in good time, and all seemed to be well.

Then it was that I discovered that before a Ukrainian play can be produced by amateur Ukrainian actors in a village hall, a tax amounting to 12s. 6d. for each performance must be paid to the authorities, this sum going to the funds of the Rumanian Society of Poets, Authors, and Composers! By this time I was sufficiently intrigued in the fate of this peasant enterprise to contribute a modest portion of the sum demanded, if only to see what would happen next, but in many cases the village is too poor to provide such a sum, even when a "full house" is assured, in which case the police prohibit the performance even after all other preliminaries have been safely surmounted.

Having paid the compulsory subscription to the society, the producer applied to the chief of the administration at Czernowitz for the necessary final permission, accompanying his application with all the relevant documents thus laboriously collected. The permit was received by return, the final rehearsals were over. The village was agog with excitement, and a packed house was a foregone conclusion. And then, at the eleventh hour, came the thunderbolt. That play, approved by the National Theatre at Czernowitz, to be performed under permit issued in Bucarest, in respect of which a tax had been duly paid to the Rumanian Society of Authors, and performed under special licence of the Chief of the Provincial Authority, was banned by—the village gendarme! And when fruitless protests were made by the entire population, the gendarme—reinforced for the occasion—declared that he had secret orders that the play was not to be allowed. The writer endeavoured to discover from which particular department those orders had come—but no oyster ever kept its secret so well as that Rumanian gendarme. He read all the permits, and shrugged his shoulders. He was extremely sorry and quite polite. But he could not and would not permit that village to witness a Ukrainian play of an entirely non-political nature dealing with the folklore of the Ukraine.

A WATER-HOLE ON THE HUNGARIAN PLAIN

Horses being rounded in for watering at a well on the greatest plain in Eastern Europe.

AMONG THE BEST FARMERS IN EUROPE

The farmyard of a well-to-do homestead in Hungary—a nation with a high standard of agricultural efficiency.

It was not always thus in the province of Bukovina. There was a time, not so long ago, when the peasants of that province—both Rumanian and non-Rumanian— were prosperous citizens of the Austrian Empire. In those days it was possible to take a cow to market without collecting a permit and the market-tax was but one or two coppers. It was possible freely to produce whatever plays one wished. But those were the days before this land passed under the Rumanian *opinshe*, and before the redrawing of the map of Europe had made it a crime to belong to a minority race.

The Bukovina province has been called "the English land", and there exists some justification for the title. For this former Austrian province is small, and its rolling valleys and well-wooded countryside are distinctly reminiscent of certain parts of England.

It is unfortunate for the inhabitants that the resemlance cannot be stretched farther, and that Bukovina is not as homogeneous in its population as is England. Less than 4,000 square miles in extent, the province contains three main, and a number of minor, racial groups. A total population of less than 1,000,000 people is entirely composed of minorities !

According to the census conducted by the Austrians in 1910, and which may be taken as accurate at that date, there were in the Bukovina 273,000 Rumanians (mainly in the southern part of the province), 305,000 Ukrainians (mainly in the Northern Bukovina), 168,000 Germans, 130,000 Jews, 36,000 Poles, 10,000 Hungarians, and handfuls of Bohemians, Slovaks, Russians, and others. The Rumanians were at that date a minority race like the rest —and like the rest enjoyed the advantages which the Austrian Empire, with all its faults and "cracks", offered to its hotch-potch of subject peoples. All minorities alike were eligible for the higher government posts, and both Rumanian and Ukrainian citizens entered the professions, the civil service, and were appointed to posts even at Vienna. Whatever sins the "ramshackle Empire" possessed, petty discrimination was not one of them so far as the Bukovina local government was concerned.

The peace settlement changed that happy state of affairs. Without any pretence at consultation with the inhabitants, the province was handed over to Greater Rumania as part of the spoils of war. The Rumanian minority, still forming considerably less than half the total population, and less numerous than the Ukrainians, became overnight members of the ruling race, while all other races were transformed into what a Ukrainian senator aptly described to me as "minorities with a vengeance". Ever since that day the grievances of those who are persecuted because of their non-Rumanian race have overshadowed all other issues ; even the agricultural crisis did not stir the average Bukovina peasant as deeply as has the national issue since the time when it was forced to the forefront by Rumanian methods of administration.

The story of the Bukovina during the last fifteen years is the story of an area long accustomed to a high standard of cultural life and well-being which is being slowly forced backwards through a century of effort to the conditions of 1834. That story is partly linked with the age-long struggle of the Ukrainians for freedom, which will form the subject of a later chapter. It bears a close resemblance to the history of the Croatian people, who, like the jig-saw of races in Bukovina, once formed part of the Austrian Empire. And because the claims of national consciousness are more insistent than the demand for greater economic prosperity, I deal with them first, before outlining the general conditions of the peasants to-day.

Two-thirds of the total population are of non-Rumanian race, and until 1919 did not speak the Rumanian language. One-third of the total population is composed of Ukrainians forming a fragment of the forty millions of that race in Eastern Europe. Because the latter constitute the largest single unit of race in the population, and also because they are as conscious to-day of their kinship with the Ukrainians living within the boundaries of Russia, Poland, Czechoslovakia, and Bessarabia as they were on the day that the last autonomous Ukrainian state was overwhelmed nearly two centuries ago, the main weight of Rumanian oppression has fallen upon their sturdy shoulders.

Every Ukrainian conscious of his nationality is liable to arrest and ill-treatment at the hands of the police at any hour of the day or night. Many have been arrested, kept in the police-posts for hours, often beaten-up—and re-leased without any charge being made against them only after their representatives have sent frantic telegrams to the Rumanian government at Bucarest.

In thus ill-treating Ukrainians, be it noted, the authorities have not the excuse that those arrested are members of an illegal organization. True, some of these victims of Rumanian rule have been members of the Ukrainian National Party. But that party is an accredited political organization, which until the general election of 1933 had three members sitting in the Rumanian Parliament ; a party, moreover, which actually concluded an electoral pact with the Government Party during many years. Regardless of these facts, its members are treated as criminals by the Rumanian police.

The real, as against the official, attitude of the authorities to the political party which represents the entire Ukrainian population of the Bukovina is well illustrated by a chart headed "Subversive Movements in the Bukovina" which I saw hanging on the wall of the office of the police adjutant at Czernowitz. This chart consisted of four "columns", of differing lengths, intended to illustrate the respective strengths of the four "subversive" movements under police surveillance in that region. The first column was labelled "Bolshevism" ; the second showed the strength of an Adventist religious sect which had apparently come under official disapproval ; the third referred to the Anti-Semitic League ; and the fourth column—the longest of the four—was labelled simply "Ukrainians". The Ukrainian National Party was not named, and apparently the chart referred to the whole of the Ukrainian population of the Bukovina.

It is scarcely surprising, after that revelation of the official Rumanian mind, to learn that the police have secret instructions to treat all Ukrainians as enemies of the state—to be watched and harried in every way possible. And in defence of that order, Rumanians point to the fact that the first article of the constitution of their country states that "Rumania is a national state . . .", clearly proving that all non-Rumanians or peoples wishing to maintain their own culture or distinct racial conscious-ness are enemies of the present-day rulers of the province.

The results of that policy have been disastrous to the unity of the Bukovina. The existence of a separate racial consciousness among the Ukrainians has been fought by the methods of police persecution familiar enough in that part of Europe ; persecution has, in turn, widened the gulf which divides the administration from the Ukrainians, who, forming 15 per cent of the population around the town of Suchava, grow steadily more numerous until they form nearly 100 per cent of the inhabitants of that section of the province north of the Pruth.

Nothing that could be done to antagonize this power-ful Ukrainian minority has been left undone. Under Austria there were 199 Ukrainian-language schools in the Bukovina, and, in addition, 5 Ukrainian high schools, 5 Ukrainian "Chairs" at Czernowitz University, 2 training schools for Ukrainian teachers, and 1 school for Ukrainian agricultural students. In those pre-war days race was no bar to securing educational facilities.

To-day not a single Ukrainian-language school remains in the whole of Bukovina province ; the Ukrainian "Chairs" at the University are no more ; the training colleges have been compulsorily "Rumanized". And it was only in the autumn of 1933, after a fight which had lasted for ten years, that the minority members of parlia-ment secured permission for the Ukrainian language to be taught *to Ukrainian children* for four hours in each week. Education is compulsory from the ages of seven to fourteen, but the lessons are given in a tongue which is never spoken in the homes of 70 per cent of the pupils. One has only to imagine the indignation which would be aroused by a proposal to abandon the English language in favour of Welsh or Gaelic in all schools in Great Britain to understand the intense antagonism of the Bukovina minorities to this state of affairs.

The Church has fared little better ; the order has gone forth that the God of the Bukovina must have King Carol as his prophet! In pre-war days the Greek Catholic Ukrainian Church was controlled by the Greek Catholic Ukrainian Bishop of Stanislav, and attached to the Metropolitan Bishop of Lemberg—both of whom were Ukrainians. Since the Bukovina was ceded to Rumania under the peace settlement, this purely Ukrainian Church has passed into the control of the Greek Catholic Bishop of Baia Mare, who is a Rumanian Church official.

Formerly every priest of the Greek Orthodox Church throughout the regions populated by Ukrainians was of that race, while the theological students conducted their studies only in that language. Now all the higher Church officials are Rumanians, while in all the most important churches, when the old Ukrainian priest dies, a Rumanian successor is appointed. In many cases the "Fathers" thus foisted upon peasant populations are renegade Ukrainian priests or Rumanians from the Southern Bukovina : men of inferior calibre who do not speak the only language which the congregation understands, but who are more Rumanian than the Rumanians and are henceforth stationed in the villages as outposts of Rumanian rule. Meanwhile the surviving national Ukrainian priests, however strong in faith and action, remain in the less attractive and poorer parishes, mostly in the mountains, without any hope of advancement. It is hardly surprising, in view of these facts, that the pre-war average of forty Ukrainian theological students preparing to enter the Church has sunk to four or five.

The constant pressure against any and every mani-festation of Ukrainian national feeling extends to the Church services—and even to activities which express the antagonism of the Bukovina peasants to Communism !

Following reports that many Ukrainians had died in the famine which was experienced in the Ukraine under Soviet Russia during the winter of 1932-33, without any religious consolation being offered for their souls, people

K

of their race living outside the frontiers of Russia desired to conduct special Masses in the Ukrainian churches for these victims of Soviet economic theories.

Permission was therefore sought and obtained for divine services to be held in the Greek Catholic Church at Czernowitz and, later, at the Greek Orthodox Cathedral, these services being intended to mark the solemn protest of the Ukrainians in Rumania against Soviet policy and its effects.

The night before these services were to take place the police notified the organizers that the "political assembly planned is forbidden by the authorities". Nothing was said in this intimation concerning church services for the dead, nor was any reason given for thus refusing to allow one branch of the Ukrainian family to offer consolation to another in an hour of tragedy for their race.

The following morning the Ukrainian senator responsible for the arrangements was informed by the priest at the Greek Catholic Church that the police would not allow the special service for the dead to be read, and that he could therefore hold only the ordinary daily service without any reference to the events which had brought a large congregation together in the church.

Following this service, the entire congregation walked to the Greek Orthodox Cathedral. There they found the gates leading to the building closed, and a high official awaiting them, supported by a large force of police, including a company of gendarmes with rifles and bayonets.

Addressing the leader of the mourners, the police chief told him that the holding of any demonstration had been forbidden, and requested him to disperse his people.

The leader answered that no demonstration was intended; that they were only marching from one church to the other "with silent dignity to honour the dead".

The police were adamant. Their orders were that the people, now swollen to some thousands, could not enter the church or hold any service. For two hours that vast concourse waited while their leaders made three journeys to interview the Prefect of Police for the city. Eventually the gates of the cathedral were opened to them and they were allowed inside—to say a Paternoster !

When, later, the leaders of the Ukrainian minority protested against this ban, the Rumanian Ministry of the Interior declared that no order forbidding the services had been issued at Bucarest. The Czernowitz police authorities, next approached, declared that it was not they, but Bucarest, which had decided the services should not be held. And there, six months after the police had stopped the services, the mystery remained.

The "drive" against Ukrainian institutions extends to village libraries, Ukrainian newspapers and books, and even to the fondness of the peasants to weave the national colours of Ukraine—blue and yellow—into their home-made clothing.

The standard of village culture throughout the Ukrainian regions, both within and without Rumania, is immensely higher than is the case in the communities which live beside them. In the Bukovina a movement was set on foot to arrange lectures and provide libraries in the distant villages. The books were confiscated, and those responsible prosecuted, sometimes within a few days of these projects being launched. The import of books and newspapers in the Ukrainian language is permitted only under licence of the Ministry of the Interior—and such licence is forthcoming only in the case of books having no relation to the conditions and problems of to-day. The volume you are now reading will certainly never be allowed to reach any of the peoples discussed in this chapter ; the fact that the Rumanian authorities cannot deny the accuracy of the statements contained in these pages will only bring it more surely under the censor's ban. For there are few things more feared, in the Europe of to-day, than the truth.

Not so long ago even more stringent precautions were considered necessary in the interests of the Rumanian state. Until 1928 there was martial law in the Bukovina. Normal political life, therefore, dates back only six years— and was not permitted until the dice had been carefully loaded against the minority peoples.

The Ukrainian districts of the Bukovina return four M.P.s to the Rumanian Parliament, of which, until the General Election of 1933, three were representatives of the newly formed Ukrainian National Party. A just electoral system, on the English model, would give that party, on voting power, at least ten members. This number was whittled down first to four, and in 1933 to one, by an electoral law which stipulates that only those parties which receive 2 per cent of the *total votes of the whole country* shall secure any seats in the Rumanian parliament. To overcome this artificial restriction on Ukrainian voting power, the party has had to co-operate with several small democratic parties in order to attain a total number of pooled votes large enough to secure any representation at all.

The reasons behind this policy of studied discrimination against the minority peoples are clear enough.

None know better than the Rumanian authorities how transient favourable frontiers may prove. Hence the constant effort, ever since 1919, to so strengthen the nationalist sentiment within the country that when revision becomes unavoidable—and even the most optimistic Rumanian Minister does not, in his heart, believe that the present frontiers of his nation can long be sustained—Rumania may escape comparatively lightly. It is with this aim in view that large numbers of Rumanian "colonists" have been deliberately planted in the non-Rumanian areas during the past fifteen years.

Further, by means of the régime of persecution which has been maintained, the Rumanian police have secured lists of all racial-conscious minority citizens. If trouble ever comes, the task of sweeping every Ukrainian, German, Hungarian, or Bulgarian intelligent enough to be labelled "dangerous" into concentration camps can be accomplished within a few hours. The minority peoples know this, and resent it. It justifies their protest that from the moment when they were included in the Rumanian state they have been consistently treated as enemies, and never approached as friends.

The economic position of the province is such as might

VILLAGE SCENE IN SLOVAKIA

Detva, showing the main street and some of Czechoslovakia's 1,800,000 peasant homesteads.

"SONGS OF FREEDOM SUNG WITH NEEDLES"

A Czech girl working the embroidery for which the peasant lands are famous.

be expected in a region in which fully three-quarters of the
total farms are of less than 20 acres in extent, while
less than 1 per cent of the area is comprised of estates of
more than 200 acres.

The Bukovina is essentially a peasant land ; there are
no employed agrarian peasants, although a few in the
smallest class, farming an acre or less "on their own",
eke out a living by working for the richer farmers. Such
workers are paid from 7½d. to 10d. for a day of ten to
twelve hours—which is, incidentally, the lowest rate of
payment for any employed workers in non-Russian
Europe.

In former times the economic mainstay of the peasantry
was corn, sugar-beet, and potatoes used in the manufacture of alcohol. Now only two sugar-beet factories are
working, and even the drink trade is none too healthy,
which may explain why the Czernowitz authorities banned
a Ukrainian newspaper, published in the Bukovina, for
warning the peasants against drink—on the ground that,
as alcohol is taxed, any propaganda against drink is propaganda against the Rumanian government !

The Bukovina participated, with other Rumanian
provinces, in the redistribution of land which followed
the war. But whereas in the Regat the Rumanian peasants
undoubtedly benefited from that reform, in Bukovina the
section of the peasantry of Ukrainian nationality found
their claims relegated to the end of the list, after the names
of Rumanian officials, doctors, politicians, and others who
hastened to take advantage of the "land racket" which
promptly developed. To those non-peasant applicants
went most of the land taken over in the Northern Bukovina,
and the land-hungry Ukrainian peasantry was left to
choose between the alternatives of remaining landless or
purchasing smallholdings from the new owners at high
prices—and by means of loans borrowed at 30 to 40
per cent interest. Many chose to buy, for the immediate
post-war years were the most prosperous the Bukovina
has known for two decades. To-day those same peasants
are saddled with mortgages and debts amounting to from
£40 to £60 per hectare.

In 1932 the Bukovina produced about 200,000 tons of cereals, including 83,372 tons of maize and 44,304 tons of oats. It was unfortunate for the peasants that the wheat crop of that season was poor, for internal prices rose temporarily owing to a prohibitive import duty, from 1,900 lei per metric ton to 6,000 lei—a reflection of the poor crop. The only effect of this fortuitous "scarcity price", however, was that wheaten flour disappeared, and *mamaliga* once more become the mainstay of life among the population.

The Bukovina is a land of dwarf farms. Only 1 per cent of its farmers own over 250 acres; 15 per cent of the farms only are in the 60-120 acre class; another 10 per cent own from 25 to 50 acres; while the remaining 75 per cent farm from $2\frac{1}{2}$ to 25 acres. Many of those holdings are the property of Rumanian colonists, transplanted from the Old Kingdom to regions formerly occupied exclusively by members of other races.

Having visited the farms established by "colonists" in Yugoslavia, Bessarabia, and the Bukovina, I had formed the opinion that both the standard of building and the standard of husbandry were distinctly lower than those of the native communities in the same districts.

And when I travelled north from Czernowitz to visit one large Rumanian settlement in the Northern Bukovina, the same fact was undeniable. The colonists, mostly ex-soldiers from the Rumanian army, and many of them, as they frankly confessed, knowing nothing about farming when "settled", had managed to turn a fertile valley into a very good imitation of a city slum. Each had received the usual free gift of ten acres of land, together with implements, fruit trees, and £40 per family in cash; advantages which they may be said to have earned for their services to their country during the war, but which find no counterpart in the attitude of the same government to the minorities among whom the colonists now dwell.

The Ukrainians do not appreciate the presence of these "aliens" in their midst, but they are a tolerant people, and the two races get along well enough, partly due to a common dislike of the tax-collector. But lurking behind those new farms is a question-mark which may one day have to be answered : if and when the political future of the minority regions in Rumania comes up for discussion, those settlers will count in the statistics by means of which the Rumanian government will strive to prove that even the Northern Bukovina has a "mixed" population, and one sufficiently Rumanian to entitle that country to remain its guardian.

It is of interest, therefore, to place upon record the comment made to me by a Rumanian colonist, a migrant from the south : "We were sent here to make this land Rumanian, but living among the Ukrainians, and learning farming from them, we are, many of us, speaking only the Ukrainian language. In fact, we are fast becoming Ukrainians ourselves."

Meanwhile, the nearer problem remains—the grievance voiced to me by many Ukrainian smallholders, who said : "Rumania does everything for her own colonists and nothing for us. Yet we, the original inhabitants, *are* the Bukovina."

What is life like in that land for the average non-political peasant who rises with the sun and sleeps after its setting? Let a typical peasant of the Bukovina, who offered the hospitality of his home to a travel-stained foreigner, answer the question.

CHAPTER XI

A PEASANT SPEAKS

I MET him in the *yarmerok*, or market, at Czernowitz (which the Rumanians call Cernauti), one Monday, whither he had travelled with his farm-cart laden with produce—geese, fowls, eggs, and vegetables—from his farm some forty-five kilometres north of that city.

Tall and dark-skinned, with dreamy blue eyes which hinted at an understanding beyond that of the peasants hawking their wares around him, he first attracted my attention when I heard him speaking in the German language to a foreign visitor. I enquired the price of the produce spread out on the ground at his feet, bought some eggs, and we thus got into conversation.

He was, I discovered, a Ukrainian from Northern Bukovina who had migrated in pre-war days to the United States. There he had worked for a time on a German settlement in the Middle West, learning the language of his employers. American farmers were prosperous in those days, and eventually he became the owner of his own farm, and attained a "comfortable" competence. But the patriotism and pride of race which is so strong in the hearts of the Ukrainian people never allowed him to forget the fertile valleys of the far-off Bukovina he had left, and every week, during ten years spent in the great Republic of the West, he added something to the savings which would one day allow him to return and settle down in the land where he was born.

The Great War came, and the son of Ukraine grew rich in the process of producing food which was desperately needed by the Allied nations. Peace followed strife, and out there on his Middle West homestead he scanned the newspapers, hoping against hope that at last, with the collapse both of the Austrian and Russian Empires, a united Ukraine would become an established fact. "During those days," he told me, "the picture of my father's farm in the Bukovina was encircled in a garland of flowers picked and sent to me by my brother."

The world leaders met at Paris. Nations rose and fell according to the decisions taken at their meetings; millions went to bed one night citizens of Austria and Hungary, and awoke to find themselves recorded in the reference books as Poles and Czechoslovaks, Yugoslavs, and Rumanians.

The Bukovina, as has been stated, passed from the benevolent, if autocratic, control of Austria into the both corrupt and autocratic control of the Rumanians. The Ukrainian exile read of the changes in the newspapers which reached his American farm. With the war over and his people in Europe facing a new life, the call of home became stronger, and early in 1920 he sold his farm in the United States and took ship for Hamburg.

Back in Czernowitz, he exchanged his pile of dollars for Rumanian currency, and looked around for a farm in the region from which he had originally come. There he found twenty-five acres of fertile soil close to the home he had originally left, paid over his savings, and settled down to erect a new farmhouse more in keeping with the American standard he had become accustomed to, and to wrest a living from the land.

When he left the market-place at Czernowitz that day, he invited me to go with him and spend the night at his farm. And sitting in the main room of his farmhouse that evening, with a couple of dozen Ukrainian villagers for audience, the peasant who knew the world gave me a picture of life in one corner of peasant Europe.

"It is all bad," he began. "Wheat used to be our best crop. Before I went away, and since I returned, a peasant could grow rich on wheat, for our land is fertile, and the Ukrainian peasant is a good farmer. Sugar-beet paid almost as well as wheat. Now nothing pays any more. Wheat brought in nearly £2 per 100 kilos in 1928. In 1932 the price fell to 8s. 4d. per 100 kilos ; to-day it is around 15s. for the same weight, with a maximum of £1.

"The selling price of maize has fallen by 60 per cent in the same five years. What that means to us peasants may be judged when I tell you that in 1928 it needed only 50 kilos of corn to purchase a pair of shoes ; to-day 150 kilos are needed."

He held out a leg encased in a pair of good quality top boots.

"I brought these back from New York with me," he continued. "I wear them when going to market and on feast-days. At other times I wear shoes I made myself ; none of us can afford to buy now.

"Or take livestock," he hurried on. "We were paid 1s. 3d. per kilo live-weight for pigs in 1928. Now the price is 6d. ! A calf sold for 8d. per kilo live-weight before prices fell. Now you are lucky if you can get 3d."

He opened a drawer in the table at which we were sitting and pulled out a soiled notebook.

"Here's the story of the Bukovina in the world depression," he said. "My account book. I learnt to keep accounts in America. Examine these pages and you will find that, after working fourteen hours a day on a piece of the best land in this country, my income is down, all round, to one-fifth of what it was. Every thousand lei has become two hundred. But the taxes haven't fallen ; we still pay land tax, house tax, a tax on the sale of all produce ; we are, most of us, too poor even to buy matches and salt, but my farm-cart is taxed ! Every man in this room is working six months in the year to pay taxes and six months for his family. Am I right ?"

A murmur of assent from the peasants standing round the walls showed that all agreed with the returned exile on this point—a sore point in the Bukovina to-day.

I interpolated a question concerning food.

"You are to be a guest in this house for to-night," he answered. "You will see for yourself what we eat. So far as food is concerned we are rich, for in this village and a thousand like it the peasant is putting under his belt chicken and meat which in better days he sold for export.

The depression has robbed us of boots, of oil and salt, of all the purchasing power we had. I have not spent ten lei on tobacco for the past month, and I am classified as a middle-peasant. But no depression can rob the Bukovina of food, for these valleys form part of Europe's larder."

Supper that night consisted of *mamaliga*, potatoes, and milk. *Mamaliga*, the main food of millions of peasants throughout Eastern Europe to-day, is a type of maize "bread" made by placing flour and salt in water. When the mixture reaches boiling point, it is thoroughly stirred with a wooden spoon or stick until it has attained a thick constituency and cuts like bread. It is left over the fire until it "sings", and then served, being apportioned into slices with a thread.

At 4 a.m. the next morning my host roused me from slumber. He was already dressed and about to feed the livestock; after which we were to depart for the fields.

Not only was the whole village awake, but I found that most of its inhabitants had already left for the day's toil. Many had five miles or more to travel to any section of their land, and in summer, with a total absence of machinery in the village, an early start was essential.

The women went to the fields with their menfolk; here as elsewhere in the peasant lands the women work as hard and as long as their menfolk. The farmhouse at which I was staying bordered on the main road, and as I sipped the glass of homemade wine offered to me as a guest, groups of women and girls were hurrying past the open door, barefooted, with kerchiefs tied round their heads and carrying long-handled hoes, food for the day—and often infants as well.

My host was fortunate in that half his land adjoined the farmhouse. This was planted with maize and sugar-beet, and both crops were more flourishing than any that I had seen in the Balkans. Indeed, the standard of husbandry in the Bukovina would not disgrace a German peasant; there is the same sense of order, the same methodical cultivation, the same determination to utilize every inch of available ground. Compared with wide stretches of the Regat to the south, this land was a Garden of Eden.

I mentioned this opinion to my host as we surveyed his crops.

"Our land is well farmed," he conceded. "For that fact we can thank, first of all, the skill of our people, and, secondly, the traditions left behind by the Austrians. The whole standard of farming in the Bukovina is higher than in Old Rumania, just as we are, or were, a century ahead of the Rumanians in civilization. I say 'were', because I am not alone in the opinion that the handing over of these new territories to a backward country like Rumania has set them back—Transylvania, Bukovina, and Bessarabia alike—for at least a hundred years.

"I admit that the fact that our exports are down by more than half has nothing to do with the government. That is due to world causes, and, in any case, the Bukovina is probably too small to support its present population of nearly one million in comfort. But look at the effects of the change of régime upon our culture! Or upon our roads!"

He dropped the hoe with which he had been working and straightened his back.

"Under Rumania there are now only two agricultural training colleges in the whole Bukovina. But for the skill that is a tradition among us Ukrainians, and handed down from father to son, this land would sink to the condition of Old Rumania—which would mean a decline in efficiency of at least 50 per cent.

"And this," he added, "was done by the peacemakers without any desire on the part of the majority of the population to join in with Rumania. Why, even many Rumanians living under Austria cried out against the crime."

As I listened, I recalled the everyday phrase, which I had heard from the lips of peasants a hundred times since I had reached the Bukovina : "To be under the Austrian boot is better than to be under the Rumanian *opinshe*."*

---

* An *opinshe* is the Rumanian name for a peasant shoe.

A SUMMER SCENE IN CENTRAL EUROPE

Czechoslovakia makes hay while the sun shines.

IN THE LAND OF THE PEASANT

The village of Zazriva in Czechoslovakia—a typical landscape in that well-farmed land.

"The Austrians were autocratic but just," continued the peasant. "They demanded taxes, and spent a fair proportion of our money here in the province. To-day the tax-collectors collect all we have, and the Bukovina never sees the money again. It is all spent in the south. We get no roads, no drainage, no health services, nothing !

"We hear that the landowners in the Old Kingdom never pay their taxes. If we cannot pay ours when they are due, there is a double lot owing next time. It goes on and on, until the debt has become so large that it can never be paid, and the peasant is ruined."

His daughter came to the edge of the farmyard to call us to breakfast. It was 7 a.m. Back in the main room of the farmhouse his wife had prepared a meal consisting of *mamaliga*, beetroot soup, eggs, a garlic-laden salad, and rye bread.

That peasant home was well built and spotlessly clean, with whitewashed walls and an overhanging thatch of straw modelled into designs at its apex which would have done justice to many a week-end cottage of the wealthy Londoner. Inside, the beds, table, chairs, and two chests of drawers piled with the home-made linen at which the Ukrainians excel, spoke of comparative affluence in those parts. But from without only the large barns in the farmyard indicated wealth : every homestead in that village of some two hundred houses was spotlessly white ; with their windows framed in gay blue paint and their farmyards enclosed in the fences which are typical of the Ukraine, whether it be outside Kiev, or on the Bessarabian plains, or here in the kindlier Bukovina. There are few, if any, peoples whose villages are so picturesque, or speak so eloquently of the energy and initiative of their inhabitants.

Over the meal, the wife gave her views concerning life in the Bukovina.

"We work fourteen hours a day in the fields, and we have no money," she said. "All we receive for our work is enough food for our family. If I need matches, salt, oil, or the farm needs a new scythe, we must either find a shop which will take something in exchange—a pig, some chickens, or eggs it is usually—or go without. A kilogramme of oil for my lamp now costs me sixty eggs. It is too much, for to sell the eggs I must walk to Czernowitz, or take the horse out of the fields for a whole day. It is not worth it, just to get some oil, so we sleep when it is dark.

"Have you shown him our matches?" she asked her husband.

The peasant smiled and shook his head. Then he took from his broad belt a flint, a home-shaped piece of steel and a piece of queer substance which looked like a fragment of sponge. It was a variety of moss gathered in his fields which, when dried and a spark is applied to it, will smoulder slowly. You can light a fire with it if you are skilful ; it is simple to light tobacco with the aid of this "slow fuse".

"We don't have to talk about it," said the peasant, "because it is illegal. Matches are taxed, and the use of this moss reduces their sale. But a good many of us are using it to-day. One must have a means of making fire, and when it's flint and steel or no light, well, we risk the penalties."

The penalty, I discovered, was usually a fine of from 1,000 to 5,000 lei, equal to the value of two or three cows !

That morning I spent in the fields near the village. Everywhere the crops were good, and everywhere in that remote valley the peasants were out hoeing the soil. Hour after hour, as the sun climbed up into the blue dome above them, those rows of bent backs went on scratching the surface of the earth which is their only friend. No learned professors or government advisers came to help them. Nor did they need that help, for those peasants are the sons of peasants, with the "smell of the earth in their lungs when they are born", and the love of it in their hearts. To them the life on the land is the finest of all ; they satisfy that definition which says that "a true peasant is he who is content to remain a peasant".

But in addition to being peasants, they were Ukrainians. And to be a Ukrainian who intends to remain a member of that race and speak its language does not make for an easy life in these days when the flag of "Greater Rumania" floats over the Bukovina, and when the Austrian police-man has been replaced by an overgrown Rumanian military garrison. If the Ukrainian population of the Bukovina could only forget their own history, and be content to become "gipsies", speaking only the Rumanian language, they might have shared the spoils of war, and the average debt owed might not have stood as high as it does in 1934.

Over a midday meal in his farmhouse—with meat on the menu because it was not worth taking pigs to market any more—I put to that couple my last question.

"What are the problems which, first and foremost, interest the peasants of the Bukovina to-day?"

It was the wife who answered.

"First, the question of free cultural development for those of us who are of Ukrainian race, particularly in the sphere of education and a share in the government of the province. We shall not rest until our own schools which the Rumanians have closed are reopened and our children once more taught by their own teachers and in their own language. Secondly, the plight of the peasants. Times are bad, as you have seen, and we wait anxiously for days that will restore to us some of the money we do not see now. And lastly, taxation must be reduced, and some of the money taken from us spent in the Bukovina instead of at Bucarest. This land needs roads, sanitation, health services, more schools. But, above all, it needs the chance of decent life for its people who now find the burdens almost unendurable."

That woman had known the United States when the standard of life in that country was at its highest. Evidently she read my thoughts, for she added, "Don't take my word for it. Go and ask our neighbours."

It was a Sunday, and the opportunity to do so came when I met the younger men of the village at the Institute. There were half a hundred of them in their club-room, and when I put my question they conferred together before replying. Then the spokesman answered, and his answer named the same three points put—significant fact—in the same order!

I bade them farewell, and set out to return to Czernowitz. On the way I stopped at another village, and thus it was that before leaving the province I met the Grand Old Lady of the Bukovina.

She was eighty years of age, and lived with her husband in a peasant home which typified a hundred thousand more. The couple had four married daughters and a horde of grandchildren living in the village. The old peasant worked the same five acres that he had farmed in the days of the Austrian Empire, or rather he worked it with the help of his wife.

That Grand Old Lady toiled beside her husband on the soil. She attended to the vegetable garden, the pigs and the poultry. She baked the bread—and good bread, too. She kept their two-roomed cottage spotless. She did the family washing. She gave advice on any and every subject impartially to all her daughters and their husbands. She made most of the clothes for her husband, herself, and her grandchildren. And, having attended to these small matters, she "looked after the children for her daughters on Sundays". Although slightly embarrassed, I was therefore scarcely surpr sed when she offered me a couple of the children to bring back to England if I wanted them !

Grand people, those unknown peasants, living and dying far from cities, and tilling the same soil from generation to generation. Asking in return only a house, food, and security. Important people, too. More important, in the last analysis, than most townsmen, for without their labour the cities and towns could not exist at all.

Thus ran my thoughts as I approached Czernowitz once more, to be held up on reaching the main square of the city by a cordon of Rumanian troops drawn across the road. Beyond, I saw that the whole square had been roped off and was filled with spectators, kept in their appointed place by rows of troops and police, the latter looking more militaristic than the soldiers in their brown and black *pickelhaubs*. From the war memorial which stands in the centre of the square a red carpet had been stretched down the steps.

A military band entered the square, playing some martial air and followed by more troops, behind whom walked a procession of men and women in civilian attire.

From the man standing next to me I learnt that they were a deputation of local railway officials, parading to lay a wreath on the war memorial. It was all very impressive for the visitor who had not ventured out of the city, and who knew nothing about those peasants and their problems. But for anyone who had asked a few questions, there was one jarring note in the proceedings—the memorial itself. Designed by a Rumanian sculptor, and executed with skill, it depicted the Rumanian bull standing over the outstretched and inert figure of the Austrian eagle, and stamping on its defenceless body. Evidently tact is not among the virtues possessed by those who advise the Rumanian government on such delicate matters.

The spectacle of the various high officials of the administration, all clad in uniforms as gorgeous as the full-dress magnificence of a British Field-Marshal, lost something of its glamour when one remembered that simple statement heard from the lips of the peasants upon whose toil Czernowitz lives : "Better to be under the Austrian boot than the Rumanian *opinshe*."

Which will survive the other in the lovely Bukovina— the resplendent Rumanian officials or the power of the peasant? To-day the Rumanians have their chance if only the government will rise to the heights demanded by its destiny. But to-day passes—and to-morrow belongs to the peasant.

CHAPTER XII

IN the shops of Budapest they sell little jig-saw puzzles which show first Hungary as it is to-day and, when pieces of the puzzle representing the territories torn from the kingdom under the peace treaties and handed over to Czechoslovakia, Rumania, and Yugoslavia are added, the Hungary that was.

Mistaken—indeed indefensible—as the dismemberment of the ancient Hungarian nation is now generally admitted to have been, it would probably, but for monetary and economic difficulties, have had a beneficial effect upon the standards of life in the countryside of that country. The full resources—scientific, technical, and agricultural —of a thoroughly efficient European nation have for fifteen years been concentrated on a population reduced to something over eight millions, of whom 60 per cent are engaged in agriculture. Moreover, the Treaty of Trianon has been answered by a recrudescence of Magyar patriotism, affecting all classes, which has united Hungary in a common cause shared by prince and peasant. Yet another beneficial effect of military defeat has been the inauguration of a certain measure of land reform for the peasants which might have been delayed for a generation or more but for the introspective mood which has afflicted the Hungarian peoples since the dismemberment of that country.

Hungarian revisionist propaganda, ably conducted by one of the most proud and educated peoples in Europe, has become a by-word. The world depression, the plight of agrarian Europe, the tariff-jungle which has grown up in recent years, the plight of the minorities, and the general unrest which the passing years do nothing to dissipate—all these developments are ascribed, if one listens to the soothing words of Hungarian diplomats, to the iniquities of the infamous treaties and the compulsory exile of the Habsburgs from the castle overlooking the Danube at Budapest. That propaganda, however, differs from many of the inspired statements circulating in post-war Europe in one important respect ; it represents, not the aspirations of an ambitious government, but the deepest convictions of the Hungarian people. Right or wrong, it remains a fact that the average peasant, tilling his five acres, or working from dawn until dark on the fields of some estate-owner for a wage of 1s. a day, believes implicitly that the afflictions which have come to Eastern Europe may be traced, in the first instance, to the wrong perpetrated in 1919, which split what had always been a compact economic unit into rival and antagonistic states, and thus paved the way for the bad times which have since visited all the peoples of Central Europe alike.

In pre-war days the predominantly agricultural lowlands of the Danube basin and the forest-clad and highly industrialized mountainous reg ons exchanged each other's produce. The Hungarian peasant was able to sell his crops at fair prices to the industrial populations, from whom they bought, in turn, the necessary implements, clothing, machinery, and timber required for their farms and homes. This ideal economic unit assuring a smooth exchange of goods over the territories of historic Hungary was destroyed by the peace treaties, and there have since been erected thousands of miles of customs barriers which prevent any resumption in that two-way traffic in produce and goods which, before the partition, benefited not only the industrialist but also the whole peasantry.

In the light of this patent fact, and ignoring the delicate political issues involved in effecting any drastic revision, is it so strange that the average Hungarian peasant sincerely believes his present poverty is due more to the treaties than to the internal policy of the Hungarian government ? Those same peasants are still waiting

for the secret ballot promised by the Horthy régime
following the disastrous Bela Kun episode, and much
criticism has been levelled at the present rulers of Hungary
for delaying the introduction of this elementary reform.
But it may well be that those peasants are right who assured
me that the mass of the agriculturists would continue to
support the governing party whether elections were
conducted by open or secret ballot, believing as they do
that the peace treaties have produced for their country a
situation in which no Hungarian political party could
effect any lasting improvement without sweeping territorial
changes.

Peasants may exist who believe that the present
frontiers of their country can be maintained, and who
would be content that it should be so. If so, the writer
did not meet them. Every agriculturist questioned on this
point during a journey from one end of the present-day
Hungary to the other, whether estate-owner, smallholder,
or labourer, expressed the view that this question of frontiers
lies at the very root of the economic problems affecting
the Danube basin—and as unanimously demanded
"justice".

This general acceptance of the views of the ruling class
may, to a certain extent, have been inspired from above.
The maps, showing Hungary before and after the war,
which have for years been displayed on many houses,
lamp-posts, and in public places up and down the country,
are evidence of the fact that the population has not been
permitted to forget Hungary's "unhealing wound". But
such intensive propaganda counts for more in the cities
than the countryside. The faith of the countryman in
treaty revision as a cure for all ills springs from his injured
national pride and the instinctive promptings of his
conservative soul.

From the viewpoint of the economics of a predominantly agricultural state, there is abundant justification for the belief that, without revision, Hungary is
condemned to perpetual poverty. That nation, in pre-
war days, satisfied almost the entire needs in agricultural
produce of the Austro-Hungarian monarchy, with a

total population of 52,000,000 persons. A fraction over 75 per cent of her total crops were sold within the borders of that Empire, free of customs duties or tariff control, leaving a balance of 25 per cent which was exported to foreign countries.

That former internal market is now sheltered *against* Hungarian exports by tariff walls and other restrictive devices. To quote figures which are readily forthcoming to all enquirers at Budapest, of the territory of pre-war Hungary, including Croatia and Slavonia, totalling 325,411 square kilometres, the Treaty of Trianon took away no less than 232,578 square kilometres, reducing Hungary to 92,833 square kilometres. In other words, 71 per cent of the total territory of pre-war Hungary was handed over to the Succession States.

Had the former Hungarian territories continued to absorb the produce of the Magyar kingdom, the economic effects of dismemberment, at least, would have been minimized. Such was not the case. Compared with the 1913 figure of 75 per cent of all agricultural produce consumed within the monarchy, by 1929 the Succession States, with populations swollen to 84,000,000 and covering double the pre-war territory of the Austro-Hungarian monarchy, were accepting only 59 per cent of Hungary's exports—and that figure is a percentage of a total much reduced. The remaining 40 per cent of exports in that year went to more distant countries and showed smaller profits owing to the high cost of transport, notably to Germany (11·50 per cent), Switzerland (4 per cent), Italy (6·86 per cent), Britain (3·37 per cent), and France (1·19 per cent).

The effect of this dislocation of Hungary's natural markets may further be illustrated by the figures relating to wheat, her main item of agricultural export, which, together with flour, represented over 22 per cent of her total exports in 1929. During that year the average price of wheat at Budapest was 3s. 6d. per quintal (equivalent to about four bushels) cheaper than the price of wheat at Liverpool. The Hungarian farmer received at that time about 30s. per quintal for wheat. By the beginning of 1934

the price had fallen to an average of 8s. per quintal.
Similar difficulties affected the important Hungarian
livestock industry, which was hampered not only by
tariffs and quotas, but by health regulations issued in
neighbouring countries in respect of the import of live
animals and meat.

Reporting in January 1934 on Hungarian economic
conditions to the League of Nations Financial Commission, Mr. Royall Tyler, the League financial representative at Budapest, stated that "it is becoming more and
more difficult for Hungary to sell her produce abroad at a
profit. Her former markets being to a great extent closed
to her, she is obliged to go farther afield, and in the
pursuit of sound foreign currency to sell in distant markets
at rates that are in reality unremunerative."

The post-war years have indeed been for the four and
a half million Hungarians engaged in agriculture one long
fight with adversity, and the end is not yet. Following the
World War, attempts were made to restore the agricultural
industry, shattered by the conflict, the Bolshevist interlude,
the Treaty, and the bankruptcy of the whole nation.

Not until 1927, when the Hungarian pengo was placed
upon a sound basis with the aid of foreign credit, did the
outlook become slightly more hopeful.

At that time Hungarian agriculturists, possessing no
capital of their own, were contracting loans abroad at 10
per cent interest, a rate which, if high, was not then
impossible in view of the prices ruling in the world wheat
markets. Much of the money thus raised went in equipping
the larger farms and estates with modern agricultural
machinery. Such a development appeared a sound investment in 1927; wheat was selling at 38s. per 100 kilogrammes, and with the aid of machinery could be produced for half that figure.

That happy state of affairs was of short duration.
Widespread mechanization in the United States and
Canada caused a break in prices, and soon American-
grown wheat was being offered at from 5s. to 8s. per 100
kilogrammes; it could be delivered to Vienna or Prague
for less than 12s. Then it was that the chill wind of

adversity began to blow across the Hungarian plains, for the estate-owners and peasants of that nation could not produce it on their less highly mechanized and smaller farms for less than 17s. to 25s. per 100 kilogrammes.

The repercussions upon Hungarian agriculture were swift and severe. Between 1926 and 1927 the wheat-farms lost from 66 to 76 per cent of their entire income. Land declined by 75 per cent in value in the same twelve months, while mortgages granted earlier and based upon 25 per cent of the estimated value of a holding suddenly represented 100 per cent of the depreciated value.

Faced with this catastrophe, for it was little less, both estate-owners and peasants were powerless. It was not their fault that debts shouldered with comparative ease in 1925, when the price of wheat was 48s. per 100 kilogrammes became "bad" in 1932, when wheat had fallen to 10s. Nor could those peasants justly be reproached with having over-borrowed earlier, for, in comparison with the peasantry of other countries, the Hungarians possess less capital and less machinery per acre than most well-farmed nations.

The position facing the Hungarian government bore some resemblance to the Reparations situation which faced the League at the same date ; either concessions must be obtained or the next step would be repudiation—or revolution.

Creditors, fearful lest prices should further decline, invoked the aid of the Courts to secure something from the wreck. The peasants could not pay, and there arose a demand for wholesale foreclosures. To avert a panic, the government prohibited the seizing of any farm or property except in those cases where the creditor was a foreigner. Financial interests representing international creditors pressed for repayment of debts, choosing to sacrifice outstanding interest in order to secure a return of capital. The result of this "run" on Hungary was a disastrous decline in that nation's credit.

One more fact concerning those debts may be mentioned, illustrating the plight of all the peasant countries. At the time when this question of agricultural debts became

urgent, the total indebtedness involved was four milliards
of pengos, an amount representing twice the pre-war
debt of Hungarian agriculture, whereas the amount required every year for interest and amortization represented *three times* the pre-war figure. It is clear, therefore, that the financial plight of rural Hungary is due
partly to the collapse of world prices, which made the
maintenance of interest payments impossible while wheat
was grown at a loss, and partly to the onerous terms
on which Hungary secured loans abroad following the
defeat and partition of that country.

Meanwhile, as agricultural prices declined, industrial
prices rose, and the consuming power of the farming
community was reduced to vanishing point as the cost
of manufactured goods rose to 30 per cent *above* the
pre-war figure, while that of agricultural produce and livestock fell to 5 per cent *below* the 1914 level. The familiar
"scissors" price-process, noted in a former chapter, was
once more in evidence, and in Hungary the "scissors"
were wide open—leaving a gap between the value of
manufactured goods and farm produce which even the
richest peasants could not bridge. Apart from textiles,
needed for clothing, the villages became self-contained and
the peasants settled down to wait for better times.

The Hungarian government is seeking to ameliorate
these conditions by an internal moratorium on debts and
tax arrears, by reducing the rates of interest, by the
provision of improved seed, and by agricultural schools
and intensive education—a modern note in connection with
which is the broadcasting of popular instructive lectures,
received in each village on an official wireless receiving set
operated usually by the village schoolmaster. In addition,
by introducing a system of standardization, and by
dividing up the country into regions according to the
character of the soil, and limiting the produce in certain
areas chiefly to the products calculated to yield the best
result, efforts are being made to place Hungarian husbandry once more upon a profitable basis. Such measures
are at best palliatives, however, which may assist the
agriculturists but cannot remedy matters until Hungary

A MORAVIAN FARMHOUSE

Exterior of a typical peasant dwelling in the village of Hroznova Lhota, Czechoslovakia.

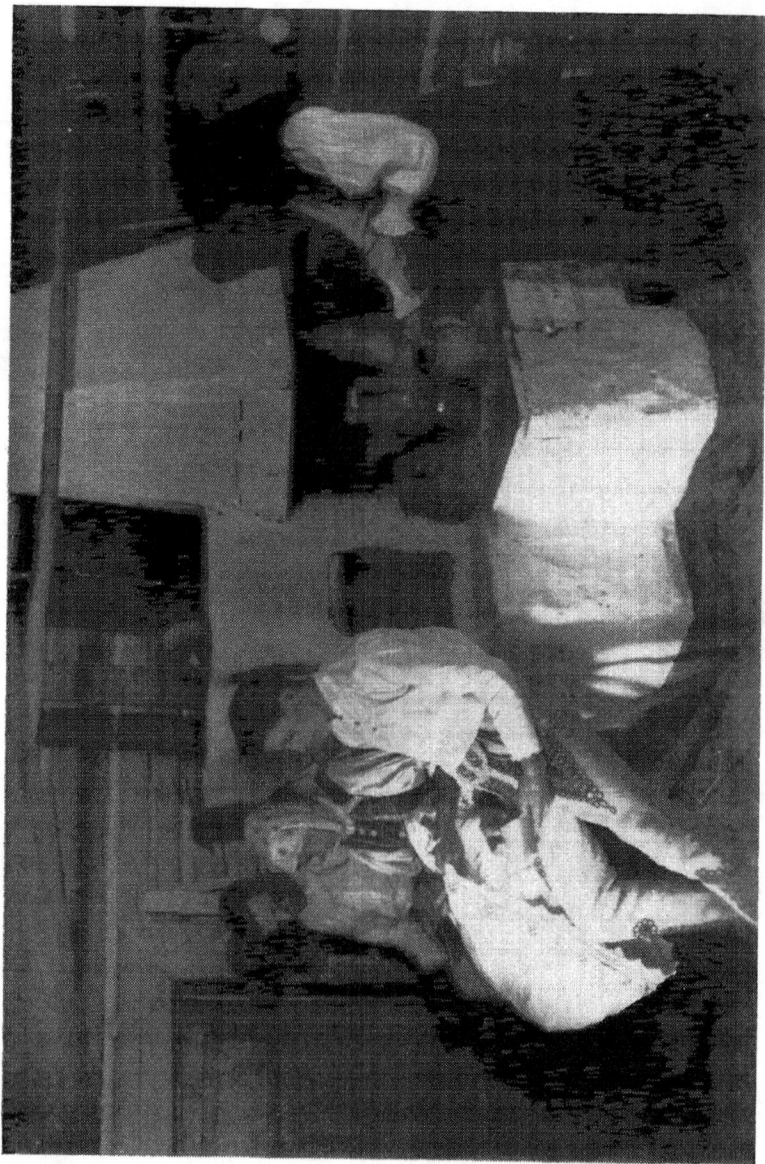

PEASANTS AT HOME

The living-room of a peasant farmstead in Slovakia.

is provided with alternative markets for those she has lost.

Despite the suggestion implied by the great efforts made, through agricultural circles, clubs, and special libraries, to instruct the peasants in modern farming principles, the standard of Hungarian husbandry, and the skilful care lavished on the broad acres of the Danubian plain, have long been a pattern and an inspiration to agriculturists throughout Eastern Europe.

The harvest of 1933 was excellent throughout the region, and would, in normal times, have enabled Hungary's rural population to pay their debts and attain a standard of living at least equal to that of 1914. Unfortunately 1933 was not a normal year, and the labour invested in those vast wheatfields brought no return in dividends. Both the 80 per cent of Hungary's peasants, who since the land reform carried out after the war have owned their holdings, and the 20 per cent who remain landless agricultural workers, benefited little from an average yield of twenty-eight bushels of wheat per Hungarian acre. True, food in general is cheap, and the peasants, whether owners or labourers, do not go hungry. On the other hand, the shortage of cash among the peasant classes is as acute as in neighbouring agricultural countries, and difficulty is experienced in renewing clothing or in purchasing any commodity for cash. Compared with the prosperous times of 1925 and the two following years, the standard of living has fallen by over 50 per cent, and it is to-day below the 1914 level. As elsewhere, poultry, dairy products, and eggs form the currency of the villages.

The dislocation of markets due to the Treaty of Trianon and the depression caused a reversal of the progress which Hungarian agriculture as a whole was making in the years immediately preceding 1929. During those years many farmers stocked their farms with modern equipment and raised their land to the maximum point of efficiency. When economic conditions changed a reaction set in, with the result that by 1934, although 50 per cent of the farms and smallholdings had electric light installed, the primary agricultural equipment had been very largely worn out and not replaced.

The same tendency was noticeable in the case of live-stock, many farmers being unable to maintain the number of animals purchased in better times, a fact which has tended to still further depress the market price of live-stock already lowered by high customs tariffs in most European countries.

The same conditions, arising out of similar factors, apply to other crops upon which the agriculturists, and especially the smallholders, depend for a substantial portion of their income. Maize, potatoes, sugar-beet, wine, vegetables, and poultry have all contributed to the fall in agricultural incomes.

There is, however, yet another factor, quite apart from either the world crisis or the mistakes of treaty-makers, which accounts for the undoubted poverty which the visitor finds in the Hungarian villages. Expert enquiry has revealed that twenty English acres is the minimum land necessary to form an economic unit capable of support-ing a family according to Hungarian standards. In the past the majority of smallholdings in Hungary have been below this minimum in extent, and the post-war land reform did not perceptibly change the average area of land owned by individual peasant families.

Hungary differs from most of the countries and regions discussed in this volume in that there still exist wide differences in the size of farms, holdings varying from "dwarf farms" of five acres up to estates of enormous extent. At one end of the agricultural scale are the jobbing labourers who hire their services to estate-owners while their families cultivate their own small plots, while at the other are the combined domains of the Esterhazy family, the various branches of which own a total of many hundreds of thousands of acres. The purely peasant class varies in its wealth and possession from the smallholder with five acres to the normally prosperous peasant farming 100 to 150 English acres of his own soil.

The total extent of arable land in present-day Hungary amounts to 13,860,000 Hungarian acres (a Hungarian acre is equivalent to 1.4 British acres). Of this total, 7,600,000 Hungarian acres, or about 55 per cent, are peasant holdings, while the rest are composed of estates. Prior to 1919 the area of the present Hungary represented by large estates was considerably greater. Following the war and the Bela Kun régime several laws were passed by the Hungarian Parliament, by which, partly in the form of a general property tax, and partly by expropriation, the government secured control over 1,259,613 Hungarian acres, equivalent to approximately 1,800,000 British acres, for the purpose of redistribution.

This land was utilized partly for the building of cottages to house war veterans and widows and orphans of the peasant class, for the creation of communal pastures, and for the formation of smallholdings. 692,011 acres were allocated to a total of 403,980 persons, as "dwarf" holdings, and a further 28,000 acres were reserved for the creation of nearly 300 model farms in all parts of the country. Expropriation of landed property was carried out by full payment of the value of the soil being made to the former holders at the actual market price. That the reform did not fully meet the requirements of the landless peasantry is shown by the fact that Hungarian official estimates admit that 20 per cent of the agricultural community was still landless at the beginning of 1934— a condition which is a natural corollary of the continued existence of the large estates with their semi-feudal conditions of labour.

The writer visited one such typical estate near Budapest, conditions on which were of a higher standard than those in more remote parts.

The highest paid worker on the estate was the manager, who had received £13 10s. a month in 1928, but whose salary had been cut to £3 10s. a month in the autumn of 1933. Day labourers on the estate were paid 1s. a day, while the regular male workers, who formed the bulk of the staff, received no cash wages whatever and were paid entirely in kind. This payment consisted of 1,600 kilogrammes of grain per year, twenty-four kilogrammes of salt, one pig with offspring, and the produce of three acres of arable land and of the garden attached to each cottage. In addition each worker received housing accommodation, electric light, and free fuel, and the services of a doctor when necessary. The wives and children were employed in the fields during the harvesting season and paid 1s. a day, the amount earned in this way representing the sole cash income of these families in the course of a year. The similarity between these conditions and those which existed in the Russian estates in Czarist days was heightened by the custom of extending to large families the right to take up and work extra land on a basis of one-third of the crop for themselves and two-thirds to the landowner.

The actual houses on this estate were of quite a reasonable standard of construction, being single-storey, plaster-and-thatch cottages, containing kitchen and either one or two additional rooms. In one of the houses, occupied by a labourer, his wife and six children, accommodation consisted of a small kitchen, in which hens were mothering their chicks in the warmth of a stove, and a bed-living-room containing three beds and a table at which four members of the family could sit simultaneously. The children took it in turns to sleep on the floor—two each night—and the family was living on a diet of bread and bacon-fat. The conditions pictured in the case of this home were reproduced in other cottages on the estate. All of them were, according to British standards, overcrowded, and in all of them there was an abundant supply of religious pictures and texts on the walls, reminding one that "a peasant people without belief in God is inconceivable, for they see what they consider His acts every day of their lives".

It should be emphasized that the conditions on this estate were definitely above the average of what remains of feudal Hungary. Nearer to the Rumanian frontier I found estate labourers living in straw and mud hovels consisting of a single room and in every way inferior to the corn barns alongside. All these landless workers, both in times of depression and abundance, share one common bond whatever their immediate conditions: they are tied to the estate on which they work and kept subservient by the necessity for retaining a home for their families, and their complete dependence on the employer is obvious.

The changing fortunes of a larger section of Hungary's rural population—the 55 per cent of smallholders—is illustrated by the earnings of a peasant family which farms fifteen Hungarian acres of good land—twelve acres of which are devoted to wheat and three acres to vegetables and fruit. The average yield of the wheatland is seven quintals per acre. Assuming the smallholder received the average price for wheat of 30s. per quintal in 1928 and 8s. at the beginning of 1934, and assuming that the peasant markets the whole of his wheat (actually the produce of at least two acres is stored for providing bread for his family), his gross income from this main crop would have been the equivalent of £36 in 1928 and £10 10s. in 1934!

Actually the latter cash sum was insufficient to pay interest on mortgage and annual taxes, hence the moratorium on agricultural debts which has now been in force in Hungary for over two years. More important than cash, however, that peasant, and tens of thousands of others farming about the same area, earn by their year's work all the food needed for their family except salt. Bread, bacon, poultry, vegetables, maize, lard, pork, and eggs were all produced on that smallholding, making it next to impossible accurately to measure the real income of that family in terms of currency.

It is, perhaps, as well that the urge to survive is strong within the hearts of mankind, for the lives of the peasant family are hard, even in Hungary. True, roads and railways are excellent—in vivid contrast to other agricultural nations—and medical and social services are highly developed. Education is compulsory up to the age of fourteen years, and abundant facilities exist for agricultural education. But tradition and habit ensure that those small two-room homes dotted about the Hungarian countryside shall be well filled. The average peasant family consists of the couple with from two to four children. Usually the grandparents, if living, share the home. As a rule the old peasant very seldom hands over the management of his farm to his son until he is entirely disabled for further work; old habits and the love of the soil die hard, and account for the fact that the average age of the Hungarian husbandmen is high.

During the spring and summer, all the adults, men and women, work from earliest dawn until sunset, with but short interruptions for meals brought by one member of the family to the field. During the winter work is at a standstill apart from tending the animals, and the time is utilized for cutting wood, making implements and embroideries, and basket-making.

In return for their labour, they enjoy the privilege which belongs to every peasant-owner—most of them go from the cradle to the grave without once buying a meal in their lives. Everything they need for sustenance is provided by the farm itself.

In a typical village community in the neighbourhood of Esztergom I visited both the homes of independent farm workers, employed on local estates but living in homes rented by themselves, and the village storekeeper. Both the men and women inhabiting the two-room cottages of this village were employed in the fields and vineyards of the neighbourhood and received the almost universal wage, in Hungary, of 1s. a day. They were living on bread, bacon, cabbage, potatoes and beans, with meat or chicken once a week. Agricultural unemployment was heavy in this little community of 2,600 people, as it was during 1933 in all parts of Hungary. For some months, until the money ran out, the workless were helped by public constructional works undertaken by the government. But these had stopped, and the workless were dependent for their maintenance upon the help of their families and the charity of their neghbours.

A very usual system of payment in this and other villages was for peasants to assist the owner of a field during the sowing and harvest season, the resultant crops being divided half to the owner and half to the peasants helping in the cultivation. Peasant clothes were noticeable for their absence—in Hungary near the urban centres the village

girls are slowly forsaking the picturesque traditional costumes in favour of the gaily coloured fabrics turned out
by the textile mills.

The story of this village was the story of the Hungarian
wine industry during the difficult years. Before 1928 the
wine produced in the vineyards through which I wandered
sold at from 10d. to 1s. 2d. per litre. In the autumn of 1933
the price had fallen to 2d. per litre. If wine constituted the
perfect diet those peasants would have been well fed.
With the gap between industrial and agricultural prices
steadily widening, and the rates of interest on mortgages
reduced only from an average of 13 per cent to 8
per cent, the standard of living had suffered a drastic
fall. The women were even making their own soap at home,
and the business at the village store was, the storekeeper
informed me, mainly confined to sugar, salt, matches,
tobacco, and oil. The storekeeper was himself too poor
to run up debts, but the co-operative shop, the only other
store in the village, was owed over £200 by that one small
community.

The village storekeeper in another village produced
his books to show the effects of the depression—and,
of course, the iniquitous tariff walls—on the fortunes of
his peasant customers. In 1929 he sold fifty kilogrammes
of sugar a month. In 1933 the amount had fallen to
fifteen kilogrammes. Sales of coffee had fallen by two-
thirds in the same three years, while the sales of confec-
tionery, a luxury, had fallen off to the extent of 75
per cent.

"The wealthy in this village are still eating meat twice a
week," the storekeeper informed me, "but the poorest are
living on a diet of bread and onions." The village was on
the banks of the Danube, a river which in pre-war days
at that point was as busy as the Rhine. Now, in the
fifteenth year of the Treaty of Trianon, it was empty from
bank to bank and from horizon to horizon. During two
days spent within sight of that noble stretch of water I saw
only one barge making its way south.

Tahi-Totfalu is a village of 2,500 inhabitants in the
fruit district outside Budapest. Its solitary co-operative

store, forming one of over 2,000 shops operated throughout Hungary by the *Hangya* Co-operative Society, is an excellently stocked shop with a manageress born and bred in the village to whose wants she now administers. What light do the account books of that store shed on the standard of living of this comparatively prosperous agricultural community, in which the largest farm is of eighty acres in extent, and the average holding of from eight to fifteen acres?

The turnover of this store was £400 a month in 1929, and £100 a month in 1933. "Our people", the manageress informed me, "are buying only 25 per cent of what they bought in 1928, and those purchases are confined to strict necessities. Fortunately prices are low here, and to the labourer who earns 1s. a day that sum means three meals of bread and one of bacon for his entire family. But they are much in debt, and as the bad times continue, and clothing and household utensils wear out, there is a noticeable decline in the well-being of the villagers."

Multiply those instances by the total number of peasant communities in present-day Hungary, and the effects of a 50 per cent fall in the value of everything that the agriculturist produces will stand starkly revealed, inviting Europe to provide an answer for the riddle of present-day Hungary.

That answer will not be provided by the passing of the world depression, for the plight of Hungarian agriculture antedates that visitation and will survive its passing. Wherein, then, lies the solution? Ask Admiral Horthy, and he will reply: "Revise the Treaty of Trianon." Ask the Hungarian government, and they will answer, "Give us back our lost lands." Ask the leaders of the Hungarian Smallholders' Party, which votes with the government, or of the Independent Smallholders' Party, which votes against the government, and the reply will be made in identical terms: "Repair the wrong done to Hungary by the Treaty." Ask the peasants themselves in their crowded two-room homes from which they go forth to long days in the fields—homes the poverty of which seems strangely removed from considerations of high

THE HEART OF THE PEASANT-LANDS
A village scene in Slovakia.

A HUTZULIAN WEDDING

Hutzulians—members of the Ukrainian nation—inhabiting the Carpathians, pose for their photograph after a village wedding.

politics—and the answer you will get will but echo the words of the Regent of that country : "Revise the Peace Treaty."

Whether or not a Hungary restored to her former glories would, *ipso facto*, mean better times for the peasants of that land is a moot point. Probably the economic Pacts, concluded at Rome in March 1934 between Italy, Austria, and Hungary, and aimed at encouraging the freer exchange of goods within the area of the three nations named, offer more solid and immediate hope of improved economic conditions to the Hungarian peasant than anything that can be hoped for, in the early future, from treaty revision. Nevertheless, the return of the ex-Hungarian lands will remain the alpha and omega of Hungarian policy ; the economic plight of that country has never raised the same depth of national feeling.

Viewed by independent eyes, other changes and reforms would seem to be needed before the people of Hungary can know real prosperity. A drastic lowering of tariff walls, not only to the limited extent foreshadowed by the Rome agreements, but, as laid down by the Stresa Resolutions, throughout Central and Western Europe, is the most important. A further and more radical distribution of land is needed, so that every one of those labourers working under almost feudal conditions in 1934 may have the opportunity to become economically independent. A world rise in the prices of agricultural products must be achieved to enable the Hungarian nation to pay its external interest and debts with the same quantity of agricultural produce that sufficed to discharge her obligations as a debtor in 1928. Some reform of the international credit system, and the relinquishment of exaggerated hopes which spread unrest in Central Europe—all these things must come to pass, and not only the revision of the territorial clauses of the Treaty of Trianon, before the rich Hungarian plains will again yield prosperity to the peasants of that nation.

It is, however, difficult to get a Hungarian peasant to admit as much. For economics and statistics are dry things,

M

and the wrong inflicted on Hungary is nearer home and never allowed to be forgotten. Moreover, Hungarians living in Transylvania, and other Hungarians from the lands ruled by the Serbian dictatorship, do at times go back to their homeland with news of the conditions of petty tyranny and persecution under which the Magyar "exiles" are living in Rumania and Yugoslavia to-day.

It is simple to answer that conditions are much the same in all the Eastern European countries. The writer, who has seen the eyes of a Hungarian peasant, living in Transylvania and compulsorily transformed into a Rumanian, light up on hearing news of Budapest, can at least understand the feelings which tug at Hungarian hearts when they think of those of their race now living under peoples who are definitely their inferiors. Peoples who, while cutting them off from their national and cultural heritage, have, except in the case of Czechoslovakia, nothing to offer them in return.

Having travelled not only from end to end of Hungary at the darkest moment of the world depression, but also from one end to the other of each of the lost territories, I can vouch for the fact that whereas the standard of husbandry in Hungary is steadily rising despite all handicaps, the standard of farming and the living conditions of the peasants in the ex-Hungarian regions, owing to neglect and maladministration, is just as steadily falling.

If that fact seems to support the hopes and desires of the whole Hungarian nation, and therefore appears to be suspiciously like Hungarian propaganda, I would point out that the responsibility for it rests not with an impartial observer, who is merely recording what he saw with his own eyes, but with those governments who have so gravely misused the opportunities to increase in stature, well-being, and contentment which the war brought them.

CHAPTER XIII

POLAND AND ITS PEASANTS

IT is always of interest to take stock of a country after a period of change. Poland has now been an independent Republic for fifteen years—years during which the Poles faced the task of reconstruction and consolidation after the war, a Bolshevik invasion, and, more recently, the world agricultural crisis.

The main problems confronting the rulers of the new Poland in 1919 were the future of agriculture and industry, the financial position, and the question of the minorities within the new state, especially their future relations with the six millions of Ukrainians forcibly incorporated in order to extend Poland's boundaries in the east.

The first three of these questions were legacies of the war and the territorial changes which brought Poland into being. Previous to 1914 the partitioning Powers (Russia, Austro-Hungary, and Germany) had absorbed at least 90 per cent of the agricultural products and manufactures of the Polish territory. With the re-emergence of an independent Poland those markets were closed. New markets had to be found for her goods and a living assured for a population numbering over 30,000,000 people. At the same time it was realized by the leaders of the new state that the real cause of the previous partition of the country had been due to divisions among the Polish people themselves—particularly to the rivalry between nobles and peasants.

One of the first tasks undertaken, therefore, was to enforce a measure of land reform which, in Poland Proper, went a long way to levelling up the inequalities between the estate-owners and the peasantry. Huge areas of land, formerly the property of the governing Powers, also came into the possession of the Republic, while the right of expropriation was used to draw further land into the area of redistribution, especially in Western Poland, formerly ruled by Prussia. In that area the new government utilized their legal rights to dispossess German landowners who refused to yield up their properties without compulsion. While undoubtedly the Poles of Pomerania lived under heavy handicaps during the German régime, in many instances the expropriation of land owned by those of German race had the complexion of an act of petty vengeance which created fresh wrongs in righting old ones.

The coming of the world depression enabled the government to carry a step further its plans for the conversion of large estates into smallholdings. In 1933 Count Zamoyski, possibly the largest landowner in Poland, was obliged to surrender 125,000 acres of land in lieu of settlement of overdue taxes, cash payment being impossible at the prices then ruling for agricultural products.

This Zamoyski family is reputed to have expended during the war at least one million pounds sterling on financing propaganda for a free Poland, and in disbursements for the maintenance of the Polish Legions in France. That fact did not save their broad acres when the Polish tax-collector was asked to wait for his money.

In the same way the Branicki family, owners of Jan Sobieski's palace at Willanow, were called upon to surrender a large tract of land. It is a somewhat surprising fact that the Polish government shows no gratitude towards these great hereditary families who in the past were responsible for the greatness of Poland—a greatness of which they are proud and which they take every opportunity of impressing upon the younger generation to-day.

Jan Zamoyski, founder of the family of that name, was the great chancellor of King Stephan Batory, possibly the greatest king Poland ever had, while Jan Sobieski, from whom the Countess Branicki is descended, nursed the nation to a pitch of military power which has never since been equalled, even under Marshal Pilsudski.

If this lack of gratitude for past services arose from a desire to improve the lot of the landless peasants the steps taken to dispossess such families could be placed on the credit side in an analysis of Poland's first fifteen years of new and vigorous national life. Evidence is not lacking, however, that the freeing of land for the peasantry is not the whole story. The treatment meted out by the Pilsudski Party to Jan Paderewski is even in Poland considered disgraceful, while the story of Witos, Poland's peasant leader and probably the greatest peasant figure in the world to-day, reveals the same ingratitude. Witos fought side by side with Pilsudski throughout the war, and while his career as Prime Minister was certainly not a success, for a variety of reasons, the subsequent persecution of this Polish patriot, ending only when he fled to Czechoslovakia for sanctuary, will remain a blot on Pilsudski's escutcheon.

Poland's ingratitude towards many of her greatest sons has, however, resulted in a measure of land reform greater than would have been achieved in other circumstances. Since 1919 more than 500,000 new farms have been established, enabling over three million additional people to be settled on their own holdings.

In 1930, the last "good year" for Polish farmers, that country exceeded the agricultural production of 1922 by 9,000,000 quintals of wheat, 15,000,000 quintals of rye, 3,000,000 quintals of barley, and 5,500,000 quintals of oats. Side by side with this "drive" for increased corn production, the government encouraged the development of stock-breeding. To-day Poland is the third largest pig-breeding country in Europe. Only Russia breeds more horses. She is fourth on the list of cattle-producing countries, and every year exports 50,000 tons of eggs collected from farms all over the country.

The oncoming world crisis dealt the resurgent agriculture of Poland a heavy blow. "Agriculture plays such an important part in the economic life of Poland that the effects of its depression cannot but be generally felt," stated M. Auguste Poplawski, chairman of the Crédit Foncier, in a report made to the Economic Committee of the League of Nations in 1931.* "The farmer who is deprived of his profits tends to restrict his own requirements and those of his business to a minimum. He only does what is strictly necessary and no longer devotes himself to the intensive cultivation of his land."

Two years later the position of Polish agriculturists showed no improvement. "The year was a disastrous one, and the financial plight of the agricultural community is about as bad as it could be. The index of agricultural prices is still at its lowest point since the depression began," stated the *Economist Commercial Review* of 1933.†

Such a state of affairs could not but have serious results for a nation in which half the total area of land is devoted to arable farms and 64 per cent of the total population engaged in agriculture. A nation in which, out of every pound's worth of exports, between 11s. and 12s. worth is accounted for by sales of agricultural produce or timber, industry providing only 40 per cent of the export trade.

In a very real sense, therefore, those 18,127,380 hectares of arable land within the frontiers of Poland constitute the real wealth of the country. That wealth is represented by food for the peasants and their families, by national revenue needed to maintain the swollen armed forces of the most militaristic state in all Europe, and to subsidize Polish industry, and—equally important —by reserves of man-power which can be called upon in times of national emergency.

The calls made upon the slender resources of the sturdy Polish peasantry are to-day more onerous than the demands which faced those same smallholders in days when they were citizens of Imperial Russia, and of the Austrian and German Empires—and free Poland was but a dream in the hearts of her children.

---

* *Agricultural Crisis.* Vol. i, p. 253.
† *Economist Commercial History of* 1933, February 17, 1934, p. 21.

The acid test for Polish agriculture is rye, the crop which provides bread for the rural population and the output of which exceeds, in good years, the requirements of the home market. The average price of rye at Warsaw fell by 60 per cent between 1928 and 1931, while the world price dropped still more steeply, so that by the latter year the price obtainable in the world market covered only about 60 per cent of the cost of production.

Despite efforts made by the government in Poland Proper to ameliorate conditions for the smallholders, the peasants were, at the beginning of 1934, in debt to the state and state institutions to the tune of over 4,000 million zlotys (about £100,000,000 at par). Taxes were heavily in arrears. Farms are constantly being sold up, and 99 per cent of all holdings are under mortgage to the state agricultural banks. The peasants had the bare necessities of continued life and nothing more.

Symptomatic of the losses sustained by producers is the fact that the rush for land which occurred during the early years of the Republic has ceased, and at the moment the authorities have far more land on their hands in the purely Polish territories than they know what to do with. Here may be mentioned a particularly sound piece of work which is being carried out in the draining of the Pripet marshes, an area of 7,500,000 acres of land, hitherto unproductive, in Polissia. This wasteland is being reclaimed, and it is hoped that when work is completed it will be possible to settle 200,000 families where formerly no blade of grass grew. Experiments already made on reclaimed areas suggest that the region may be suited to intensive dairy-farming, a branch of agriculture which is little developed. Unfortunately, this work of reclamation in a region inhabited by members of the Ukrainian race is being used as a pretext to settle Polish "colonists" in Polissia rather than to make land available for the native inhabitants.

In that little-known region bordering the Russian frontier life for the inhabitants is severe, especially during the long months of winter. No one who has not visited Polissia can visualize the privations endured by the population owing to the physical conditions of the land. At the end of each winter cattle are reduced to moving skeletons. Horses, having exhausted their winter supply of fodder, are propped up in their stalls in the hope that spring may arrive in time for them to be carried to the pastures before death releases them from their sufferings. The peasants themselves are often in little better plight; mere skeletons racked with fever and malaria, their clothes skins and rags and their foot-coverings of bark cut from trees.

Throughout Poland those peasants employed on the remaining large estates are paid partly in cash and partly in kind. There is also a regular scale of "purchase by barter" drawn up by local authorities which is enforceable at village shops. Thus 169 kilos of rye, or 33 kilos of pork, will purchase ten enamel cooking-pots, while 103 kilos of rye, or 22·6 kilos of pig, will purchase 10 kilos of soap.

It was hoped, at the time when the agrarian reforms were instituted, that it would prove possible to increase the income of the peasantry to a point at which they would prove the mainstay of Polish industry. Economists estimated that if every peasant were provided with the means of spending an extra 30s. a year on manufactured goods the results would mean boom conditions for the factories of the Polish state. Unfortunately, the crisis has turned such comforting calculations into idle dreams; the standard of living among the agricultural population is to-day as low as any in Europe. The village hall is, except in the more highly developed Ukrainian regions under Poland, the exception rather than the rule. Cinemas, of which there are less than 500 in the whole country, are non-existent so far as the majority of the population is concerned. Roads are in an appalling condition. Education has been developed in Poland Proper, but it is doubtful if, even in the most favoured regions, facilities have kept pace with the growing thirst for knowledge of the peasants.

Taxation remains at an oppressive level, making the poor peasant poorer, and preventing progressive spirits among the large landowners from doing anything to improve the lot of their workers. I asked an official of the Polish Ministry of Finance if he could give me a list of all the taxes demanded of the peasant and estate-owners. "It is impossible," he answered. "I do not know the answer to that question myself, and it would take days to get the facts." He volunteered the information, however, that less than 5 per cent of the farm holdings in the eastern, southern and central regions were paying their way at the present time, and added that every quintal of grain sold on the markets is being produced at a net loss of from six to eight zlotys. Even so, the actual facts prove that official to be an optimist!

Many of the farmers still make a small profit from the breeding of pigs for the bacon industry, and from cattle-raising, those being the only branches of Polish agriculture which have yielded any profit whatever during the past three years. The cattle and pig breeders are now losing their favoured position owing to the introduction of quotas in many of the countries which were, in the past, Poland's best customers for animal products.

The average profits of the "middle" class of peasants, owning from 25 to 40 acres apiece, amounted to 143 zlotys in 1929, and were replaced by a net loss of 947 zlotys in 1931. The average loss incurred by all classes of food producers, from the smallest to the largest, in the latter year, amounted to 664 zlotys—a figure which makes manifest the plight of the rural population.

Despite the critical position of her greatest industry, Poland has by means of an elaborate system of export stimulants, preferential railway rates, subsidies, bounties, credit guarantees and the rest, managed to show a favourable trade balance for each of the past four years. The profit on the total foreign trade, both industrial and agricultural, was (in millions of zlotys) 411 in 1931, 222 in 1932, and 133 in 1933, the figure for the last-named year being made possible only by the fact that exports to Britain greatly exceeded imports from this country.

It was, nevertheless, found necessary to resort to a large internal loan in October 1933, the subscribing of which reminded observers of the collection of monies in Palestine in the days of the Romans.

Every citizen was expected to subscribe according to his or her means and no one was permitted to escape. Tax-collectors made a schedule of citizens owing unpaid income tax, and then those figuring on the lists were politely invited to subscribe to the loan for amounts in proportion to the amount of taxes overdue. Refusal to do so was met with the intimation that no leniency would be shown in the matter of tax arrears.

Civil servants were obliged to devote one month's salary to the loan, as did all government employees and officers of the armed forces. At special meetings of these classes, convened in order to approve subscriptions totalling one month's salary per person, the loan was unanimously supported—a fact scarcely surprising, as it had become known that any opposition would mean dismissal.

The result was eminently satisfactory to the government, the total subscriptions amounting to 340,000,000 zlotys. But the manner in which that sum had been attained did little credit to Poland, and was responsible for a number of stories revealing the cynicism with which the Polish people viewed the operation.

It was reported at Warsaw, for example, that a man had been found dead with a placard pinned to his chest bearing the letters "P.N." These letters stood for *Pożyczka Narodowa* ("National Loan"), but they were interpreted by unwilling subscribers to the loan as meaning *Pod Naciskiem* ("Under the Screw"). Again, on the evening of November 11, 1933, a statue commemorating Poland's fallen heroes was unveiled. This represented a gladiator stricken to death in the arena raising himself on his elbow to draw his last breath. The ribald people of Warsaw declared that it represented the Polish people dying under the burden of taxation.

It should, in fairness to the government, be added that the disturbed financial conditions in other countries, and the growing confidence of the Poles in their own currency, caused a rise in Polish government securities following the issue of this loan. Bonds offering a yield of 15 per cent in the autumn of 1933 were selling on a 10 per cent basis by February 1934,* with the result that many of those who had subscribed unwillingly to the National Loan of 1933 decided that after all they had made a good investment.

The Polish peasants may well wish that their own fortunes could be linked more directly with that of their government, for the problem of credit facilities has dogged the footsteps of the peasantry ever since the days, following the war, when the destruction wrought over the Polish lands was liquidated almost entirely out of the resources of the smallholders themselves. From that effort, which exhausted the resources of countless small farmers, Polish agriculture has never completely recovered. Debts piled up, and the impoverishment of both state and people prevented their conversion into long-term loans. In 1931 the amount of such long-term agricultural indebtedness amounted to 42 million dollars, whereas in 1914 the long-term indebtedness of the same territory had been over 410 million dollars.

The shortage of capital placed the peasantry at the mercy of moneylenders and forced them to sell their produce immediately following each harvest, regardless of the prices obtained, thus aggravating the subsequent depression.

The remedy for this unsatisfactory financial condition of the countryside is, obviously, for the government to take over the debts and replace them with national mortgages granted at reasonable interest. Only thus can the costs of production be reduced. But shortage of capital resources has prevented the government from coming to the rescue of the men upon whom, in the last analysis, the prosperity of the Polish nation ultimately rests. True, in February 1930 the government agreed to defer payments of taxation, and loans due from farmers amounting to 200,000,000 zlotys, but this measure did little to relieve a desperate situation, and it is clear that

---

* *Economist,* February 3, 1934.

debts will remain the bugbear of the majority of peasant homes in that country during the years immediately ahead.

Unfortunately, the Polish character is not such as to excite sympathy with the plight into which the world depression has landed the most important section of the nation.

The besetting sin of the Pole is chauvinism. A century and a half ago, before the partition of their country, that race had a glorious historical tradition to remind them of their greatness. During the period of captivity they excited the sympathy and admiration of the world. To-day they cannot forget that they are the salt of the earth. Having obtained their independence despite taking up arms against the very Powers which made their freedom possible, they have the *toupet* to scoff at their liberators and consider them as pawns in the Polish political game. Every Pole with whom the writer has ever talked considered that any Englishman, Scot, Welshman, Frenchman, or American would be privileged if allowed to adopt Polish nationality! Yet those same Poles have no gratitude in their natures, either as a nation or individually. Confronted with their national pride, or their exasperation over the simple fact that the Ukrainians of Eastern Galicia prefer to remain Ukrainians instead of assessing Polish nationality at its true worth, as estimated by Warsaw, one is reminded of Sydney Smith's remark that "gratitude is a sense of favours to come". In the Polish Press one comes repeatedly upon a perversion of Cavour's remark: *Italia fara di se*—but with *Polonia* interpolated for *Italia.*

Their spleen at the beginning of 1934 was mostly vented against France, the nation which has done more for them than any other—in money, men, ammunition, and in the diplomatic world. But their ingratitude to the United States is equally black. It was the relief rushed to Poland by Hoover which saved that nation from Bolshevism and starvation. To-day the Polish peasant, instructed by his "betters", will inform you that the supplies which America sent were rotten and were

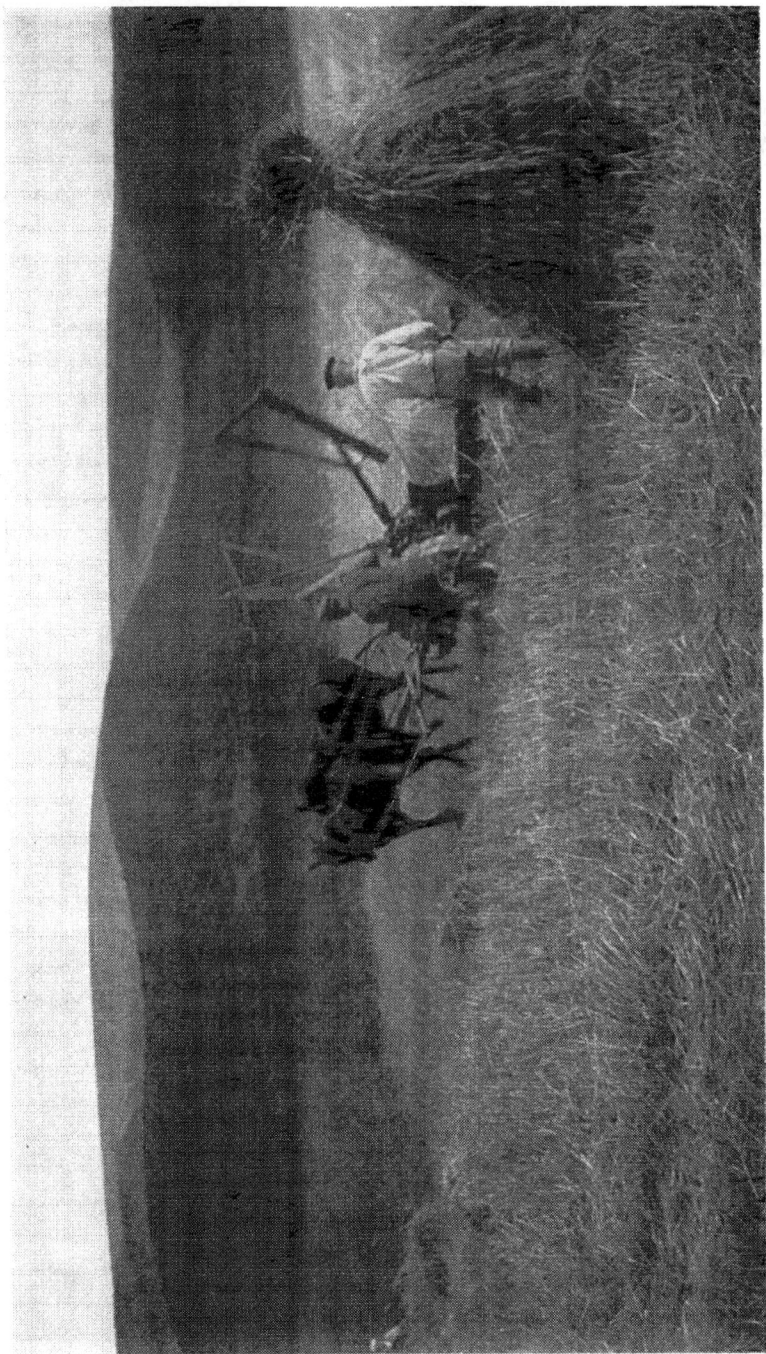

"SWORDS INTO PLOUGHSHARES".

Gathering the harvest on a former battlefield near Novogrodek, in Poland.

WHERE POVERTY IS UNIVERSAL.

Peasant women outside their wooden homes in a village "street" near Bialystok, Poland.

dumped on the Poles to get rid of them, and that Poland was charged an exorbitant sum in good dollars for this "relief".

Until recently Germany was, however, the *enfant terrible*. Nothing that that nation did was right. They were held up as perjurers and liars. The failure to ratify the Commercial Treaty of 1931 was taken as a direct insult to Poland. It was not until Hitler came into power, and the shadow of a Nazi *revanche* loomed over the diplomatic scene, that Poland made a friendly gesture to her western neighbours.

The man behind this policy of intransigence, and whose person typifies the chauvinism of the whole nation, is Marshal Pilsudski, virtual dictator of the country, and idol of industrialists and peasants alike. The fact that a whole nation of food producers, reduced to beggary, have blamed every conceivable "villain of the piece" except the man who is their virtual ruler must be almost unique in the story of modern Europe. Nevertheless, the fact is true, and must be recorded. Pilsudski is easily the most popular man in all Poland; it is doubtful whether any other national leader, not excluding Hitler, is so popular in his own country as this old, tired, Polish patriot who got the fever of Polish might into his blood during the years of captivity and has never been able to get it out again.

Pilsudski is more popular than any film star, and the receptions accorded to him on the rare occasions when he is seen in public would make Greta Garbo jealous. The public trust him implicitly, even though they do not trust the gang of politicians and industrialists around him.

It is one of the tragedies of Poland that this national leader is almost completely out of touch with his people. Although the papers are read to him every day, he learns little from them of what the Polish people are thinking, for they contain no news unfavourable to the government. And the condition of the people, and especially of the peasants, does not seem to worry the "big hats" of that government overmuch.

Colonel Slawek, twice Premier, and next to Pilsudski the most powerful man in Poland to-day, is more concerned to make Poland invincible in the military sphere than in mitigating the appalling conditions in which more than half the people of that state are living.

The threat to policies which would again expose the Polish people to the risk of slaughter on the battlefield will come, if it comes, not from the group dominated by Colonel Slawek and his cronies which meets at the Café Europejska in Warsaw each evening, but from the country districts that would be called upon to provide the cannon-fodder. Already, in the south-eastern districts, peasant risings have taken place and been suppressed with great ferocity. Warsaw only hears that, perhaps, eight persons have been killed for firing on the police, when the actual figures of casualties are well over a hundred.

Jew-baiting as a pastime is spreading, and the fact that the peasantry are still suffering from the usurious rates charged by the Jews for loans will cause it to grow year by year. This Jewish question has, indeed, been called "the greatest minority problem in Poland".

Next to the Jewish problem, which affects every region of Poland, and has been intensified by the presence of many refugees from Germany, the denial of justice and the disregarding of pledges given to the Ukrainians of the eastern territories—a nation within a nation, numbering over six million peasants—is the question which promises to exercise the most profound influence upon Polish internal affairs. Those Ukrainians remain united in spirit with their blood-brothers living in ad-joining lands, and are determined to resist by any and every means the aspirations of Polish chauvinists, who are quite unequal to the mental strain of understanding why anyone fortunate enough to be living in their brave new Poland should not wake up each morning with the words "Long live Pilsudski!" on his lips.

Poland faces other racial and foreign problems. Many even of the Polish inhabitants of Pomerania and Pomorze, former German territories, have assured me that life was far happier under the Reich, and taxation less oppressive. The relations of Poland with Lithuania over Vilna have long been an open scandal—a scandal which Pilsudski cannot now end by compensating Lithuania at the expense of East Prussia as he is known to have contemplated before the *rapprochement* between Poland and Germany.

Soviet Russia lies in uncomfortably close proximity to Warsaw, while Herr Hitler's reputed aims of eastward expansion do not lighten the task which faces Poland's diplomats.

Of all these problems, however, the most crucial is likely to prove the harvest gathered by Polish chauvinism in the lands peopled by peasants of Ukrainian race which now form the eastern regions of that country.

Adjoining those other Ukrainian regions under Soviet Russia, Rumania, and Czechoslovakia, and united to them by stronger ties than any that governments can forge—bonds of common brotherhood and common struggle against oppression going back for centuries— the Ukrainians at present living under Polish rule have, and always will have, more in common with those other submerged territories than with Warsaw. The eyes of the Ukrainian people of Eastern Galicia look east, not west. They are a separate nation forming an integral part, not of the Polish Republic that oppresses them, but of the Greater Ukraine—the nation that nobody knows. Let us, therefore, turn from Pilsudski's Poland to consider the post-war history and conditions of the Ukrainian peoples as a whole.

CHAPTER XIV

THE NATION THAT NOBODY KNOWS

LOOK for the Ukrainian state on the map of Europe and you will not find it. Yet there is abundant evidence that the Ukraine still exists, six hundred years after the independent Ukrainian dynasty disappeared from Europe, and nearly two centuries after the last autonomous Ukrainian state, allied to the Russian Empire, was annexed by that nation in 1764. Between the Pripet River in the north, and the old frontier of Rumania in the south ; between Przemysl and the River San in the west and the River Don in the east, there are living to-day a homogeneous population of some forty millions of Ukrainians.

Those Ukrainians, more numerous than the Poles, more virile and cultured than the Rumanians, more loyal to their national ideals even than the Czechs, form the most romantic nation in Europe—the nation that nobody knows.

Distributed by the post-war settlements between Soviet Russia, Poland, Rumania, and Czechoslovakia— with more than half their population included within the boundaries of Red Russia—without any prominent national leaders to appeal on their behalf at the bar of world opinion, treated as troublesome "minorities" by governments aggrandized by the peace treaties, or flayed by the Bolshevist flail, the Ukrainian people have, by their energy, initiative, and loyalty to their ideals, shown how strong is the instinctive unity of their race.

Enjoying independence under their own princes from about the year A.D. 800 until 1340, when the Polish king Kazimir the Great occupied Eastern Galicia and extinguished Ukrainian freedom, for generations the Ukrainian people have clung with more devotion and stubbornness to their national ideals than any other submerged people in Europe. For centuries, Pole, Muscovite, and Austrian sought by every means available to autocracies to extinguish the spark of Ukrainian nationalism, without success. The end of that period found the Ukrainian peasants holding fast to their own language, their own culture, and their desire for freedom. The Russian and Austrian Empires passed, the map of Europe was redrawn. Still no independent Ukraine appeared to symbolize the age-long struggle of that race for the right to control their own destinies.

That struggle is waged with non-violent "weapons" by each separate branch of the Ukrainian family. The traveller to Lemberg, or Brest-Litovsk, Czernowitz, or Kishinev will find the Ukrainians united by the same bonds of language and culture. They are among the most skilled husbandmen in Europe. Ninety per cent or more are peasants, tilling the soil and content with the rewards thereof. One hundred per cent of them cherish in their hearts the hope that the day of deliverance from alien rule will come, and the Ukrainian family will be united and independent—free at last from the bondage of alien rule.

That day nearly came in 1919. In that year, when the map-drawing season was in full swing in Europe, many Ukrainians believed that, at last, with the collapse of the Austrian and Russian Empires, the servitude of centuries was about to be ended and the Ukrainian nation would reappear on the maps of post-war Europe. Events decided otherwise, but it is the opinion of the writer that the formation of an independent Ukrainian State was only postponed; a nation numbering forty-three millions of people, united by common bonds of history, language, culture, and purpose, is unlikely to remain submerged indefinitely under the rule of more backward peoples.

On the day that Europe's largest and most homogeneous minority attains the status of nationhood, a dramatic change will be seen in the maps of Eastern

N

Europe. The area populated by the Ukrainian race totals nearly 750,000 square kilometres, or over three times the area of Great Britain.* The existing frontiers, under which members of the Ukrainian race are distributed between four nations, are entirely political, and correspondent to no divisions—ethnographical, economic, or social—in the Ukrainian family. The peasant belonging to the Ukrainian territory now under Soviet Russia speaks the same language, is a member of the same Church (distinct from both the Russian Orthodox and the Roman Churches), and bases his philosophy on the same democratic conception of life as the Ukrainian peasant tilling the soil in the Bukovina, or the peasant who pays his taxes to the Polish government in Eastern Galicia. Moreover, so brightly does the flame of nationality burn throughout the Ukrainian regions that, after centuries of subjection, peasant disputes are often settled by the judgment of the head-man of the village according to the ancient laws of the Ukrainian peoples handed down from the days of independent Ukraine. Only in Southern Ireland does there exist the same reverence for the historical past ; the peasant in Western Ireland, just as the peasant in Eastern Galicia, refuses to recognize changes wrought by alien rulers, and doffs his hat to the descendant of native chieftains who may be as poor as himself.

The forty-three millions of Ukrainian race alive to-day are distributed in the Ukrainian territories, and abroad, as follows :

---

* This figure is made up as follows:

	Square Kilometres.
Ukrainian territories within the Union of Socialist Soviet Republics, including the Soviet Ukraine, the Central Black Soil area, the North Caucasian area, etc.	582,584
Poland (Eastern Galicia, Volhynia, and Polissia)	121,041
Rumania (Bukovina and Ukrainian part of Bessarabia)	17,264
Czechoslovakia (Podkarpatska Rus)	14,673
	735,562

Ukraine under Soviet Russia ..	25,364,000*
U.S.S.R outside Ukrainian Soviet Republic	8,450,000
Rumania (Bukovina and Bessarabia)	1,160,000†
Czechoslovakia (Podkarpatska Rus and Slovakia)	550,000‡
Ukraine under Poland	6,876,000§
Canada	430,000
Elsewhere, including U.S.A. and Far East	1,000,000

The territories peopled by this peasant race are among the most fertile in all Europe: the Ukrainian lands now under the Soviet Union and the plains of the Central Black Earth region of Russia yielded up the fruits of the soil in such abundance in pre-war times that these regions were known as "the Granary of Europe". To the richness and fertility of their lands may perhaps be traced the fate which has kept the Ukrainians in subjection for centuries, and caused both their numbers and their homes to be decimated in wars between rival alien peoples who desired to secure or retain the rich prize which the Ukrainian territories represented in the pre-war world.

Wheat, maize, sugar-beet—but above all wheat—these crops the Ukrainian lands have poured out in

---

* According to official Soviet statistics for 1931, which show that 80 per cent of the total population of the Soviet Ukraine are Ukrainians. Of the balance, 9·2 per cent are Russians and 5·4 per cent Jews. The Ukrainian Socialist Soviet Republic comprises about 20 per cent of the total population of the U.S.S.R.

† Official Rumanian statistics give a lower figure, but these are suspect for political reasons.

‡ This territory was included in Czechoslovakia after the war by agreement with Ukrainian organizations in the United States and the Great Powers. Official Czech statistics give the total population of the Podkarpatska Rus territory as 725,350. About 70 per cent are, therefore, of Ukrainian nationality.

§ The Polish census of 1931 showed a Ukrainian population within the Polish frontiers of only 4,800,000, but this is almost certainly an under-estimate, due to the methods by which the census was taken. For instance, the census of 1921 recorded only 2,680,550 Ukrainians in Eastern Galicia, whereas the Austrian census of 1910 for the same region recorded a figure of 3,208,092 Ukrainians. Taking into account both war losses and increase in population, the influence of political considerations upon the Polish figures can clearly be seen.

abundance throughout the last century and before. Rich mineral resources—coal, iron, manganese ore, and oil—exist, and have recently been developed by the states in control.*

In addition to this fertility and mineral wealth, the Ukraine occupies a strategic geographical position, dominating the Black Sea area, and lying across the natural highway from west to east, which invests it with a pivotal position in the European balance of power.

The prize was, indeed, so rich that only a strongly armed and aggressive people could have maintained their position against the rising tide first of Muscovy in the north and Poland in the west, and, later, of the expansionist policies of Czarist Russia, on the one hand, and the Habsburg Empire on the other. The Ukrainians —and this was the real cause of their misfortunes— were neither warlike nor aggressive; they were and are one of the most cultured and democratic peasant races in Europe, desiring only to be allowed to live on their own territories undisturbed. To that fact they owe their early disappearance from the map of Europe. Placed between the upper millstone of the Russian Empire and the nether millstone represented by Poland, and, later, Austria, the Ukrainians lost first their independence, then their autonomy, and finally their national unity. The creators of a great empire, and the cradle of an early civilization far superior to that existing in the lands surrounding them, fell prey to more powerful neighbours, and "disappeared from history" to endure generations of serfdom.

With their "disappearance" began the romantic fight, waged without weapons but never abandoned until this day, for the resurrection of the Ukrainian nation. That irredentist problem, indeed, played a prominent part in the politics of Eastern Europe in the years immediately

---

* According to official Soviet statistics, between 20 and 25 per cent of the entire agricultural production of the U.S.S.R., nearly one-fifth of all the industries of the Union, over 55 per cent of the metals, 76 per cent of the coal, 89 per cent of the coke. 77 per cent of the iron ore, and 80 per cent of the sugar produced within the Soviet Union are found in the regions of that country populated by the Ukrainian race.

before 1914, and remains still, fifteen years after a post-war "settlement" which ignored every relevant fact, the most important of many factors responsible for the unsettled condition of that part of the world.

Under the growing might of the Russian and Austrian Empires, which had absorbed the Ukrainian territories, not only the right of nationality, but even the Ukrainian language, was suppressed. In 1863 a Russian Minister of the Interior declared that the Ukrainian nation and the Ukrainian language alike "never has existed, does not exist, and never can exist". Thus began a conspiracy designed to refute even the elementary fact of the very existence of the Ukrainian people.

The ambitious statesmen of the two Empires found little difficulty in denying even the plainest fact. Since in the interests of Russian and Austrian unity it was necessary, nothing was simpler than to deny the existence of a people whose leader, the Cossack hetman Bohdan Khmelnitzky, had been one of the prominent free rulers of Europe during the seventeenth century, as the correspondence which passed between the Ukrainian Cossack state and Oliver Cromwell, still preserved, records.

To smother and defeat the repeated attempts of the Ukrainians to secure control of their own affairs, which it would have been inconvenient to grant, all that was necessary was to deny that such a thing as a Ukrainian existed! So, until 1914, the Ukrainians living under Austria in Eastern Galicia and elsewhere were labelled "Ruthenians", while the Czars insisted that the inhabitants of the Ukraine under Russia were "Little Russians".

The new and recently aggrandized states which have become the successors of the vanished Empires have profited by their example : in the Ukraine under Poland to-day you will find it very difficult to meet many Ukrainians if you rely upon the authorities for guidance, despite the fact that a great Ukrainian co-operative movement exists side by side with numerous Ukrainian newspapers. And despite the further fact that some six and three-quarter millions living in that country habitually speak the Ukrainian language in daily life. It is so much more convenient, perhaps, for a government which has broken its twice-pledged promises to grant autonomy to the Ukrainian regions merely to seek refuge in the statement that many of the Ukrainians are actually "Ruthenians" —a nation which, like Ruritania, never existed outside the fertile imaginations of nineteenth-century statesmen !

If anything could explode once and for all the declarations of interested politicians, it would be the history of the Ukrainians at the moment when, following the downfall of both the Russian and the Austrian Empires, the recognition of their claim to nationhood seemed in sight.

"Europe's Unknown Nation" had, when 1914 dawned, long been waging an heroic struggle for survival as a racial unit against two of the most powerful Empires in the world. The unifying and centralizing policy of the Czars, and the repressive policies of Austria, had alike failed to break the Ukrainian will. Every effort to turn Ukrainians into Russians had failed. Unknown as are the details of that struggle to the Western world, no greater or more heroic fight has ever been waged by a conquered people against their alien overlords in the whole history of Europe. Two hundred years after the last autonomous Ukrainian state disappeared from the map the Ukrainian of Kiev felt a greater affinity with his brother of Kishinev, in Bessarabia, or of Lemberg, under Austria, than he did with the Russian from Moscow or Tsaritsin. The Ukrainian peasant living in the Bukovina might have been a citizen of Austria, but in his heart he was still a member of the Ukrainian race, looking upon the Austrian official as a foreigner, and upon the Ukrainian from Russia as a brother in adversity.

Chaos swept over Russia in 1917, and with it came the opportunity for which generations of Ukrainians had waited. A Ukrainian Republic was proclaimed at Kiev, and when, a year later, the Austrian Empire followed the Russian Empire into dissolution, the Ukrainian provinces of Austria proclaimed their independence in a Western Ukrainian Republic, and, on January 22, 1919, announced their union with their Russian brothers in the nation of Great Ukraine. On that day the blue and yellow national colours of the Ukrainian people were once more seen in Eastern Europe, and forty millions of people heralded the day of liberation.

The new Powers that rose out of the ruins of the old Empires proved, however, quite as predatory as had the Muscovite and Polish nations at an earlier day. The war, indeed, while it had placed Eastern Europe in the crucible, had actually strengthened some of the forces most antagonistic to a free Ukraine, notably the Polish landowners in Galicia, a class which had, under Austria, consistently opposed every whisper of reform in that province. The Poles, now raised to the dignity of a nation, were too blinded by their chauvinism to recognize the claims of others to justice or freedom when these claims clashed with the interests of the Polish Republic. Nor did the Rumanians, whose own bondage was sufficiently recent, one would have thought, to suggest sympathy with other races in a similar plight, behave any better. The dictates of wisdom, statesmanship, and justice were alike disregarded in favour of extending the boundaries of "Greater Rumania" by any and every means available.

In these circumstances, it was a matter of days before the newly announced Ukrainian Republic was fighting for its life. It fought so doughtily for survival that, had the rulers of the world not been overwhelmed with other and greater problems during that time, the spectacle of this democratic and liberty-loving peasant race, isolated amid hostile nations, lacking in equipment, munitions and supplies, resisting not for months, but for years, the forces of annihilation on a series of fronts, might well have convinced the architects of the new Europe that some recognition was due to Ukrainian national claims.

Great and urgent as were the problems confronting the peacemakers gathered at Paris, the stubborn defence of their claim to independence put up by the Ukrainian people did not pass unnoticed there. The British delegation at the Conference, especially, openly favoured independence for the peoples bordering upon Soviet Russia, and especially for the Ukrainians. Had the British view found support, much unrest which exists in Eastern Europe to-day would never have arisen, and the Ukrainian race would have been making their contribution to the peace and stability of that area as a rich and prosperous "buffer"-state between Soviet Russia and the West.

Those were, however, the days when the military adventurer and the freebooter brought off surprising *coups*, and discovered the fatal secret that if one could arrange a *fait accompli* it stood a very good chance of being accepted, and the loot left in the secure possession of those bold enough, and determined enough, to seize it.

While the battle of words continued at Paris, therefore, it was the sword and the cannon that were writing history in the eastern regions of Europe. And the principal victims of the era of freebootery were the Ukrainians. Unable to withstand pressure from all sides ; armed only with a just cause and the patriotism in their hearts, the Ukrainian Republic disappeared from the map of post-war Europe before the first of those maps was drawn.

In 1923, Greater Ukraine capitulated to the forces of Communist Russia, and became a member of the Union of Soviet Socialist Republics : the strong national feeling of the Ukrainians in that territory preventing the Russians from robbing it of its identity.

The region inhabited by Ukrainians west of the Soviet frontier—Eastern Galicia, Volhynia and Polissia—fared even worse. It was occupied by the newly created Polish armies as early as 1919, on the now well-tried method of presenting the Great Powers with a *fait accompli*, and, despite demands from Paris that the Polish troops should withdraw from territory to which they had no racial or other right, the Poles refused to quit, proceeding to consolidate their hold on the conquered lands.

Better informed than were other delegations, the British representatives at Paris urged that a High Commissioner should be appointed to protect Ukrainian interests, a solution which would at least have provided that people with a neutral "observer" to give evidence on their behalf during the fateful years ahead. This modest demand was rejected, however, as was a further proposal contained in a "Statute for Eastern Galicia" which would have accepted Polish occupation of this territory for a fixed term of twenty-five years, subject to a measure of autonomy being introduced at an early date.

Throughout the diplomatic discussions which followed, the Poles, assured of French support, refused to withdraw, even though they had not the hardihood, before that assembly of the world's statesmen, to pretend that the territories occupied by their armies were inhabited by "Ruthenians " ! On the contrary, while grimly holding to their gains, they offered to guarantee a liberal measure of "Home Rule" for the Ukrainian people thus brought within their borders—thereby setting the diplomatic stage for one of the most cynical and flagrant betrayals in history.

It being clear that nothing short of armed intervention could secure the withdrawal of the Polish armies, and none of the war-weary nations being willing to assume the task, the *impasse* was finally ended by a decision taken at the Conference of Ambassadors in 1923, by which the Ukrainians of Eastern Galicia were left to their fate within the State ruled by their ancient foes, the Poles : not, however, before the representatives of that nation had implemented their promises of Home Rule by signing a treaty which recognized, in the words of Mr. Bonar Law, then Prime Minister, "that the ethnographical conditions make autonomy necessary in that region".

Fate was no kinder to those Ukrainians who formed 99 per cent of the population of the Northern Bukovina, and a great part of the inhabitants in the former Russian province of Bessarabia. As these territories adjoined areas occupied by peasants of Rumanian extraction, it was perhaps natural that statesmen at Bucarest should, without worrying overmuch about the rights of other people, include them in their vision of "Greater Rumania".

The fact that in 1918 the Ukrainian section of the Bukovina had declared its union with the West Ukrainian
Republic, and that, subsequent to the Russian revolution,
Bessarabia proclaimed its independence as a Democratic
Moldavian Republic, while the overwhelmingly Ukrainian
parts of that province desired to be incorporated in the
newly formed Great Ukraine, governed from Kiev, did
not deter the Rumanian government from carrying its
plans into effect. After all, had not the Poles shown how
it could be done ? And who would say that the Rumanians
were slow to learn the art of the freebooter when rich
territories were waiting to be seized?

Once more democratic ideals proved powerless against
aggression reinforced by bayonets. The Rumanian troops
first occupied, and later annexed, the whole Bukovina,
and simultaneously occupied the province of Bessarabia.
By the Treaty of Paris, signed on December 9, 1919, the
Great Powers formally recognized both these territories
as Rumanian. Soviet Russia did not prove so amenable,
and upon maps hanging up at Moscow one may still find
Bessarabia shown as Russian territory, with the inscription "In Rumanian military occupation", but the U.S.S.R.
had too many troubles at home to contest the issue, and
with the signing of a pact of non-aggression between
Moscow and Bucarest in 1933, that Power may be said
to have accepted the *status quo* which planted the
Rumanian colours on the right bank of the Dniester
River, and transformed "green Kishinev" into a Rumanian
provincial capital.

In none of the territories outlined above, be it noted,
were the desires or wishes of the population taken into
account, either by the predatory Powers or by the statesmen who eventually accepted the new frontiers. On the
contrary, in the Ukraine under Russia, Eastern Galicia,
Bukovina, and Bessarabia alike, the Ukrainian populations
had given clearest possible evidence of their desire for
self-government by bringing autonomous Ukrainian
governments into being at the earliest opportunity.
Those governments were suppressed, and their leaders
killed or imprisoned, not by the action of the peoples

whom they represented, but by foreign bayonets. The disappearance, once more, of the independent Ukraine corresponded to no change in the opinion of the Ukrainian peasants, but was due to foreign invasion : the Ukrainians, lying in the track of the world war, with their menfolk weary after four years of fighting with the Russian and Austrian armies, and unable to secure munitions or other means of defending their national rights, capitulated to hunger and machine-guns.

The free governments dissolved, but the aspirations which had brought them into being remained unsatisfied, and have continued to grow more intense from that day to this. "We were weak in 1919, and we believed President Wilson when he said that he intended to make the world safe for democracy," said a Ukrainian leader to me recently. "Next time we shall be strong. And we shall make no mistake."

Out of over forty millions of Ukrainians in Eastern Europe, only half a million were consulted, even by proxy, concerning their desires. The rest were handed over, like cattle, to the tender mercies of the armies which had camped on their peasant fields and occupied their cities. The solitary exception was the case of the 550,000 Ukrainians who occupy the territory known as Podkarpatska Rus. Formerly Hungarian, and lying west of the Bukovina, the destination of this territory was settled in agreement with the Ukrainian emigrant organizations in the United States, whose acceptance of the claim put forward by Czechoslovakia to the region was officially sanctioned by the Treaty of Saint Germain (September 10, 1919), signed by the United States, the British Empire, France, Italy, Japan, and Czechoslovakia, in which the latter country agreed to "constitute the Ruthene territory south of the Carpathians . . . as an autonomous unit within the Czechoslovak State". The same treaty laid it down that the territory should possess a provincial legislature, and that officials should be chosen as far as possible from the inhabitants of the territory.

Alone among all the Ukrainians, this remnant around

Podkarpatska Rus, which under Hungarian rule had remained among the most backward and poverty-stricken of all Europe's peasants, have found sanctuary within the frontiers of a democratic state, and thus escaped the persecution and repression which has been the common lot of other members of their race, both within and without the frontiers of Soviet Russia.

The methods by which both Poland and Rumania has sought to break the nationalist spirit of the Ukrainians within their borders are dealt with at length elsewhere in this volume. In this outline of the recent history of the Ukrainian people, however, the post-war condition of the Ukrainians of Eastern Galicia may fittingly be referred to, if only because they have, under Poland, been called upon to remain true to their race and ideals through a martyrdom as terrible as anything that modern history can record.

This was the "pacification" of that province by the troops of Marshal Pilsudski in the autumn of 1930, when, following repeated demands made by the Ukrainians that the Polish government should redeem its promise—twice guaranteed—of autonomy for the Ukrainian regions, the Polish authorities launched a veritable reign of terror, carried out by both troops and police, against the scattered communities of Ukrainian peasants.

Admitting the Polish contention that rick-burning and other crimes against property had occurred in Eastern Galicia, due to political discontent among the Ukrainians, it remains true and indisputable that the Polish authorities, instead of attempting to discover the individuals responsible and bring them to trial before a recognized court, proceeded to use all the weapons of an organized and supposedly civilized government in carrying out a campaign of mass sabotage and mass torture inflicted upon a defenceless peasant people.

In dozens of Ukrainian villages, in the districts of Lemberg, Stanislavov and Tarnopol, priests and peasants were brutally flogged in hundreds, women mishandled, cottage homes unroofed, schools closed, peasant co-operatives looted, libraries destroyed, and ruinous

A UKRAINIAN PEASANT GIRL

Typical of a race which has survived generations of repression and still demands freedom.

EASTER MORNING IN THE UKRAINE

Peasants gathered outside their Church in an Eastern Galician village.

requisitions for foodstuffs levied upon village communities whose only "crime" was that their inhabitants spoke the Ukrainian language. When the author visited some of the victims of this "mission of pacification" two years later, their bodies still bore the scars inflicted by the Polish *gendarmes* and soldiery, while village co-operatives and institutes contained furniture smashed by the representatives of Marshal Pilsudski, and religious pictures which had been torn up and cast underfoot by those same agents, intent, it seemed, upon stamping out by brute force everything which typified Ukrainian culture.

The troops thus unloosed upon a defenceless civilian population systematically destroyed both public and private property owned by the Ukrainian peasants, without any attempt being made to discover those guilty of the rick-burning outrages which were the official "justification" for this wave of medieval terrorism : a fact that caused many observers to incline to the view that the Ukrainians were being punished, not for rick-burnings, but for having the temerity to address an appeal to the League of Nations for those rights which Poland was pledged to grant, and which had been consistently refused.

During the three months between June and September 1930, at least 20,000 Ukrainians were arrested and thrown into prison, including sixteen of the twenty-six representatives of the Ukrainian National Party in the Sejm, the Polish Lower House, while, following the action of the Polish police in turning back doctors and others who attempted to go to the assistance of the maltreated peasants, many of the victims died of their wounds.

A feature of the "pacification" which strengthened the view that it was a blow aimed at the national consciousness of the Ukrainians was the destruction of national costumes and peasant embroidery in the homes raided. Similarly, Ukrainian co-operative stores and creameries, forming part of the most highly developed peasant co-operative organization existing anywhere in Europe (Denmark only excepted), suffered heavily.

Reading-rooms and educational organizations were raided, and a heavy blow struck at the whole peasant culture, unique in Eastern Europe, which the Ukrainian people have built up during generations in bondage. That peasant culture which is the especial achievement of the Ukrainian race is a century ahead of anything existing in the non-Ukrainian regions of either Poland or Rumania, and represents more surely than anything else the triumph of Ukrainian spirit of national unity against the forces of centralization and disruption alike.

News of the "pacification" reaching the outside world, the Poles were constrained upon to recall their Uhlans, and the "pacification" ended. But the squadrons of Polish cavalry who rode out of Eastern Galicia left behind them a heightened hatred between Ukrainians and Poles.

If, in fact, the "pacification" was intended to browbeat the Ukrainians into silence, the terrorist campaign was a complete failure. For events have proved that the Ukrainians of Eastern Galicia, who, in common with their brothers elsewhere, have kept the light of patriotism burning through the long night of serfdom, and through generations of Russian and Austrian rule, do not intend to be intimidated by Polish troops, however ruthless their methods, into forgetting Poland's broken pledges. Or into allowing the world to forget.

For a few dramatic months, within the memory of those Ukrainians now living, the Ukraine was free. The husbands and brothers from those peasant homesteads knew the glory of fighting and often dying in the struggle to maintain their hard-won independence against Communism. If they did not die in the uniform of the Ukrainian National Army it was only because in 1919 the Ukrainians were too poor to afford uniforms, and Europe was in chaos all around them. The Great Ukraine existed not on paper but in the hearts of its people. And none who know those sturdy peasant hosts can deny that, in the hearts of Europe's largest "minority", free Ukraine exists to this day.

The Ukrainian is a philosopher with a knowledge

of history. If he tolerates the manifold injustices of his life to-day, the victim of Communist ideology, of Polish chauvinism, of Rumanian tax-gatherers and corruption, it is because he believes the day will come when he will be free of those things : the day when Europe's Unknown Nation will write its name large on the maps of Eastern Europe, and justice will finally be done to a peasant people who have fought to preserve their national identity with a tenacity, courage, and indomitable will that knew not defeat.

The Ukrainians have been called "the British of Eastern Europe". The name fits. Like the British race, they have by their industry and enterprise created a culture and civilization superior to those which surround them. And, like the British, they have the fatal defect, from the point of view of their adversaries, of never knowing when they are beaten.

For six hundred years, with one brief interval as an autonomous state linked with the Russian Empire, they have fought to remain Ukrainian. They have preserved their own distinctive language, their own Church, their own clothes, their high standard of husbandry. And, at the end of that fight of centuries, as at the beginning, they face the world undaunted alike by poverty, persecution, and repression—demanding the right of forty-three millions of people having a common stock and a common life to rule themselves. That demand may be resisted for a year, a generation, or a hundred generations. But at the end of that time the Ukrainian peoples will still be asking for their freedom. And there will be neither lasting peace nor the reign of justice in Eastern Europe until that right is granted, and the alien troops withdraw, leaving the Ukraine to control its own destinies and enrich all the peasant lands by its example.

CHAPTER XV

THE UKRAINIANS LIVE ON!

THE standard of farming and the general cultural level of the Ukrainian population at present incorporated in the Polish state differs as completely from the conditions in Poland Proper as do conditions in France or Germany. If Poland is no longer that "hell of peasants" which the Italian Pacichelli described in the seventeenth century, it is still, judged by Western standards, politically and culturally inferior to the Ukrainian territories of Eastern Galicia and Volhynia, Polissia and Podlashia.

Approaching those eastern territories of Poland (and western territories of the Ukraine) from Czechoslovakia, one finds east of the River San the same grey, cold plains which have been described as the typical Polish landscape —but with an important difference. Entering the Ukrainian regions the housing standard improves. Every Ukrainian cottage, however small, is enclosed in a fence, symbolical of that individualism and love of home and the soil which lie at the very roots of the Ukrainian temperament. The spick-and-span appearance of even the poorest villages reminds the traveller that these Ukrainians are, jointly with the Hungarians, the best husbandmen in Eastern Europe. Had that not been so the Ukrainian territories would present a very different picture to-day, for the lands east of Przemysl were devastated in the World War more completely than any other region in Eastern Europe, and the restoration of those territories has been one of the miracles of the post-war years.

Eastern Galicia, the largest and most important of the Ukrainian provinces within the frontiers of Poland, comprises a territory of 7,849,183 hectares, of which no less than 96 per cent is productive land. The population of the province, according to the census of 1931, was 6,207,662, of whom 88 per cent are peasants. Of the remaining 12 per cent of the population, the greater part live in the small towns which predominate in that region, and are engaged either in the cultivation of land on the outskirts of those towns or in catering for the needs of the peasants in the surrounding countryside. If this further class is classified as agricultural, the percentage of the entire population of Eastern Galicia engaged in that industry exceeds 90 per cent.

The climatic and natural conditions of the province vary widely in different areas. Within its borders are found high mountains, damp peat plains, a dry grain belt, and the district of Zalischyky, which, with its extremely moderate climatic conditions, has been called "the Galician Riviera". Some of the districts, such as Nadvirna, Dolyna, and Kosiv, have only 10 per cent of arable land; Bohorodczany, Kalush, and Stry have from 20 to 30 per cent of arable land; while others, such as Zbarazh, Tarnopol, Terebovla, Skalat, and Horodenka, have from 75 to 80 per cent of arable soil. The most fertile district of Eastern Galicia is Podilla, a strip of country with a very fertile black soil predominantly devoted to grain, and the only part of Galicia where wheat is produced for export. Here, also, are grown the more delicate fruits, and wine, also general fruits, sugar-beet, and tobacco.

The distribution of the whole area according to the latest figures shows that approximately 50 per cent of the land is arable, 20 per cent devoted to hay and meadows, 25 per cent forest, and 5 per cent to other crops.

It remains a paradox that this fertile region, inhabited by the most efficient peasant people which Eastern Europe has produced, should lag behind the achievements of agriculturists in other lands. That paradox may be directly traced to the backward conditions under which the peasants have been forced to labour, not only by the Polish authorities but under Austrian rule before 1918. Its causes may be found in the small area of land held by most of the peasants, areas too infinitesimal to permit of efficient farming, and to governments which for centuries have made no effort to improve the economic standing of the Galician peasantry.

The average yield from each hectare of Galician land sheds such a lurid searchlight on the neglect and depression from which the province has suffered that the figures may justly be quoted, together with the figures for certain other countries, in order that a comparison may be made.

Average yield per hectare in percentages of 100 kilogrammes.

1929. Eastern	Wheat.	Rye.	Barley.	Oats.	Potatoes.	Sugar-beet.
Galicia ..	11·5	10·8	10·6	10·6	100	203
Poland	13·6	11·8	11·9	10·7	116	255
Czechoslovakia	16·9	16·6	18·8	14·3	116	249
Germany ..	21·3	18·8	20·8	16·4	168	309
Rumania ..	11·6	12·0	13·3	10·6	91	152
World average ..	12·9	12·8	11·5	12·6	121	220

These figures reveal that Eastern Galicia ranks, in so far as the average yield of crops is concerned, only with such countries as Rumania, which occupies a low place in the world scale of farming, while in no case does the average yield of crops equal the world average, although that average is "weighed" by the inclusion of many countries with an inferior standard of farming. If a comparison is made with such highly developed nations as Germany or Czechoslovakia the result is a still more damaging indictment of those who have been responsible for the nurturing of the Ukrainian territories under review.

Cattle-raising and pig-farming are closely connected with peasant life ; in Eastern Galicia the big estates do not play any important part in this branch of agriculture, which is almost entirely in the hands of the peasants. The Ukrainian values a cow beyond all things, and will keep one even on a holding not large enough to justify the maintenance of animals at all. In 1929, 65 per cent of cattle owners possessed one cow, 27 per cent two cows, and only 6 per cent three cows or more. How greatly the ownership of milk cattle is appreciated in these small homes is revealed by the further fact that on 35 per cent of all peasant holdings in Eastern Galicia in 1929 there existed one cow and no other cattle or horses whatever.

This point is further illustrated by official statistics showing that there exist in Eastern Galicia 18·2 horses to every hundred peasants, 24·8 pigs, 6·3 sheep, and 36·6 cattle. The tendency of peasant holdings to increase the number of cows and the amount of milk production continues, the milch cows forming 68 per cent of all cattle in the country, while oxen account for only 1·9 per cent.

Horses are not raised for sale to any extent, the Galician type being too small to be sold for military purposes or exported. In recent years efforts have been made to raise the sturdy Hutzulian highland horses for export, but with only partial success. The recent census shows that less than 20 per cent of the horses in the territory were suitable for military requirements, this low percentage being due to the fact that very little attention has been paid to breeding—which also accounts for the low milk yield of cows.

On the overwhelming number of peasant holdings poultry-raising and egg-production play the most important part in the peasant's budget. With the ready money thus secured he pays, in normal times, his current accounts—one reason why the export of eggs from Eastern Galicia, especially to Germany and Britain, attained such high proportions before tariff barriers and other artificial means of restriction caused a contraction in this trade.

The explanation of these conditions may be traced to two facts—the small size of the average holding and the neglect of such aids to efficient farming as agricultural education, government research stations for the improvement of seed, cattle-breeding, etc., and the provision of agricultural credits.

In the past the greater part of the arable area of Eastern Galicia has been composed of large estates. While it is true that the possessions of the great land-owners have tended to diminish in recent years, the stranglehold which they imposed upon the region following the downfall of the free Ukraine in the seventeenth century is not being relaxed speedily enough to meet the needs of a growing rural population.

Prior to the war, 40 per cent of the land area was in the possession of large landowners, this figure having fallen by only 4 per cent in the previous eighty years. On the other hand, during the same period the number of peasant holdings had increased from 511,714 to over two millions! It is clear, therefore, that in the course of those eighty years the 60 per cent of the total area which represented peasant holdings had been divided to one quarter of the size considered adequate in the middle years of the nineteenth century to maintain a family. This sub-division resulted in an alarming growth of "dwarf" holdings which, even under the most scientific cultivation, were quite inadequate to mitigate the extreme poverty of the peasant owners.

In 1914, prior to the re-incorporation of the territory within the Polish state, no fewer than 42.6 per cent of all peasant holdings were of under two hectares in extent. Holdings that could keep one horse only as working power (between two and five hectares) accounted for a further 37.5 per cent. Add those two figures together, and it will be seen that in Eastern Galicia, at that time, a fraction over 80 per cent of all "farms" were of less than twelve English acres—a figure that needs no comment.

At the same date, two-thirds of the estates were in the hands of the Polish nobility. This class remains to-day the representatives of big ownership, and only by the splitting up and redistribution of a proportion, at least, of their wide acres can the landless Ukrainian peasant hope for an improvement in his economic condition. In addition, some tenth of the estate areas were, in 1914, owned by Jewish landlords who had bought them from bankrupt Polish owners and who subsequently became big landowners, chiefly because they had invested their money in agriculture. These Jewish landlords the Ukrainian peasantry regarded as temporary proprietors of the soil, and those same peasants still hope that it may be possible to buy out the Jewish landowner, who is usually in no way tied to the soil, sooner than the Polish landlords. The peasant is quite aware of the fact that the latter are often sincerely guided by their nationalist feelings and family traditions when refusing to part with any of their inheritance, in direct contrast to the Jewish landlords, who will readily sell to any peasant who can pay the market price for the land.

The condition of the peasant during the post-war years, far from improving, became very much worse. By 1921 the percentage of dwarf holdings up to two hectares had risen to nearly 60 per cent of all peasant farms, this further division of peasant holdings bringing in its train additional pauperization of the peasant class. Nor was this process confined to the dwarf holdings. Larger peasant farms suffered in the same way.

This fact is the most important of all the economic problems confronting the Galician peasant. The starvation line looms steadily nearer with the passing years, and still the authorities at Warsaw are content to allow things to drift, and leave Pilsudski's cavalry and police to suppress any evidence of discontent.

The remedy for this, Eastern Galicia's most pressing problem, lies along one of two roads—emigration, or the breaking up of the big estates. Emigration before the war was twofold : the migration overseas for permanent settlement in the new world, and the seasonal migration of peasants who went abroad to earn money, intending to return to their native land. Estimates show that up to 1909 some 470,000 persons emigrated from Eastern Galicia to the United States alone, while the total Ukrainian emigration from that province cannot be placed lower than 700,000. The seasonal migration from Eastern Galicia was in pre-war years directed chiefly to Prussia, and amounted to 200,000 agricultural labourers a year. This annual trek served as a safety-valve for surplus peasants.

In the post-war years, overseas emigration has diminished, and during the period between 1924-1929 only 60,000 persons left Eastern Galicia permanently, most of them going to the Argentine. This number includes a large number of relatives of earlier emigrants. Seasonal migration during the same years was confined chiefly to peasants who went to France to assist in gathering the harvest during the summer months, and has not exceeded 30,000 persons.

The virtual cessation of both overseas and seasonal emigration had a very marked effect on peasant conditions, and has resulted in the still greater impoverishment of the Ukrainian peasantry. Ukrainian farmers who have returned after years spent in the United States have assured me that the fall in the average standard of living of the villages, compared with twenty years ago (and prior to the world depression), amounted to at least 40 per cent. This is the price which the Ukrainians in Poland are paying for the absence of any concerted scheme to ameliorate conditions in that territory.

The natural increase of the population, the acute shortage of land at any price which the peasant can afford to pay, the impossibility of landless peasants earning money in industrial centres, and the closing down of emigration—these factors together have brought the Ukrainian peasantry, not only of Eastern Galicia, but also of Volhynia, to the verge of nation-wide catastrophe.

Half-hearted attempts have been made to remedy matters by the purchase and redistribution of land. During the ten years ending 1929, 227,000 hectares were made available for peasant settlement, representing 10 per cent of the area of the estates in Eastern Galicia. Unfortunately for the Ukrainian peasantry, the prime consideration in the minds of those responsible for this modest degree of reform was the colonization of purely Ukrainian regions by Polish settlers, thus changing the racial character of a purely Ukrainian region, and, incidentally, presenting Europe with a further minority problem for the future.

No figures are available revealing the nationality of the persons who benefited by the breaking up of estates, but if it may be assumed that Roman Catholics represented Poles, and Greek Catholic and Orthodox buyers represented Ukrainians, the statistics show that 53·4 per cent of the land thus freed was given to Poles, who formed 47·6 per cent of the total number of persons benefiting by this modest measure of reform. Remembering the acute land shortage which exists among the Ukrainian peasantry in all districts, it is difficult to resist the contention of the peasants that the prime purpose of this land reform was to strengthen the Polish element in Eastern Galicia to the disadvantage of the natives. The position of the Ukrainian peasantry after this redistribution had been brought to a standstill by shortage of money remained precisely what it had been before it was carried out ; the few thousands of peasants who benefited were not sufficiently numerous even to offset the natural increase in population for the years concerned.

The second factor which helps to elucidate the low yield of crops per hectare in the Ukrainian regions under Polish rule concerns the neglect of agricultural education. Throughout this ancient Ukrainian territory there is not one government school teaching in the Ukrainian language. The solitary agricultural college open to peasants who speak only their mother tongue is one maintained by the Ukrainian *Prosvita* society, a society which has done excellent work in maintaining the cultural traditions of the Ukrainian people. Even the number of Polish agricultural schools in Eastern Galicia is insignificant, there being only five schools and one agricultural college.

Czechoslovakia, with approximately the same number of peasants as there are in Eastern Galicia, has 1,247 agricultural schools, attended yearly by some 40,000 peasants' sons. When this figure is compared with the almost total absence of agricultural education facilities in Eastern Galicia, a further reason for the poverty of Ukrainian peasants becomes manifest.

Were there no demand for educational facilities, it would be possible to apportion at least a little of the blame for this state of affairs to the lack of enterprise on the part of the peasantry. In the Ukrainian territories under review, precisely the reverse is the case. The standard of intelligence found in the masses of this virile, democratic people is considerably higher than the average, having been nurtured through centuries by a keen sense of national pride.

In dozens of Ukrainian villages, consisting of perhaps two hundred homes, the writer has found village institutes and libraries built by the peasants themselves without outside assistance—each peasant family contributing the value of so much wheat for the purchase of materials and so many hours' labour to the task of building. In many of these institutes 80 per cent of all the members could read, and kept themselves informed concerning events by studying the Ukrainian newspapers.

This high percentage of literacy may be traced to the fact that, under Austrian rule, there existed 3,600 primary schools teaching in the Ukrainian language. Following the incorporation of the territory within the Polish state, even this measure of free cultural development has been denied to the inhabitants of Eastern Galicia and the other Ukrainian provinces. By 1934, only some 123 schools teaching in that language remained open—five in Volhynia and the balance in Galicia. All the rest had become bi-lingual, teaching the more important subjects in Polish.

In view of these facts, it is hardly surprising that Warsaw should consider it unnecessary to provide university training for the sons of Ukraine. True, the Polish Sejm, in 1922, passed a bill providing for the inauguration of a Ukrainian University in Eastern Galicia, but the authorities evidently regarded the gesture as sufficient, for no university has materialized. The annual expenditure of Poland for the provision of university facilities for six million Ukrainians is confined to the maintenance of two

Ukrainian "Chairs" at Warsaw University, costing 63,490 zlotys in 1934. The total number of Ukrainian students who secure university training in any one year is little more than two thousand—this for a people who have, by their own initiative and out of their own resources, raised themselves to a standard of cultural development unique in Eastern Europe.

Another phase of that cultural development is seen in the existence of a strong co-operative organization, through the channels of which flow almost 50 per cent of the entire retail trade of Eastern Galicia and Volhynia. This co-operative movement, which, in many villages, numbers 100 per cent of the inhabitants among its members, was developed, and is still maintained, entirely by the peasants. When, in 1930, the Polish authorities spread suffering and ruin over wide areas of the Ukrainian lands, the account books recording the indebtedness of individual members were, in many cases, burned or confiscated, on the pretext that such books could not have been kept by the peasants themselves, and that the co-operatives were obviously, therefore, in league with trained agitators.

Remembering this fact, I made a point, when making random and unannounced visits to these all-peasant stores in various parts of the Ukrainian regions, of inspecting the books. Without exception all were in perfect order, and, for the previous quarter, had been "audited and found correct" by working peasants.

The destruction of account books during the "pacification" might have resulted in the financial ruin of the whole co-operative system, but for one fact. That fact was the innate honesty of the Ukrainian peasant. Immediately the Polish troops were withdrawn, those concerned voluntarily came forward and admitted the amounts of their indebtedness to the village stores. Actually the only lasting result of this unprovoked interference with one of the most remarkable and highly organized co-operative units in Europe was a brief dislocation of business due to the destruction of furniture and fittings, and the withdrawal by the Polish government of the permits formerly granted to the Ukrainian Co-operative to sell tobacco.

The cultural difficulties of the Ukrainian peasants in Volhynia have been even greater. Their condition under the Russian Empire was, if anything, worse than the conditions of their compatriots living in Eastern Galicia under Austrian rule. Following the return of Marshal Pilsudski to supreme power in 1926, a determined effort has been in progress to drive a wedge between the Ukrainians in the two provinces.

In the years after the war the co-operative and other Ukrainian national cultural movements centring on Lemberg began to spread northward into Volhynia, where there existed no educated class to direct the strivings of the peasants for betterment. Since 1926, the Polish government has firmly opposed every development calculated to unify the Ukrainians of the north with the members of their race in Eastern Galicia, even to the extent of starting counter-movements labelled "Ruthenian", in the pious hope that with the passage of time the people of Volhynia would overlook the racial bond linking them with their blood brothers in the south.

The peasantry in Volhynia own, on average, larger holdings than those existing in Eastern Galicia, but their educational and cultural standards are definitely lower than in the neighbouring region. For a time, developments directed to overcome the lower standard resulting from Russian rule were rapid. This process was, however, brought to a standstill by the attitude of the Polish authorities, culminating in the suppression of all Ukrainian secondary schools, and all but five of the Ukrainian primary schools, in the province. In 1932 came the final blow—the total suppression of the educational institutes founded by the Ukrainian *Prosvita* society.

Evidence gathered on the spot makes it clear that the Polish authorities, in their zeal to damage Ukrainian organizations, and the strong movement for Ukrainian nationalism existing in Volhynia, even went to the extreme of deliberately turning a blind eye to such communist sentiment as existed there. Nevertheless, communism as a political force in this once Russian territory is declining, while Ukrainian nationalism gathers strength. Thus the Polish authorities were forced, in their "war" on Ukrainian ideals, to fall back on fining co-operative stores five pounds whenever they could find one which had not provided customers with a spittoon as required by law! Unbelievable as it is, many fully authenticated instances of such petty persecution exist.

Every obstacle which ingenuity can suggest has been pressed into service to hamper the growth of Ukrainian organizations. In countless cases where peasants have prepared the necessary plans for the erection of village institutes and co-operative stores the government officials have arrived at the village to investigate the matter (at a cost of 200 zlotys), only to refuse permission for the store to be opened just as frequently as any shadow of an excuse can be suggested for doing so. On many of these occasions the Polish authorities have revealed the real reasons behind their objections by stating frankly that if the community concerned will resign from membership of the Ukrainian Union of Co-operatives at Lemberg, and join the Polish Co-operative Union, no obstacles will be raised. Despite this calculated campaign, which has lasted for seven years, more than 500 co-operative stores linked directly with the parent organization at Lemberg exist in Volhynia alone, and 120 more had been established and closed by the authorities.

Fear of the influence of educated Ukrainians from Galicia on the masses in Volhynia is at once a tribute to the cultural standard in Eastern Galicia and an admission that the Polish authorities intend, if possible, to continue their policy of ignoring the Ukrainian demand for autonomy and to treat the Ukrainian territories as colonies of Poland. Even the Ukrainian Anti-alcoholic League has been refused permission to pursue its activities among the Volhynian peasants, on the ground that any success gained would be against the interests of the Polish drink monopoly!

Both in Eastern Galicia and, even more, in Volhynia, any person attempting to talk with the peasants concerning these things is liable to arrest ; indeed, numbers have been arrested. Even the most distinguished foreign observers are not immune. British journalists have, in recent years, become so accustomed to police interference with those of their number who sincerely try to maintain touch with peoples and their opinions, that most of them accept this annoyance as inseparable from the performance of their duties. What is one to think, however, when a distinguished member of the British House of Lords, who visited Eastern Galicia at the invitation of Ukrainian friends, finds himself pilloried in the Krakow press as "a most unmannerly lord"—the grounds of the attack upon his good manners being that he had actually visited peasant farms in the Lemberg district without first asking the Polish authorities whether they would like him to do so !

How does the individual peasant fare in this land, torn with political and racial strife ? The poverty existing among the Ukrainian people is clearly proved by the evidence set out in this chapter. One further fact may be quoted here—the savings deposited in Ukrainian savings institutions in Eastern Galicia, to which nearly all peasants belong, amounted at the beginning of 1934 to five and a half million zlotys, or almost exactly one shilling per person in English money.

To achieve this measure of well-being the nameless millions who inhabit those scattered thatched settlements dotted about the Galician landscape live lives as hard and stern as anything known in modern Europe. The traveller who is early astir may see the women and younger children leading horses or carrying tools to the holdings at 3 a.m. in the spring and summer mornings ; the men more often sleep where their work finishes and rise where it begins. The only break in days of constant toil are those made necessary by the rains of winter (when there is weaving and carpentry to be done in the cottages), and by the holidays of Christmas, Easter, and the anniversaries of the poets and heroes of the Ukrainian people.

One other habit of the Ukrainian peasantry may be classified under the heading of recreation. In normal

A GRANDMOTHER OF THE MOUNTAINS
An aged Hutzulian peasant woman "snapped" in Eastern Galicia.

REPRESENTATIVE OF A FAMOUS RACE

A peasant "elder" of a village in the Ukrainian territory now under
Poland.

times the peasant looks forward to market-day and to the chance for gossip represented by the visit to a town. Even if he has nothing to sell he will make the journey in order to buy salt or oil—products which he could purchase just as easily in his own village.

The economic position of the peasantry, such as it was, has been completely undermined by the world agricultural crisis. What that crisis has meant to Eastern Galicia will be related in a later chapter. The middle peasant (farming about ten acres) has no net profit even in normal times, the whole of the crops raised being needed to feed his family. The lowest class of peasant—the dwarf-holder—was fortunate if he could keep his family alive, and more fortunate still if he could find employment for himself on a nearby estate, leaving wife or sons to look after the small farm.

The average wages paid by the estates to their workers amounted to from 8d. to 1s. per day for men and 5d. to 8d. a day for women workers—that was before the oncoming depression brought salary "cuts" to the Galician plains equally with judges, M.P.s, and civil servants in Great Britain. By 1932, the highest wage obtainable even in harvest times was 7d. a day for men and 5d. a day for women.

Despite the fact that the average market value of the food needed to maintain a peasant family of four amounts to about 4d. a day, it is scarcely surprising, in the light of these figures, to find that the standard of living of the middle class of peasant has fallen to the standard of the lowest class, while the plight of the smallholders at the bottom of the social scale was at the end of 1933 catastrophic. Eastern Galicia at that date was a land of barefooted men and women, roads falling into decay, and moneyless homesteads. In the case of all except the richest peasants the only cash income was secured by selling eggs and milk. In village after village the answer to an enquiry concerning cash resources was, "Not one groschen in the whole village." Former Ukrainian settlers in the United States and Canada, who had returned after the war hoping for better times in the homeland, showed me their clothes—made from the skins of dogs and goats.

"The story of Eastern Galicia," said one peasant, "is soon told. We raise cattle and pigs for the debt-collector. We raise food to keep ourselves alive. We use eggs as the only currency left. It is six months since I saw one zloty in this village. We cannot go on."

The strain of life is leaving its mark upon many of the older generation, hardened as they are by lives of toil. By some miracle the children have escaped the worst. It is typical of the progressive ideas which animate the Ukrainian people that in quite small villages one will find a crèche in the village hall, presided over by a Ukrainian peasant-girl, where the mothers leave their children while at work in the fields. Little groups of children up to three years of age, and looking every bit as intelligent as the average city child, may be seen sitting in circles on the floor, drinking milk, singing Ukrainian lullabies or sleeping.

The economic conditions in Volhynia are, if anything, even more severe than in Galicia. There are fewer large estates and fewer landless peasants. Every family has enough to eat, but the system of tax-collecting is more severe than in Galicia, repression of Ukrainian organiza- tions more general, transport more difficult, and the disposal of crops, with but few co-operative stores, almost entirely in the hands of speculators. There are, indeed, great possibilities of development in Volhynia if and when the present oppressive coercion of the Ukrainian inhab- itants ceases. Until then the conditions of the 92 per cent of the population represented by peasants must remain backward and hopeless.

Meanwhile the homogeneous mass of Ukrainian peasants, whose territories march side by side with those of Poland Proper from the borders of Czechoslovakia to the extreme north of that country, nurse their traditions, their national pride, and their sense of solidarity with their brothers living under Soviet Russia, Rumania, and Czechoslovakia.

Looking across the plains on which they dwell they

are conscious of the rich promise of lush pastures and fertile soil—promise unfulfilled because governments, for their own purposes, have determinedly plotted to keep these areas as backward as possible. How otherwise explain the fact that when Ukrainians living in the United States offered to open and maintain agricultural colleges in Eastern Galicia and Volhynia for the benefit of their compatriots, the proposal was vetoed by the Polish authorities, with the result that numerous experienced Ukrainian experts, anxious and willing to go to the help of their countrymen, are barred from Poland?

That nation, as reconstituted by the peace settlement, had enjoyed one spell of power over Eastern Galicia before 1919. In 1340 Kazimir the Great, King of Poland, occupied the Galician principality following the extinction of the free Ukraine. Later, in 1569, further slices of the Ukrainian territories were incorporated in the Polish kingdom, only to pass again into the hands of the Ukrainians when the independence of that state was re-established in 1651. The struggle between Polish ambition and Ukrainian patriotism continued right up to the fall and partition of Poland itself, when, as has already been related, Galicia was annexed to Austria and other Ukrainian territories incorporated within the Russian Empire

The first period of Polish rule over the Ukrainian regions adjoining her eastern ethnographical frontiers reduced them to complete economic, social and cultural ruin. The Ukrainian nobility (boyary) were either Polonized or exterminated, the middle-class was destroyed; the Ukrainian cities were Polonized and church properties plundered. The Ukrainian peasants were deprived of personal liberty, converted into serfs, and became the absolute property of the Polish nobility. Such were the blessings which the first period of Polish rule brought to the Ukrainian people. The blessings of the second period of Polish rule, which has now persisted for fifteen years, are equally dubious when viewed through impartial eyes.

Ignoring the patent fact that just as the Ukrainians struggled to re-establish their free state in the seventeenth century, so they are still struggling, with undiminished energy, to secure control of their own lives three centuries later, the Poles, in seeking the suppression of Ukrainian nationality and ignoring the economic plight of the Ukrainian people in their care, are repeating the very mistakes made by their ancestors.

And the Ukrainians, who stood by the grave of one Polish state, remain inflexibly determined that sooner or later justice shall be done to a harassed people, and that, by the road either of autonomy or separation, they will free themselves from the shackles of a new and even more intolerant Poland.

CHAPTER XVI

CZECHOSLOVAKIA—A SUCCESSFUL EXPERIMENT

AGRICULTURAL Czechoslovakia, stretching its length from
the eastern frontier of Germany to the borders of Hungary,
often seems to the traveller accustomed to agrarian land-
scapes to have been fashioned out of the best of all peasant
nations. Not that the plains and valleys of Europe's most
successful post-war creation are markedly different from
those of less prosperous lands—Karel Čapek, travelling
in Andalusia, could awake to think himself in his own
Czech countryside—but there is an orderliness, a sense
of well-being, about the villages of Czechoslovakia,
reinforced by modern well-kept roads, which tells its own
tale—a tale of good government, of an industrious peasantry,
a high cultural standard, and benevolence on the part of
those officials in whose hands rest the administration of
that smiling countryside. In short, the Republic of
Czechoslovakia has already earned its place among the
best-governed countries in Europe.

The present state of affairs did not just happen;
much had to be accomplished before the new state could
boast of 1,618,710 peasant proprietors.

In the days of the Austro-Hungarian monarchy, the
valleys and hillsides of Bohemia, Moravia, Slovakia, and
Sub-Carpathian Ruthenia (the provinces of the Austro-
Hungarian Empire which to-day form the Republic of
Czechoslovakia) were regions where the big estate, the
wealthy landowner, and the game preserve flourished.
Between 1924 and the present day about one-third of the
total area of the republic has been expropriated under the
Land Reform Laws, most of which has been handed over
to the peasants.

Although Czechoslovakia occupies only the fifth place among the thirteen European states which have introduced land reform movements since 1920, the thorough and systematic manner in which the redistribution has been accomplished constitutes one of the major events recorded in agrarian Europe during the past decade. That social transformation continues—for although 1,700,000 hectares have already been transferred to peasant ownership, more land was still becoming available at the beginning of 1934, and not until two further years have passed will Czechoslovakia's agricultural reform be complete.

That reform has been put into effect by a whole series of laws, the first of which came into force in 1919. Under this original decree, peasants who owned less than twenty English acres of land were enabled to purchase such additional acreage owned by the large landlords, church or state as they or their families had previously held on lease for a period of not less than twelve years. Under this law an area of about 100,000 hectares passed into the possession of the smallholding class which had previously worked the land as tenants.*

Later in the same year the Law of Expropriation was introduced, decreeing that henceforth no owner of land should lease, mortgage, or divide his property without the consent of the Czech Land Office. Under this law 150 hectares of cultivated land, or 250 hectares altogether, remained the owner's free property, but in certain exceptional circumstances the amount of land thus permitted to remain uncontrolled was extended to 500 hectares.

The amount of land expropriated under this law amounted to 3,963,000 hectares—equal to 28 per cent of the total area of the country—of which about one-third was cultivated land and the remainder forests, etc.

Having taken over one-third of the entire country, the Czechoslovakian government faced the task of redistributing the land thus made available. For this purpose

---

* It is interesting to note that more German than Czech farmers took advantage of this law. The average price paid to former landlords for the whole country was 1,800 Czech crowns per hectare.

two further laws were passed—the Act of Compensation of 1920 and the Law of Allotment of the same year.

The first law laid down the terms and prices of compensation to be paid to the former owners, the amount paid per hectare varying according to the size of the expropriated land and the length of time during which the landowner had held it. Compensation was paid either in cash or by Land Bonds carrying interest at 4 per cent, with $1\frac{1}{2}$ per cent amortization per annum.

The Law of Allotment dealt with the thorny problem of redistribution of the lands thus freed for the peasants. The state was empowered either to retain the land for its own purposes or to distribute it to the small peasant class, landless persons, late employees of the estate expropriated, and former soldiers. The difference between the price paid for the land and the amount paid by the new proprietors, limited to 42 per cent, was used for compensating former employees of the landowners, for the expenses of the Land Department, and to make good losses in income tax, while applicants for the small farms thus created were granted credit up to a maximum of 90 per cent of the price of their holdings.

This agricultural "reformation" not only made possible many schemes for social betterment, including the erection of new housing estates, schools, and parks, but dictated the pattern of the new agrarian Czechoslovakia which has since come into being.

Former extremes between great estates and small-holdings disappeared ; "dwarf-holdings" of less than five English acres decreased in numbers, while holdings of from 25 to 100 acres multiplied. To-day only 31,000 farms in the whole country exceed 100 acres in extent, and the preponderance of the large estate over the small farm has been done away with for good.

A further result of this redistribution of land was the creation of the so-called "residual farms" comprising the residue of expropriated lands after small parcels had been allotted to individuals or co-operative bodies. These "residual farms", averaging 100 to 200 acres, have been allotted to former employees, officials, leaseholders, and other qualified persons. In Czechoslovakia, where more than 86 per cent of all farms are of less than 25 acres in extent, these holdings rank as important farms.

In 1933, two years before these land reforms are expected to be completed, 5,386,043 persons out of a total population of 14,735,000 were engaged in agriculture, forestry, and fisheries. Of this total, about one million are still numbered either among the landless, and employed for wages, or are the owners of "dwarf-holdings" who work for larger farmers in addition to cultivating their own small fields.

The industry which has yielded the Czechoslovakian farmer a higher standard of living than that found in most agrarian countries, and which is responsible for the fact that, despite the cutting up of large estates, agricultural production is still rising in that country, is amply confirmed by statistics.

Thus those five million villagers scattered from the German frontier to the Ukrainian borders of the east own, between them, 748,000 horses, 4,500,000 head of cattle, 3,000,000 pigs, and over 1,000,000 goats—this last a surprising figure, for the author spent many days on the farms of Moravia and Bohemia and cannot recollect having seen one goat !

Between them those Czech and Slovak farmers grew, in 1932, 14,600,000 quintals of wheat, 22,000,000 quintals of rye, 15,000,000 quintals of spring barley, and 17,000,000 quintals of oats—quantities which, with the exception of maize, make Czechoslovakia independent of foreign imports of corn for the feeding of her teeming urban populations. The fact that the country has in normal years a favourable trade balance (amounting to 1,351,000 Czech crowns in 1931) is largely due to the balance maintained between agricultural production and industrial activity.

From the peasant's point of view, however, Czechoslovakia consists of four distinct countries—Bohemia, Moravia, Slovakia, and Sub-Carpathian Ruthenia (the Podkarpatska Rus region)—and the conditions differ between one province and another scarcely less than between one nation and the next in other parts.

Thus the yield of grain per hectare in Bohemia is nearly twice as high as in Slovakia, and almost three times the yield in the still poorer Podkarpatska Rus territory. The nature of crops, and the architecture of the village home, varies hardly less as one travels east through the countryside, while methods of cultivation, and the general standards of education, are considerably higher in the purely Czech regions than in Slovakia, a fact which is at once an indictment of past Hungarian governments and a tribute to the persistent efforts of the industrious Czechs to improve the conditions in Bohemia during the days of Austrian rule.

Culturally, however, the various provinces of the Czechoslovakian nation are more united than are many other agrarian nations of common stock. One finds within the frontiers of that state no such sharp divisions as those which separate the various branches—Serb, Croat, and Bulgarian—of the Southern Slav race.

The climate of Czechoslovakia varies according to the height above sea-level. Thus the higher parts of Slovakia and Ruthenia are cattle-raising regions, while the climate of Southern Slovakia and those Ruthenian (or Ukrainian) districts which adjoin the Hungarian Plain permits the cultivation of maize, tobacco, and vines with success.

About 18 per cent of the total cultivated area of the country is devoted to sugar-beet and 36 per cent to corn. The smaller farms created since the war produce less wheat and sugar beet than did the former estates. On the other hand, more rye and potatoes are now grown. Cattle and pig-breeding has also increased, over 90 per cent of the livestock in Bohemia being bred on holdings of under 100 acres.

Current statistics reveal that in the country as a whole both the amount of cattle and the area under corn has increased during the past six years, while production has not suffered in any department through the drastic transformation of the economy of the countryside under the Land Reform Law.

In former days, before the depression became at

once the cause and the excuse for every ill, two crops yielded a safe and sure income for the peasant homes of Czechoslovakia—hops and sugar-beet. In those valleys was grown all the sugar needed for the whole Austrian Empire. Now that empire is no more, and its former territories have been cut up into lands separated by unclimbable tariff walls, sugar is not the profitable crop that it was, although hops are reported, from Prague, to be standing up well to the bad times—as well they may when the prestige of Pilsener is remembered.

What has happened to the Czech farmers who formerly "banked" on sugar-beets to pay their household bills is revealed by a single sentence in the last annual report of the National Bank of Czechoslovakia, which reads : "It was necessary to reduce the area devoted to sugar-beet cultivation by an additional 21·5 per cent." During the good years which preceded the world slump, that nation utilized 32·6 per cent of its total production of sugar for sweetening its own food, and exported 67·4 per cent. After four depressing years, Czechoslovakia is consuming 10 per cent less and the exports have fallen to 44 per cent of the reduced production. It is extremely doubtful, in other words, whether sugar-beet, despite one development to be mentioned later, is now yielding the Czech farmers more than one-third of the income which flowed into their pockets from that crop in 1928.

Notwithstanding the general decline in incomes, the legatees of the land reforms applied in Czechoslovakia since 1919 are still to be numbered among the fortunate agriculturists of Europe, for, in addition to the redistribution of the land, they dwell in a country affording the peasant markets easy of access for his produce and an abundance of cheap factory goods for his money.

In so far as the western regions of the country are concerned, it would, indeed, be incorrect to imply that agrarian betterment waited upon the formation of the new ceate. The present high standard of agriculture in the stzech regions has its roots in the eighteenth century, when Ce "Patriotic Agricultural Society" was founded as a thntre for reform and betterment. About 1850 the growth of industry in the cities caused a flow of labour from countryside to factory. Wages rose, and sons sent home money to their parents in the villages. Thus it came about that machinery appeared on the farms many years before such implements had even reached the "novelty" stage in other lands. The sickle, still the universal implement in most eastern nations, was the first to go. Harrows and ploughshares were improved, and about 1870 the first sowing machines appeared on the large estates. By the dawn of the twentieth century, the average Czech peasant had become well versed in a standard of farming not markedly dissimilar to that found in Great Britain—and superior to the conditions still surviving in Poland, Yugoslavia, or Rumania to-day.

Two great crises caused by over-production—in 1820 and 1870 (when agricultural prices fell to 40 per cent or less)—failed to check for long the natural prosperity of a fertile countryside, and by the turn of the century the peasants began to buy the products of the factories and a new chapter opened in the story of Czech agriculture. In the first place, labour-saving implements were bought in the market towns ; then articles of personal wearing apparel, and for use in the home. Thus came about a state of affairs unknown in the lands around Czechoslovakia, with the exception of Germany, in which the countryman became an important customer of the industrialists.

This high standard of living is not, however, without its dangers, as recent years have shown. Once having acquired the habit of buying most of the necessities of life, the farmer, when his income began to decline after 1929, began to incur debts in order to bridge the gulf between income and expenditure, with the result that at the beginning of 1933, the estimated total indebtedness of the Czechoslovakian peasants amounted to thirty milliards of crowns !

A glance at the larder of a typical Czech farmhouse in 1928, before the world crisis depleted its variety and range, would have caused a Rumanian or Serbian peasant to grow green with envy. Of all European agriculturists, save only the German and Austrian peasant, the Czechs feed the best in normal times.

In scattered farmhouses nestling in the valleys of Bohemia and Moravia I have seen the larders bulging with pork, beef, and mutton (but especially beef), fruit, gherkins, lard (used more than butter), potatoes, cabbage, and bread. Tea is little seen, but coffee is a universal drink on the farmsteads. Bacon, sausages, ham, all sorts of pork, were available in abundance, while the ubiquitous tinned sardine and herring were found in every village store. Apart from coffee, beer is the most popular drink, which is hardly surprising, for, as every traveller in the country will remember, it is the best beer in Europe, and costs the equivalent of one penny a glass.

If one had to express the difference, in good times, between the Czech farmer and the peasant of most other lands discussed in this volume, one might sum it up in a single significant word—food ! Nothing testified more eloquently to the high standard of living enjoyed by the Czechoslovakian peasant than the weight of good things found on his table ; in this respect the country was, so far as the author's observation goes, unique among the predominantly agricultural nations.

Such was the condition of the peasantry between 1925 and 1929—the good years to which two million Czech peasant families now look back with longing.

The agricultural crisis engulfed all alike, but the mountainous districts suffered most severely, for there the fields do not yield enough to feed the families, and tens of thousands of peasants found their incomes barely sufficient to buy flour.

The famous cottage industries, which have existed from time immemorial in Northern Bohemia, formerly provided whole districts with subsidiary incomes, but the depression hit these home-workers no less hard than the factories, so that during the years following 1930 the peasant standard of living suffered a sharp contraction in all parts of the country.

Of the 38 per cent of the total population engaged in agriculture, the class which proved most resistant to the crisis proved to be the poorest class of all, save only the inhabitants of the mountain regions. These were the owners of the "dwarf-holdings" found mostly in the industrial districts—workers farming up to three acres who were normally employed in nearby factories while their wives and families managed the "farm".

Faced with the spectre of unemployment, these in-dustrialized peasants were able to withdraw on to their land, which at least yielded to them and their familieis the means of life, and saved them from dependence upon charity and state alike. The success of these "dwarf-holdings" provides further evidence regarding the social benefits of the land reforms, and has led to a movement to settle more of the industrial workers on their own "farms".

The event which brought renewed hope to the hard-pressed peasants during recent years was, however, not the multiplication of smallholdings, but the growing use of alcohol, diluted with petrol, as a fuel for internal com-bustion engines.

In most countries the primary producers still grow food for human consumption ; in Czechoslovakia they are producing it to feed motor-cars ! In the hour of greatest need, the authorities remembered that sugar-beet, potatoes, rye, and maize—in fact any vegetable material rich in starch or sugar—can be used to manufacture industrial alcohol. A hundredweight of potatoes or sugar-beet will yield an imperial gallon of alcohol, which in turn can be mixed with petrol in a proportion of 30 per cent alcohol to 70 per cent petrol. In Germany over 100,000 tons of home-produced alcohol is consumed in this way every year ; is it so surprising, therefore, that the 650,000 Czechoslovakian farmers who were officially recorded to be growing sugar-beet and potatoes in 1930 remembered this fact in their darkest hour for a generation, and, with corn, cattle, sugar, and most other products sinking to record low levels, exerted pressure to provide a new market for their products ?

The result was a victory for the peasants. To-day Czechoslovakia is the only European nation, apart from Latvia, in which the sale of petrol undiluted with alcohol is forbidden—and the price of that alcohol, as fixed by law, is 2s. 11d. per imperial gallon. By this means large quantities of sugar-beet and potatoes have been taken off the normal market and have at least yielded some profit to the producers. With petrol available in 1933 at less than 4d. per gallon (excluding duties), the victory for the peasants has been purchased at the expense of the motorist and the national revenue, for less petrol imported means less in taxation. But with nearly forty families out of every hundred engaged in producing the nation's harvests, it is natural that the peasants should play a prominent rôle in influencing public opinion.

This question of the use of alcohol as fuel affords an interesting comparison between conditions in Czechoslovakia and more politically backward nations where the peasantry, although the main pillars upon which rest the prosperity of the whole nation, have very little to say concerning either the policy pursued by the government, taxation, road development, or any of those other matters conditioning their own lives, in regard to which they remain helpless tools of fate.

The "Republican Party of Smallholders and Agriculturists" is the biggest political party in Czechoslovakia, with 46 members (out of 300) in the Lower House, and 24 senators (out of a total of 150). A. Svehla, the leader of this party, may be cited as typical of the class of intellect which will come to the fore if ever the "Green International" becomes more than a dream in the hearts of the peasant millions. The son of a former estate-owner in Central Bohemia, he is himself a practical and experienced farmer. During the war he was one of the little band which worked valiantly for Czech independence, and the land reforms owe much to his knowledge and experience. This farmer has since served his country as Minister of the Interior, and was three times Prime Minister before a serious illness caused his partial withdrawal from public life in 1929.

John Rozkosny, who founded the Moravian Agricultural Council, and many other peasant leaders, bear witness to the part which the countrymen have played in fashioning the new state. In no country in Central or Eastern Europe has peasant leadership attained a higher standard.

There is, however, one corner of Czechoslovakia to which none of the foregoing remarks apply; a territory which, far from enjoying a high standard of living, modern educational facilities, or wise leadership, was until 1919 the Cinderella region of Europe, populated by the poorest peasants to be found in the whole length and breadth of that continent. That territory is the Podkarpatska Rus region, situated at the extreme eastern end of Czecho-slovakia and inhabited by members of the Ukrainian race.

Incorporated in the Czechoslovakian state in circum-stances described in a previous chapter,* this corner of the Ukrainian lands may be divided into two parts—the mountainous region inhabited by Hutzulians (a branch of the Ukrainian family) and the plains verging on Hungary, peopled by Ukrainian cultivators.

Prior to the World War the Hutzulians in the mountains relied for their living upon two main sources of wealth—the timber industry and seasonal work on the farms of the Hungarian plains. Timber was cut and sent to Hungary. Harvesters migrated to that country and worked for pay-ment in kind, the government transporting workers and corn free of cost. Both these forms of economic activity have been brought to a standstill by the new frontier, which has left the Hutzulians separated from their former markets by an unscalable tariff wall. Attempts have been made to discover substitute markets and opportunities inside the borders of the Czechoslovakian state, but with-out much success. At the end of 1933 the position of this hardy mountain people was extremely grave—so grave that the political parties were distributing maize at very low prices in order to keep these unfortunate and innocent victims of the Treaty of Trianon alive.

The position of the Hutzulians is complicated by the fact that, although their plight is considerably worse than that of any other group within Czechoslovakia, they are a

---

* See Chapter XIV.

proud people ; too proud to ask for doles, with the result that there has probably been more genuine privation in those mountain cabins than in any other region discussed in this book.

The position of the Ukrainians inhabiting the plains is better. With good soil and a mild climate, vineyards and orchards flourish, and the peasants can at least produce food for their families.

The attitude of the Czechoslovakian government to these 500,000 members of the Ukrainian race committed to their care has justified the trust placed in the new state by the Ukrainian organizations in the United States and elsewhere when they concurred in the present boundaries, and forms a striking contrast to the cultural conditions of other branches of the Ukrainian family.

True, the Czechoslovakian government does not recognize them as Ukrainians, and prefers to label them "Ruthenians", thus reviving the name originally applied to the Ukrainians in the thirteenth century, and later revived by Austria for political reasons. True also that whereas there was not one Czech in the Podkarpatska Rus region before 1919, there are now about 34,000, mostly officials whose presence there is an interesting comment on the promise that, as far as possible, all local authorities should be recruited from the population. But these are minor points compared with the vigour with which the officials at Prague are improving both primary and "middle" education and supporting societies for adult education. There is, moreover, no restriction whatever on any Ukrainian occupying the highest office in that country, or rising to the command of the Czechoslovakian army, promotion and appointments being made solely upon merit without regard to race.

Unfortunately, this backward corner of the Ukrainian territories has produced few leaders of prominence, the intelligentsia being confined to teachers, clergy, and a few lawyers.

In the political sphere the same libertarian principles are to be observed. Full political freedom is accorded to this "minority", part of the inhabitants being adherents

A VILLAGE "INDUSTRY"
Making decorated Easter Eggs in the Ukraine under Poland.

THE VOICE OF THE PEOPLE
A mass-meeting of Ukrainians in Eastern Galicia.

of the Social Democratic Party and part to the Czech Agrarian Party. There are also groups affiliated to the Ukrainian People's organization and a minute Communist faction. Similarly, no restrictions are placed on Ukrainian plays, meetings, and other forms of communal activity.

These are, perhaps, small things, but they are nevertheless important, and reveal greater political wisdom than is usual in that part of Europe.

Yet even the Czechs, justifiably anxious concerning the unity of their country in view of its exposed position in the heart of a Europe which seethes with national hatreds, have sought to minimize the factors which tend to link the Ukrainians within its borders with their brothers in other lands. Thus although the Academy of Science at Prague has recognized the Ukrainian language as being the tongue of the inhabitants of the Podkarpatska Rus region, when the largest organization of teachers in that territory sought to register their name as the Ukrainian Teachers' Association the Czechoslovakian government refused to accept the designation as correct, on the ground, apparently, that the inhabitants were "Ruthenians".

Similar difficulties have been experienced in the sphere of religion. The Ukrainians of Podkarpatska Rus are members of the Greek Catholic communion, and were until the World War (and theoretically still remain) part of the diocese of Lemberg. Lemberg, however, is now situated in the Ukrainian territories under Poland, and Czechoslovakia does not relish the Bishop of another country having any voice, spiritual or temporal, in the lives of those within its frontiers. As a result efforts have been made to make the "Ruthenian" Church within the Czech frontiers independent of outside influences.

When all such inevitable incidents of an age of nationalism have been taken into account, however, it remains true that, in so far as their treatment of the tiny Ukrainian minority is concerned, the Czechs have clean hands. No other minority people in Central or Eastern Europe enjoy a greater degree of cultural and political liberty, or have received greater benefits at the hands of the ruling race. If those benefits stop short of the restoration of the economic advantages formerly enjoyed by the Ukrainians of mountains and plains, and swept away by the Treaty of Trianon, or the advantages this "minority" would gain by incorporation within a free and united Ukraine, it would hardly be fair to blame the new Czechoslovakian state on that score. Even a Masaryk, than whom there is no wiser ruler in all Europe, cannot perform miracles.

Faced with vociferous demands for frontier revision, the government has thought fit to stand fast by the *status quo*. But while doing so, the Czechs have at least realized that all is not well with the peoples of Podkarpatska Rus, and especially with the Hutzulians, and some attempt has been made to bring to them, the poorest peasants in Europe, an echo of the comparative affluence the Czech and Slovak peasants knew before falling prices forced all sections of the agrarian community to "cut their coat according to the cloth".

Even to-day, hard times have not affected the industry and perseverance—or the kindliness—of the peoples of that land. They are smiling in adversity, confident in their country and its future. And, conservative at heart as all peasants, their lives follow the old grooves. The ancient feast-days are still observed on every scattered farmstead.

To-day, as yesterday, each successful harvest means for the peasant an occasion for expressing gratitude to God for the blessing of his labours. Although the commandment "by the sweat of the brow shalt thou earn thy bread" is fulfilled to the iota in the course of the seasons upon every peasant holding, nobody complains of the intensive labour of the harvest. And at the end of the labour comes one of the big moments in the peasant's year—called in Czechoslovakia *obzinky*, or harvest home.

In one of the fields a patch of ungarnered corn has been left in readiness for the festival. Singing and laughing, the whole family makes a wreath, or bouquet, of corn-ears and field flowers. For does not the grain lie stacked in the barns, with another year's rains, winds, and labour behind them? The last sheaves of corn are put into a flower-trimmed cart and all the harvesters sit on top of it for the drive home.

Before the farmhouse door the peasant and his wife are waiting for the harvesters. They have prepared bread and salt—eternal symbol of the most important needs of man—and some ale, the "liquid bread" with which the harvesters have been refreshing themselves during sultry days at work in the fields. Two of the most handsome harvesters, holding the wreath, step forward and present it to the peasant and his wife to signify that the task is completed. The housewife next presents each one with a slice of bread and a pinch of salt, and the peasant dispenses drinks. Then all raise their glasses in a toast to the God of the fields, and merrymaking begins, all joining in as one family nourished for another year by the produce of the earth and the warmth of the summer sunshine.

It is a ceremony which, with local variations, is as old as the hills among which it takes place, and as universal as is the peasant himself. You may see it on the banks of the Volga, in the lands watered by the Danube, or among the hill-farms of Andalusia. Which is as it should be, for, standing in a Czechoslovakian farmyard, with my slice of bread and pinch of salt, I felt that the things which unite the farmer of Moravia or Slovakia with the farmer of Devonshire or Yorkshire are greater than the things which divide them, and that all the peasants of the world, in the last analysis, are one family, toiling down the years that the earth may yield its fruits for the benefit of mankind.

CHAPTER XVII

THE WORLD DEPRESSION AND THE PEASANT

"THE crisis is universal; it does not merely affect the European market. It affects overseas states as well as the states of Europe. It operates with unequal intensity according to the economic development of the countries, their capacity for resistance, and the relative advantages which they enjoy as agricultural producers. . . . The reason for the agricultural crisis and for its continuance is to be found in the fact that agricultural prices are low in comparison with the expenditure which the farmer must meet. The profit-earning potentialities of agriculture are weakened. Agricultural products cost a lot to produce and then fetch very little in the market."

In those words the Economic Committee of the League of Nations summed up the worst catastrophe which the peasant millions, the world over, have suffered for half a century past—a catastrophe more widespread in its incidence, and as profound, measured by human suffering, as the dislocation and hardships endured during the years of the World War.

"The severity of the present crisis is aggravated by the fact that almost every branch of agricultural production is affected," the Committee further records.* "In normal times and even during periods of partial depression, the diversity of agricultural production offers a certain margin of safety. The general balance may continue to be favourable, even if some branch or other of agricultural production is working at a loss. At the present time, almost all elements of agricultural production are affected. There are

---

* *The Agricultural Crisis.* Vol. i, Geneva, 1931.

only a few local or temporary exceptions. Hardly any country in the world, hardly any branch of agricultural activity, has escaped the general distress."

Translated into actual prices, the value of the wheat crop fell by over 50 per cent in exporting nations such as Bulgaria and Hungary, while world stocks of wheat (in millions of quintals) rose from 114 in August 1925 to 246 in the same month of 1931. The value of sugar-beet declined by 40 per cent, while stocks rose from 37 million quintals in 1925 to 87 millions in 1931.

As for other grain crops, "the market in rye, barley, and oats has collapsed in the same manner as the wheat market. This slump has been even more pronounced, and the producers have been hard hit. A considerable part of the oats, rye, and barley is, no doubt, consumed on the spot at the farms; but the producers who market a large part of their crops of oats and barley, and the districts in which soil and climate make rye the essential cereal, have found themselves in a deplorable position."*

Turning to livestock, better conditions prevailed during the earlier phases of the crisis, but prices fell steeply at a later date.

The number of cattle in Europe (excluding U.S.S.R.) was still increasing in 1929, while the price of sheep and pigs was well maintained until 1930 in the principal world markets.

In the Danubian countries with which we are here concerned, however, the position of the farmers was more unfavourable. By 1928, cattle prices at Budapest were below the 1913 level, while the price of live pigs in 1929 was only 4 per cent higher than the pre-war figure, and by June 1930 was 30 per cent below it !

"Agricultural conditions in the agrarian countries of Eastern and Southern Europe, notably in Hungary, Yugoslavia, Rumania, and Bulgaria, became considerably worse during 1932," stated the report of the Czechoslovakian National Bank for that year. "Poor crops, simultaneously with abundant crops elsewhere, and the

---

* *The Agricultural Crisis*, p. 29.

marked decrease in the price of grains, rendered the crisis more acute, caused a further reduction in the purchasing power of these countries, a still more unfavourable condition of government finances, and augmented the difficulties encountered in interest payments to foreign countries." Which is the bankers' way of saying that the cost of a pair of peasant shoes in Czernowitz represented 50 kilogrammes of wheat in 1928 *and 150 in 1933*; And that in Bessarabia, a kilogramme of maize was worth a fraction more than one farthing in August of that year!

Thus the experts in the international watch-towers summed up the main factors of the agricultural depression before the worst effects of that prolonged crisis had become manifest. What do those cold statistics mean when translated into terms of the conditions obtaining in the lands of the peasant hosts?

"I have good land, and good crops," a rich peasant in Eastern Galicia told the author. "I work fourteen hours a day, and have four children, all of whom work with me. In 1932 my profit, after growing our food and paying taxes, was £1."

"In 1928 the average price which I received for a young cow was £12," stated a Croatian farmer living near Osijek, in Yugoslavia. "The other day I took a cow to market and the highest price I could get was 45s., while eggs were selling, when you could find a buyer, at five for 2d."

"Our villages have again become self-contained units," a *chorbadjia* stated in a little Bulgarian hillside village. "My people used to have sufficient money to buy matches, salt, oil for their lamps, fertilizers and tools for their fields, boots, and an occasional luxury. Now we have no money left. The fields must do without any fertilizers. We are once again making our own boots. Luxuries are forgotten. A kilo of oil costs sixty eggs, or six chickens; it is too dear, and so in winter all Bulgaria outside Sofia goes to bed when it gets dark. Matches and salt we still get when we can exchange those things for eggs. Boots, clothing, hats, and household linen we make ourselves or go without."

At Jassy, the ancient capital of Rumania, I met a peasant

lad carrying a bundle of onions weighing nearly two kilos to the market. I enquired the price. "Two lei (1d.)," he answered. The lad had walked twelve miles in the hope of gaining that penny—and it was raining !

In Bessarabia the traveller hears the same refrain of the ruined peasant lands.

"I sold sixteen kilogrammes of maize yesterday," said a farmer interviewed at Kishinev market. "It fetched 6d. When this was a Russian land we gave *mamaliga* to our pigs. To-day my family is living on it—seven days a week."

To study the effects of the depression upon the Hungarian peasants one should turn to the figures showing the main agricultural exports of that country for 1928 and 1932. Exports of wheat fell in bulk (apart from the price fall) from 2,878,000 quintals in 1928 to 1,439,000 quintals in 1932 ; of rye from 1,212,000 to 522,000 quintals ; of flour from 2,046,000 quintals to 1,439,000 quintals. Exports of cattle dropped by 20 per cent during the same four years. Only in the case of pigs, sheep, and poultry is any increase in the bulk of exports noticeable ; evidence of the intensive efforts of the Hungarian people to find new markets to replace the old.

Though, as recorded elsewhere in this volume, the standard of farming is high in that country, and the land excellently cared for, these things count for little in an age of tariffs, quota restrictions, and depression. Had Hungary been the worst-farmed nation in Europe, instead of one of the best, that nation could hardly have suffered more severely.*

If any nation was well placed to ward off the forces of the universal depression, it was Czechoslovakia, with a large urban population within its own borders, and the accumulated reserves of prosperous years in the hands (and stockings) of its peasants.

What of the 1,618,000 farms of that pivotal country in Central Europe ? Let the official figures compiled by the Agricultural Academy at Prague tell the story.

---

* See Chapter XII.

The estimated cash yield per hectare of cornland in 1927, a good year, was 1,325 Czech crowns. In 1928 it fell to 1,080 crowns, in 1929 to 658 crowns. By 1921 the figure was down to 210 crowns, or one-sixth of the figure five years before. Still the remorseless arithmetic of the world slump wrote on. In 1932 the cash yield was down to 110 crowns per hectare, and in 1933 it disappeared altogether, to be replaced by an actual loss for every acre of corn produced in that country !

As prices fell, debts climbed. By 1933 a fall of 75 per cent in the income derived from every branch of farming was balanced by debts owing by peasants totalling 30 billion Czech crowns (approximately £185,000,000 at normal rate of exchange). And still the Czechoslovakian peasants could not make ends meet; farm-buildings went unrepaired, boots unsoled, the sick undoctored, and adults under-nourished.

Visit one of those villages which arose, phœnix-like, from the ashes of war in the Ukrainian regions now under Poland ; districts where the houses are described by the inhabitants as "collapsible" in case another upheaval comes. The refrain is the same. Net profit in 1928, £30. Net profit in 1932, £1. A cow worth £55 in 1928, and a beast of the same age and weight fetching £6 10s. in Lemberg market five years later. A good horse fetching only £5 in spring and as little as 3s. in the autumn, when the problem of winter keep must be faced.

Cream worth 2s 3d. a litre in 1928, and 6d. a litre in 1933. Eggs—the universal currency of the peasant lands —worth ½d. each. The richest farmer to be found in that well-farmed region—a man famous because he possessed a reaping machine imported from England in 1910—had an income of £60 per annum in cash, and was considered a millionaire.

The Polish Agricultural Institute at Pulawy has stated that the average farmer in Poland, or the Ukrainian territories at present incorporated in that state, was—at the price-level ruling in 1933—making no net profit whatever. In the case of some sixty farmers in various parts of Poland Proper, and the adjoining Ukrainian territories under

Poland, whose annual profit-and-loss accounts I have seen, the *average* amount of indebtedness was 1,200 z'otys (say £60), and the highest cash income, after paying taxes and interest on debts, was the instance of a family of six, already mentioned, which earned £1. To earn that sum, husband, wife, and four children rose with the sun for eight months and toiled in the fields until darkness came. From March until October their lives were bounded by work and sleep. There was nothing wrong either with their land or their methods of cultivation. Indeed, the peasant was a highly skilled worker, and his farm near enough to Lemberg to enable him to sell his milk in that city.

That family would be classified as "rich". The "middle peasants" in the same country made no profits, after feeding their families, in normal times. Now they have sunk into the lowest class.

In one Ukrainian village in Eastern Galicia, where the size of the average holding is five acres, and the village children clothed in rags scarcely less picturesque, in their very raggedness, than those seen in the peasant regions of Soviet Russia, I found the village owing a sum for overdue taxes representing at least six times its entire value. The government collectors called at every house once a week in order to make sure that no income escaped the tax net. As one villager expressed it : "We only feed our cattle and pigs in order to give more in taxes when they are ripe for sale. No matter how hard we work, there is nothing left for us."

"We cannot go on—we have no money at all." The cry is heard from priests, traders, and peasants. Nothing is spent on the roads, the state of which may be judged by the fact that the impoverished taxi-drivers of Lemberg and Brest-Litovsk will lose a day's employment rather than venture outside those cities with their vehicles. When a cart-track becomes impassable even for the slow-moving farmcart (which means when even an army tank would find the going difficult, and not before) the peasants do something about it themselves. It is either that or leaving the outlying fields unharvested.

The lives of those peasants—Polish and Ukrainian

alike—are even more grey than the winter scene on the Galician plains. Hard work, unrelieved by a single spark of hope as long as present conditions last, is the common lot. In winter their clothing is eternally damp, and their world eternally a muddy sea. In summer the human body must be strained to breaking point, lest during the coming winter they starve. If things get worse it will not affect them, for there is nothing else left to lose except the means of life itself. The peasantry who live under Pilsudski— Polish and Ukrainian alike—have been stripped to the bone.

But why continue the refrain? All the way southward from Prague and Warsaw to the borders of the Turkish Republic, and back across Eastern Europe to Brest-Litovsk and the Baltic, the story of 1933 was the same. National frontiers have no real existence in the sphere of economics in that region to-day; the Bulgarian peasant faces precisely the same problems as the Ukrainian smallholder in Volhynia; the Bessarabian wheat-grower shares his anxiety, and watches his debts pile up, in company with the Hungarian landowner and the Slovak peasant. Before the onrushing and universal poverty these peasant lands stand revealed as a single economic unit. The more watertight compartments that exist within that unit, the worse for all. The cost of the "Balkanization" of Central Europe has been paid not by governments, and only in part by industry; the main portion of that "account rendered" has fallen on the backs of the peasantry.

To appreciate fully the devastation which has swept, like a cyclone, across "the other half of Europe", however, the traveller should enquire about matches.

Matches are one of the necessities of life. Without them it is impossible, in these days when flint and steel have been banned by governments mindful of revenue derived from match monopolies, to light a fire, or bake bread, or cook food; or even enjoy a cigarette of dried grass. The poorest peasant, living on the produce of ten acres, in some valley forty miles from the nearest apology for a market town, formerly bought matches even when he could buy nothing else.

Ask about matches in Rumania to-day, and you will

in all probability—if it is clear you are not a government agent—be shown the flint, steel, and moss mentioned in a previous chapter. Matches are luxuries in rural Rumania.

Ask the same question in some village in Polish Poland, and you will be taken to a cottage and shown a fire which, if it is not mid-winter, will probably be the only fire in the entire village. When the peasants have cooking to be done, they either bring their pots to this communal flame, or use its glowing embers to make a fire in their own cottages— no matches needed.

Or watch a Ukrainian peasant in Eastern Galicia light a fire in the cooking oven of his hut. If he is lucky he still has matches, but they are expensive in days when eggs have replaced money as the medium of exchange. Before using them, therefore, he splits each match into four, longways, so that a quarter of the "head" is left on each stick. Each box of matches thus becomes two hundred ! Thus are the peasant lands fighting the world depression.

Even before the catastrophic fall in prices, world tendencies were threatening the economic welfare of the peasant regions. During the past twenty years the world demand for cereals has fallen sharply, due largely to the shifting of consumption from cereals to other forms of foodstuffs.

Compared with the years 1909-13, the annual consumption of wheat in Europe for 1921-24 declined by 4 per cent, of rye by 18 per cent, barley 23 per cent, and oats by 16 per cent. If the increase in population between these two periods is taken into account, the decline is even greater, amounting to 11 per cent per head in the case of wheat, and no less than 24 per cent per head for barley.

The belief that this drastic drop in the basic food requirements of Europe (which had occurred before the world depression precipitated an even steeper decline) is due to changed habits of diet is confirmed by the fact that since 1913 the world production of potatoes has increased by 23 per cent, of sugar by 40 per cent, wine by 21 per cent, coffee by 28 per cent, and cocoa by 13 per cent. For Eastern Europe alone the consumption of bread cereals per head has risen since 1913 by 2 per cent in the case of wheat and 8 per cent for rye. Drastic declines in consumption per head have, however, occurred in Great Britain, Germany, Switzerland, and France. And this decline in consumption has been aggravated, from the point of view of the peasant producer, by a still more drastic decline in imports of cereals due to tariffs and other fiscal measures adopted by the Western European nations.

By 1933 the import of foreign wheat into France had been totally prohibited, while there was still in existence on the Statute Book of that country an import duty amounting to 200 per cent *ad valorem*. Italy confined her purchases to one per cent of foreign wheat, admitted on payment of a duty of over 200 per cent. Germany, formerly an important market for the peasant lands, was moving swiftly towards self-sufficiency and permitting the import, under a quota scheme, of only 3 per cent of foreign wheat, with a duty of more than 300 per cent. Yet in 1923 the three nations named imported over six million tons of foreign wheat! In those ten years, not only has their native production of wheat enormously increased, but, owing to the high internal price of wheat and bread, there has also taken place a large increase in the consumption of rye, maize, and potato flour.

One is apt to think of the yield of the world's farms as being more or less constant from year to year, but in the light of the figures given above it is hardly surprising that cereal production over the whole of Europe (including Russia) declined by over 20 per cent between 1913 and 1925. That decline has, since the latter year, been intensified by the contraction of markets due to the world crisis, and by fiscal restrictions.

The latest recorded changes in European crop yields bear clear evidence of the efforts made by the peasant nations to overcome the effects of changing habits in diet, reduced markets, and fiscal barriers.

During 1932, the wheat crop increased by 11·8 per cent in Germany, 12·5 per cent in France, and 11·3 per cent in Italy. Rumania, on the other hand, registered a decline in wheat production of no less than 55·9 per cent in a single year, while production fell in Yugoslavia by 45˙9 per cent, in Hungary by 19˙3 per cent, and in Bulgaria by 17˙4 per cent.

The total crop of rye in 1932, as compared with 1931, was 25˙2 per cent larger in Germany, 12˙4 per cent larger in Poland, and 56˙8 per cent larger in Czechoslovakia. Hungary registered in the same year an increase of 60˙4 per cent in the quantity of maize harvested and Yugoslavia 41˙1 per cent, whereas Rumania's crop of maize was 10˙4 per cent smaller than the previous year.

Behind such sober statistics recorded in governmental and national bank reports may be glimpsed the frenzied attempts of millions of individual peasants to discover a crop for which there is a market, and which will yield them some profit and not a loss ; and similar efforts by the governments of predominantly agricultural nations to mitigate the effects of the world depression and growing tariff walls upon their peoples.

In a world in which both consumption and prices were falling, only taxes and the burden of debt owing by peasant-proprietors increased. Before the governments concerned were moved to take action, more than 70 per cent of all the peasant holdings in Eastern Europe were threatened by debts incurred during good years. The alternatives were, clearly, wholesale evictions and distress or emergency legislation. Wisely, those concerned chose the latter course. Unpleasant facts were shelved for a term of years by a system of moratoriums, or partial moratoriums, on agricultural debts which to-day cover almost the whole of the peasant regions.

The terms of these moratoriums vary. In Bulgaria debts are repayable in instalments over five years, the terms of any settlement between debtor and creditor being compulsorily notifiable to the Courts. Under Polish law, while distraints may still be levied under certain circumstances, the debtor cannot seize the first cow or the first pair of horses on any farm. Furniture, bedding, and household goods may, however, be taken in payment of overdue taxes, but difficulty is often experienced in finding bidders when these are put up to auction, the peasants refusing to purchase goods thus taken from neighbours.

In Rumania a five-year moratorium on peasant debts came into force on April 15, 1933. Under this law, peasants owning not more than 50 hectares of land are required to pay interest at 1 per cent per annum over the period of the moratorium, and larger owners 3 per cent. A reduction of the debt is also allowed, amounting in the case of owners of 10 hectares or less to 50 per cent. The average amount of indebtedness among the peasants of Rumania is from £25 to £50 per acre ; this among a population whose sole earning power consists of the soil which they cultivate !

Eighty per cent of the peasantry of Yugoslavia are being "strangled by debts"—to quote a foreign diplomat living at Belgrade. Faced with the problem of peasant debts estimated to total nearly £30,000,000 at normal rate of exchange, the government introduced a new law at the end of 1933, providing for the conversion of rural debts into long-term loans repayable within twelve years, and carrying interest at the rate of 4 per cent in the case of private creditors and 6 per cent on debts owing to banks— the differentiation being due to the high rates, often 25 per cent, charged on private loans in the past.

In Yugoslavia, as elsewhere, the depression has routed the machine, and the horse and ox have once more come into their own ; farm tractors purchased during the "good years" are to-day rusting in the fields because their owners are too poor to buy oil or employ mechanics to carry out needed repairs.

In Czechoslovakia, profits from farmland have, as already stated, shrunk to a minus quantity. As a natural corollary, not only have debts soared, but consumption in the peasant regions has fallen to record low levels. As one government expert expressed it, to-day the peasants are spending "only on their children and their fields". Repairs to buildings, fertilizers for the fields, and clothing or luxuries for adults are alike beyond their reach. In many districts there is not even money for doctors, and the health of the people is suffering in consequence. These conditions exist in communities which, until 1928, enjoyed one of the highest peasant standards in all Europe.

In normal times the effects of bad crops would be offset to some extent by the presence of cottage industries offering a subsidiary income. In North Bohemia fully 20 per cent of the peasants formerly had some income apart from agriculture, derived from the making of toys, glass, textiles, sabots, and other things. Between 1929 and 1933 these industries shared in the slump, and subsidiary incomes were drastically scaled down, or disappeared altogether. Thus the farmers of Czechoslovakia have suffered scarcely less than those living under more primitive conditions further east ; one more example of the world-wide character of the crisis.

The network of emergency laws thus imposed to ease the financial strain imposed by the world crisis upon the primary producers has prevented a wholesale elimination of peasants from their holdings which, but for these artificial checks, would largely have neutralized the benefits of the redistribution of land following the war, and, by placing large tracts of territory in the hands of Jewish moneylenders and "middle men", aggravated that anti-Semitic feeling which undoubtedly exists in many parts of Eastern Europe.

Private debts, however, form only one facet of the financial problem facing the peasants to-day. No device known to science can protect the penniless producer from the activities of the tax-collector in nations which are struggling to maintain their solvency in the face of an unprecedented decline in national income.

The burden of taxation is relative to the prosperity of those upon whom it is levied, and a sum total which may be paid without difficulty by a British or French agriculturist may constitute a crushing burden in countries where a cash income of £5 a year puts the lucky possessor among the wealthiest class of farmers.

When one reads that a "rich" farmer in Eastern Galicia was in 1933 paying the equivalent of £15 a year in taxes, plus eight days a year obligatory labour for the commune, it will shed little light on the burdens which the peasants are shouldering so patiently. When it is added, however, that that £15 represents even in normal years about 75 per cent of the total cash yield of twelve months' labour—in other words, that the same family works for at least eight months out of each twelve to satisfy the demands of the state—the bitterness aroused in the peasant lands by the continuing high level of taxation, in years when profits have disappeared, will be understood.

If the "rich" farmer cannot find £15 easily, it is no less difficult for the poor peasant to find the £3 or £4 needed to pay his land tax, and those other taxes which, in all countries, must somehow be met. To solve this problem without resorting to distraint, a system of "working it out" has been adopted in a number of regions, including Poland, the taxes due in certain instances being accepted in the form of free labour for so many days or weeks on roads, repair of bridges, drainage work, etc.

High rates of taxation, bearing heavily upon slender resources, and the absence of profit, account for the remarkable fall in the value of land which has been a further feature of the depression even in those nations where growing pressure of population had for decades heightened the persistent land-hunger of the people.

In the Bukovina the value of an acre of good land has fallen from £200 to less than £40, while in Eastern Galicia, where arable land in the vicinity of the cities was eagerly bought at £70 to £80 an acre before the world crisis, it can be purchased for half that figure, and there are few buyers. In more remote regions excellent fertile soil can be had for as low as £15 an acre.

With these prices ruling a peasant possessing £50 is a capitalist; for that sum he can, in Volhynia, buy two acres of good ground, erect a house for his family, and have the equivalent of a five-pound note left over for purchasing tools and seed. Having done so, however, he would be fortunate indeed if the labour of his entire family from dawn until dark enabled him to feed them and remain free from debt. A farmer who achieved that miracle to-day would qualify as a lecturer to explain how it was done!

Side by side with dwindling capital has come a return to

primitive methods of cultivation in those districts where, before the depression, conditions favoured a slow evolution to modern methods. In 1926 the petrol-driven farm tractor was just "making its bow" in Eastern Europe. One famous American firm reported sales of 200 tractors in Yugoslavia and 2,000 in Rumania for 1926. To-day it would be difficult to find a purchaser for a piece of farm machinery (outside Government experimental farms and co-operative bodies) from one end of Eastern Europe to the other ; while of about 40,000 tractors in use before the crisis, half have disappeared owing to defaults in payment and most of the rest are rotting in the fields.

In their place, the hand-scythe once more reigns supreme, with the bullock-cart for transport. The slump has even altered the fashions. Factory-made clothes remain unsold, while the ubiquitous sheep supply coats, hats, and boots for millions who, before 1928, were inclined to doff their picturesque peasant clothing for the nebulous delights of "shoddy" from Poland and boots from the Bata factory at Zlin.

Oil being a luxury, the home-made candle has come back—supplied by the same sheep who keep one's body warm and feet dry in winter. "Town"-bought furniture is carefully tended as befits relics of better days, while the menfolk have learnt anew the art of fashioning peasant-stools and benches. Even the tendency of whole nations to lift themselves off the floor—that sure guide to the standard of living in peasant lands—has been reversed. Those "setting up house" in Bulgaria, Rumania, or Poland to-day are, as often as not, faced with the prospect of sleeping on Mother Earth just as their grandparents did in the days of the great Empires.

Four years which have put back the clock of progress in that almost limitless ocean of peasant lands for fifty ! Nearly one hundred millions of men, women, and children, of the most vigorous, industrious, and valuable stock in all Europe, reduced to a state bordering on beggary by the world depression, intensified by misgovernment and excessive taxation. How are they surviving at all in their remote, moneyless hills and plains ?

In the answer to that question lies the supreme paradox of the world depression. Poorer than for generations past in almost every other respect, in one important particular millions of peasant families have been enriched by events. Unable to find purchasers in the markets of Europe for their cattle, sheep, pigs, geese, poultry, butter, eggs and the rest—often unable even to barter these things for essentials —they are eating what would otherwise go to market. It will remain the most remarkable fact of these remarkable years that the number of peasants who ate meat once a week was probably greater in 1933 than ever before.

Those peasants have little or no cash income. A census taken by the author n three hundred small farmsteads in the interior of Yugoslavia revealed that the *average* amount of actual money in the possession of those three hundred families amounted to 1s. per head. They would hand over their cattle and geese to free themselves from debt if these things were wanted. They would sell them—but in market after market four-fifths of the produce goes back to the farm unsold, while the remaining fifth barely covers taxes and commissions on the sale. So the peasants remain on their holdings, breeding their cattle, rearing pigs and poultry, growing the corn wherewith to feed those animals—and in the end serving them up in the family stew-pot on Saturday night. This fact has done more than anything else to rob the world crisis of its worst hardships, and has served to preserve the strength of the peasant peoples at a time when the physical powers of many industrial workers were deteriorating through idleness and malnutrition. The peasant lands still have their epidemics. Many countrymen still lack milk for their children because, if they are fortunate enough to live near a city, every drop of the precious liquid must be hurried off each day to provide cash for the tax-collector. But these are permanent features of life in the peasant countries; they are not attributable to the depression.

You will find almost every kind of disease and sickness in those primitive peasant houses—except malnutrition. That "disease" of civilization has been kept at bay by the simple fact that with world agriculture bordering on total collapse, these voiceless millions retain the ownership of the soil they love, and have in their hands the means of production. They may not be able to find a trader willing to exchange eggs for matches; their clothes may reveal their poverty. But they need ask no man for permission to grow the food which is needed to maintain those under the family roof, and to that task they have set their hands with undiminished energies, undeterred by political discontents, "Minority" persecution, officialdom, or the mysterious antics of money-markets and governments. Nothing reveals so truly the outstanding qualities of the peasant—his dogged individualism and genuine love for the soil to which he is attached—as this spectacle of an agrarian Europe which has gone back to the conditions of a century ago, when agriculture was not so much a national industry as a means of survival, and whole populations were absorbed in the task of growing food for themselves rather than for export.

Even so, the diet of the average peasant would not appear over-elaborate to any but the hardiest of pioneers. Your English breakfast (assuming that the reader likes bacon and eggs) this morning cost more than a Ukrainian peasant living under Poland or Rumania can make toiling fourteen hours a day for a week. Potatoes, bread and milk —with meat once or twice a week—is the main diet of the middle class of farmer in those regions.

The Croats have not managed to get back to their pre-war affluence, thanks to the heavy taxation and anti-Croat bias of the Yugoslav dictatorship. The white bread which the traveller found in every Croat home has been replaced by black. Breakfast consists of maize porridge and milk, and the midday dinner of home-made cheese, vegetables, and milk.

The Bulgarians, as befits a nation of gardeners, are living on bread, cabbage, pickles, beans and onions, with mutton, geese and poultry for special occasions.

Compared with these Balkan peoples, the Hungarian peasants are still well-off. In that country peasants working in the fields for a wage of 1s. a day live on cabbage, potatoes, beans, with bread and bacon once a day and meat or a chicken each week-end.

The rule that the peasants are feeding better than in pre-slump days applies to all the nations under review—except Czechoslovakia. The Czech and Slovak peasants have never "lived on their farms" as do the producers of other lands. In former days they produced crops for sale, and with the money thus earned bought from the cities most of the food they needed. They drank coffee. They wore boots—bearing the inevitable Bata label! With the disappearance of profits, the position was dramatically changed. A high standard of living became a liability instead of an asset. Farmers growing "eatables"—wheat, vegetables, pigs, and poultry—were still able to feed their families reasonably well, but in the grasslands and forest regions the yield of eatable crops was so low that diet suffered. As peasants they had the means of production in their hands, but one cannot eat hay, sugar-beet—or timber!

Behind the crisis responsible for this impoverishment of half Europe lie factors outside the scope of this volume, of which the most important are declining consumption, coupled with increasing production of agricultural commodities, the progress of mechanization in some nations, the lack of equilibrium between what the peasant buys and what he sells, and the dislocation caused to the agricultural markets of Europe by the Great War and the new frontiers.

This last factor has played a more important part in the history of the agricultural crisis than is generally realized.

The regular currents of trade were turned backwards. In order to provide food for the belligerents, distant countries were asked to increase their production. In the principal non-European exporting countries the area under cereals increased. New Zealand, the Argentine, and Australia at present export 350 million English pounds of butter in place of 50 millions in 1900. The production of meat in these countries is calculated at 2,000 million pounds as against 300 million in 1900. As compared with the pre-war period, the output of sugar in Cuba increased from 2·5 to 5 million tons, and in Java from 1·5 to 2·5 million tons. . . . The seriousness of the situation is enhanced by the fact that,

Peasants making baskets in an Eastern Galician village.

Delivering the baskets to a Co-operative collecting station.

sooner or later, Russia and the Central and Eastern European countries whose agricultural organization is not yet complete will appear in the market with increased outputs.*

It is the opportunity of finding markets, first for the existing scale of production, and later for the increased quantities of produce which, given remunerative prices, improved transport facilities, and a surcease from political uncertainty, can and will be grown in the peasant lands of Europe, that the millions are waiting for.

For the fact which impresses itself most sharply upon the mind of the traveller in those lands to-day, when the effects of the world agricultural crisis still lie like a pall over millions of smallholdings, is that, given encouragement, the peasants of Europe can double alike the yield of their farms, the wealth of their countries, and their own standard of living.

Those peasant homes are hungry for the products of the factory. Civilization has given many of them the sewing-machine ; motor-cars are rarities ; wireless sets and gramophones almost unknown. If the day comes when the debt load is lightened, and the effective cash income of every peasant home raised to 5s. a week, Western Europe will discover that the potentialities of the vast Chinese market are no greater than the appetite of this "other Europe" which lies at our very doors.

"We want a steel bridge to replace this wooden carriage-way over the river," said a Rumanian peasant to the writer. "We could afford to pay a fair price, by instalments, if only some steel firm wanted cows or pigs to feed its workpeople. But your firms don't do business on those terms .They want cash—and cash we have not got. So I suppose the old bridge must be patched until it falls down."

When the farmlands recover their lost credit it will be possible to inaugurate in Eastern Europe a public works programme which will eclipse the dream of the wildest Socialist who ever lived. To-day that region is largely undeveloped. For years, roads (such as they are), railways,

---

* *The Agricultural Crisis.* Vol. i, p. 18.

R

rolling stock, bridges, homes, schools, and equipment of all kinds have been wearing out. The extension of agricultural machinery, motor-bus services, and other "improvements" wait upon the passing of the depression, and the restoration of municipal and private fortunes.

These are factors which invest the future of Eastern Europe with romance. Meanwhile, only poverty thrives. And when the peasant pauses in the task of hoeing his crops to speak with the traveller of the hardships that are his lot to-day, of high taxation, debts, and the lack of roads and credit, he speaks for all the peasant millions.

Those are problems common to every part of the peasant lands. They are the problems which, sooner or later, must be solved, if the millions whose patience has been the most remarkable factor of these past years are not to take matters into their own hands and put some of their own ideas to the test. For the European peasant is thinking in these days, and the vision of power is stirring in minds evolved from countless generations of tillers of the soil.

CHAPTER XVIII

THE PEASANTS LOOK AT THE FUTURE

HE had a bent back, but must have been tall before age caused him to shrivel like the shelf of over-ripe apples which I noticed in his barn. Since he first wielded a long-handled hoe he had seen spring come more than seventy times to the thirty acres of land he tilled north of Warsaw, felt the hot suns of summer beating down on his head, and watched those same fields surrender their soil to the grip of the northern winter.

He had seen other things, too, in his eighty-four years. Life under the Russian Czar, which had been difficult for a patriotic Pole. War, which had taken his sons and spread death and destruction across the land —his own and his neighbours' acres. Peace, and the dawn of Polish freedom. He had taken fresh heart at that, only to have his optimism dashed when he was caught up in the Bolshevik invasion of 1920.

Although that visitation had lasted only a few weeks, it meant making yet another fresh start, and he was already old. But he remembered that he was now living in his beloved Poland; no more was he a member of an oppressed "minority", but a free citizen of his own state. Had not Witos, his leader, been elevated to high office in the service of Poland? Surely, when Polish peasants became famous, it meant that the night of tribulation was passed, and the dawn of a new day—the day he had prayed for since he was first old enough to think at all—was at hand.

His neighbours were equally optimistic. The new era would mean fair play for the producer, good prices for crops, lower taxation, peace, and plenty. Once more he set about the task of repairing his little home, and replanting his fields, over which the Bolshevik cavalry had swarmed on the "drive" which ended at the very gates of Warsaw.

He was still toiling away, that aged peasant, when I passed his home a month or so ago. His single working life almost bridged the years between the serfdom of old Russia and the world depression. And, as he told me, with a trace of sadness, at the end of the road he found the condition of his neighbours little better than it had been in the dark days of his beginning.

True, they were securely in possession of the soil which is life to them. They were thus able to provide their families with food. But nothing else ; before the chill winds of economic adversity all their dreams of peace and plenty had disappeared.

"For seventy-six years I have toiled on this piece of earth, paying my taxes and producing food. Fighting poverty in peace, and marching whither I was told in war. Providing children for the armies of the men who ruled us. Asking nothing of life except security—security to labour fourteen hours a day, and a little surplus at the end of the harvest with which to buy some fal-lals in the city for the womenfolk. And at the end of it all, what do I find ? An ocean of debts around me. My neighbours poorer than ever ; too poor to buy matches. Governments doing little or nothing to assist the peasant, forgetting that in these parts the peasant carries governments on his shoulders. Witos, our leader, in exile. Life still being ordered for the benefit of the cities. We peasants ignored and neglected. But let the rumours of new wars grow a little louder, and you will see a change. For wars are fought mainly by peasants. On the day that Europe believes another conflict is coming, you will find the statesmen rediscovering what fine fellows we peasants are. Actually, we are just fine fools."

Thus that old Polish farmer summed up life as he saw it after more than seventy-five years of toil. As he spoke I recalled a news item appearing in the newspapers of Europe that day, announcing that Soviet Russia had decided to issue double rations to the peasants living on the eastern frontiers of that country, as a precautionary measure against Japanese aggression.

In Europe, the time is not yet ripe for those double rations to be issued, and when that time comes, governments may learn that the bovine, "inarticulate" peasantry have been replaced by a new race of toilers who can see further than the ends of their noses.

Strange things are happening beneath the surface of the peasant-lands. The "unchangeable" peasant is changing. And the evidence of that change is revealed by the fact that the peasants are thinking for themselves, becoming politically conscious, *as peasants*, of their common interests and common destiny. They have not yet reached the stage at which the spectre of the "Green International" will be transformed into an urgent, living question. It is possible that if Rumania, say, declared war on Soviet Russia or Bulgaria, the world might again see the spectacle of one set of over-taxed poverty-stricken peasants marching to attack another set of toilers, whose interests were identical with their own. Possible, but not so probable as it was in 1914, and becoming less probable with each passing year.

Several factors have conspired to set the peasant masses thinking. The most important, of course, the European War, and its aftermath of disillusionment. Just as the peasants as a whole probably lost more by that war than any other class, so the heaviest burden of the world crisis of 1929-1934, expressed in terms of individual hardship, fell not upon governments, bankers, or industrialists, but (in Eastern Europe, at all events) upon the peasant masses.

Peace, taxation, social betterment, political freedom, prices, debts—these six things are stirring the peasant mind to-day from the Baltic to the Black Sea. The peasants are nationally minded without being nationalist; they demand facilities for their children to be nurtured in the culture and the language of their forefathers. Most earnestly of all, they desire peace, not only because they have no longer any doubt that war is against their interests, but, equally

important in assessing the future prospects of those who
till the soil, because they are conscious that war spells
death and destruction to all their plans for an improved
standard of living and to the whole democratic conception of peasant life. "Whoever wins the next war, the
peasant will lose it," said a Bessarabian farmer to me—
and one hundred millions of European peasants echo
that sentiment.

The peasant is chafing under systems of taxation
and banking which, whilst often absorbing all, and more
than all, his surplus, bring him nothing in return. He
is critical of the bureaucracies which he carries on his
shoulders in many lands, and of governments which
seek to redress every deficit in the national accounts
by subjecting the peasant masses to another "turn of
the screw". Under Poland, for example, one of the main
grievances of the peasants—Polish and Ukrainian alike—
was the fact that, owing to the creation of a match monopoly, the cost of matches was suddenly doubled in 1930
—at the very moment when money was most difficult
to get, and many peasants could not afford to purchase
matches even at the lower price of former years.

The mountains of debts owed by the peasants of all
countries are not troubling the debtors overmuch for
a significant reason. Ask any peasant, owing perhaps the
equivalent of £300 on ten acres, what hope he has of
ever being free from debt, and he will say, "Never."
Hint that he may, in that case, have his farm taken from
him, and he will reply quickly with the same word.
No peasant, however deeply he may be in debt, believes
that any government will dare to authorize the large-scale
expropriations which would be necessary if payment was
to be enforced within any reasonable time. That way
lies revolution, and governments know it. The utmost
that may be anticipated by anyone cognizant of conditions
in the agricultural east of Europe is the eventual funding
of these debts through some agricultural banking structure, which will take them over at rates of interest low
enough for the debtors to make annual payments for
interest and amortization.

You may hear it said in Vienna that wine, Protestant-ism, and Hitlerism go together, while beer, Catholicism, and Conservatism are similarly linked—Conservatism, in that land, being expressed by loyalty to the Habsburg clan.

In Eastern Europe generally, no section of the peasants, whether Catholic, Orthodox, or Protestant, subscribes to the theories of dictatorship. The politics of the awakening peasantry may best be described as Conservatism with a difference. Not the Conservatism of the old estates and the open ballot, the "rigged" elections or the Divine Right of Kings, but the conserv-atism of ancient ways of life, customs, and habits.

Search Europe from one end to the other and you will not find any people more suspicious of change than the Bulgarian peasant communities. Nor will you find a people more truly democratic in their ways of thought and in their respect for authority. Throughout the peasant regions this brand of democratic conservatism is growing in strength, and may eventually exercise considerable influence on events.

For that which the peasants wish to conserve is not the fortunes of states or governments, but the fortunes of the peasant himself.

Listening to question and answer at political meetings in the villages of Croatia, Rumania, Poland, and other lands, I have found myself marvelling at the informed mind and grasp of detail shown by men and women in these isolated communities. To mention but one instance, a discussion on "The Gold Standard and the Peasant", held in the *Prosvita*, or educational institute, of a village in Volhynia, attended by some two hundred peasants, who had none of them travelled more than ten miles from that isolated community since 1918, was followed by a general debate, the standard of which was far higher than similar debates to which I have listened in the city of London.

This insight into world affairs may be attributed, in most cases, to the fact that a majority of the peasants now not only read newspapers, but discuss their contents with an eagerness unknown in the world of cinemas, gramophones, and wireless. As one agricultural professor expressed it: "The peasant often takes a long time to learn very little. But, once having learnt it, he never forgets." The European War and its aftermath taught them a lot, and they are still learning.

What, in their hearts, do the peasants want? It is a question needing more than one answer.

Producing more wealth than they consume, they want a voice in the spending of that wealth; which means an extension of social services, and participation both in the levying of taxation and in the allocation of the revenues which they provide.

Forming an absolute majority of the inhabitants of the predominantly agrarian states, they demand freedom to express their opinions, freedom to elect their own representatives, and consideration for their views when elected, in place of government in the interests of crowned rulers, presidents, bankers, industrialists, militarists, or urban minorities. In a word, they demand that the welfare of the peasants comes first instead of last, not on the ground of their economic contribution to the states concerned, but in accordance with the principle of "the greatest good for the greatest number". (Their repudiation of any purely materialistic conception of government is shown by the fact that their political parties are in almost every case known as *Peasant*, and not *Agricultural* or *Agrarian*, parties—to the cultivator the man is more important than the soil.)

Conscious of the evil effects upon family happiness, and economic prosperity, of wars and rumours of wars, they would welcome an end of national fears and rivalries, and the ushering in of an era of co-operation between nations, in which the products of industry would once more flow to the farms—and food would command a fair price in the cities.

But more important than these considerations, and, seen through peasant eyes, the inevitable first step towards their attainment, is the liquidation of the evil results of the peace settlements. There can be neither justice nor social betterment for Croats, Ukrainians, or Hungarians while millions belonging to these races remain under the heel of states which deny their just national aspirations, ignore their deepest and most profound feelings, and regard them as colonies to be exploited in the supposed interests of the ruling race.

Territorial revision may be a thorny subject, but it is a living issue in the peasant-lands. What, assuming that the peoples were consulted on the question of an adjustment of national frontiers, would that revision involve?

In the case of those peasants who already live under governments of their own race, the transformation they would make could be carried out without affecting their neighbours. In the case of those tillers of the soil who to-day comprise the often-persecuted "minorities" of Eastern Europe, the achievement of their ambitions would begin with wholesale and drastic revision of existing frontiers. For it is an amazing fact, frequently and bitterly placed before the traveller in those regions, that with the possible exception of Poland Proper and Czechoslovakia the peasants of Eastern Europe were never consulted when the maps of the post-war Europe were being drawn at the Versailles and other peace conferences.

To the peasants, the revision of the treaties is not a political question at all, but an act of elementary justice. They realize the strength of the forces arrayed in defence of the *status quo*; they know that the fight may be long. But they also know that the end is not in doubt, and that the existing frontiers have "put back the clock" in Eastern Europe for two generations.

It is an unfortunate fact that the aftermath of the territorial changes which followed the war in that region has clearly proved those decisions to be against the true interests of the peasantry. With all its faults and weaknesses, the Austro-Hungarian Empire enabled the races within its borders to develop a certain national life of their own. It gave to them security, markets, and justice. The Succession States, with the sole exception of Czechoslovakia, have provided them with none of these things, and, in place of them, have sought to eliminate racial differences and national aspirations by force.

The inexorable logic of facts compel the independent investigator to admit that, after fifteen years, it has been clearly proved that, of all the changes incorporated in the treaties concerned with Eastern Europe, only two— the creation of Czechoslovakia and the satisfaction of Poland's demand for independence—can be placed on the credit side of the account, and the re-emergence of a free Poland was sullied by the promptitude with which that nation denied similar justice to the Ukrainians of Eastern Galicia, Volhynia, and Polissia.

All the rest of the territorial changes, affecting Transylvania, the Banat, Croatia, and the Slovene territories, Macedonia, Dobruja, Bessarabia, Bukovina, and those Ukrainian regions under Poland, have merely permitted reaction, neglect, and persecution to flourish more abundantly.

Between 1919 and 1921 millions of Ukrainians, Hungarians, Germans, Croats, Slovenes, Macedonians, and Bulgarians were bundled into this country, and that without the smallest regard for the wishes of the peoples concerned—indeed, often against their expressed desires —as though they were cattle rather than human beings. Race, national consciousness, and ambitions were alike ignored. From that initial mistake flows much of the pent-up bitterness which simmers beneath the surface in Eastern Europe to-day.

There have always been "minorities" in that region, and there always will be ; for it would defy the wisdom of a Solomon so to draw the lines of frontiers that, in Transylvania, for example, all the Hungarians were on one side and all the Rumanians on the other. The ethnographical soufflé was baffling enough in 1918 ; to-day it is far worse. The nations which then aggrandized themselves have, during the interval, deliberately striven to "so scramble the eggs that no one will ever unscramble them". Rumanians from the old Regat have been sent as "colonists" to Bessarabia and the Bukovina ; the

Transylvanian cities remain Magyar while the country around them is more solidly Rumanian than ever. Ten years ago the population of the Nashitze district of Yugoslavia was over 90 per cent Croat; by 1933 the percentage had been brought down to only 60 per cent by Serb settlement. Even Eastern Galicia, which has been solidly Ukrainian since the dawn of history, has its Polish settlers.

Although usually spoken of, and treated as, minorities, it is actually incorrect to speak of either the Ukrainians now living under Poland, Soviet Russia or Rumania, or the Croats and Slovenes in Yugoslavia, as minorities. They are homogeneous peoples inhabiting the lands which their ancestors have occupied for centuries. In some cases, such as the Ukrainians, they are not only of a higher cultural level than, but actually outnumber, the races which to-day oppress them.

The only true "minorities" are the little "pockets" of population of distinct race found dotted throughout Eastern Europe—Germans in Rumania and Czecho-slovakia, Bulgarians throughout the Balkans, and, of course, the Jewish inhabitants of the region.

Were the dispossessed peoples—Ukrainians, Croats, Slovenes, Macedonians, Hungarians, Montenegrins, and Bulgarians—ruled by peoples of equal cultural and social development to themselves, the minority problems of Eastern Europe would never have constituted the danger to the peace and stability of peasant Europe which they have assumed. Had the peace treaties been expressly designed to flout the unwritten law that "Western" peoples should not be placed under "Eastern" civiliza-tions, and to ensure that self-determination should never be extended to the peasant, those documents could scarcely have created a more unfortunate position.

Overshadowing the political grievances of the peasants as a class, however, is the question of the persecution in certain areas.

"Clear out the Rumanian *opinshe,* and then we will consider what our policy is as peasants," a farmer in Bessarabia declared to me, when I suggested to him that there existed a bond of common interest between the Rumanian peasants of the Old Kingdom and those brought within the frontiers of that country by the peace settlement. If that view is commonly held throughout the "minority" regions, it is the fault of governments which saw in their extended boundaries, not opportunities for fostering the welfare of all their peoples, but only additional opportunities for self-aggrandizement, larger armies, and predatory taxation.

The result is that these minority peoples are to-day linked in a new "Little Entente", of which few statesmen have ever heard, but which is united by the bonds of a common hatred for those who have controlled their destinies during the past fifteen years. And unless all the signs are deceptive, history will date the awakening of the peasants of Eastern Europe, *as a class*, to the formation of that common front, utilized, in the first instance, to secure freedom from persecution.

The events responsible for this regrouping of peoples are set out elsewhere in these pages. Every attempt to secure redress of grievances long borne in silence has been met with more repression, more arrests and more prison-cells. The "Western" and democratic conception of government, has, for fifteen years, been battling with the "Balkan methods" favoured by Poles, Rumanians, and Serbs—rule by naked force.

The facts concerning that unseen conflict are no less a threat to the tranquillity of Europe because the victims are defenceless peasants and the police squads of Pilsudski, Carol, and Alexander II are able to report, upon all occasions, that the situation is well in hand.

At the end of 1933 thousands of persons, mostly peasants, were incarcerated in the prison-houses of Eastern Europe for the "crime" of refusing to deny their nationality. Any man possessing the calibre of a national leader within the "minority" ranks walked in danger of his life, and was liable to be "removed" by methods redolent of the Chicago gangsters at the first opportunity.

An army of police spies and *agents provocateurs*—

THE SPIRIT OF THE PEASANT-LANDS
A Ukrainian peasant woman beside a wayside shrine in Eastern Galicia.

paid out of taxation raised from the peasantry—flood the countryside; in Czernowitz there are some 10,000 spies, out of a total population of 120,000, while in Lemberg there are nearly as many employed in keeping that Ukrainian territory safe for Poland! All letters posted to England from "minority" regions are subjected to censorship. Any foreigner who is in touch with the people immediately finds himself under suspicion, for there is nothing the governments concerned fear more than *vox populi*.

Faced with these conditions, some of the minorities have, in turn, achieved a degree of national unity and organization which has badly scared the governments concerned. More than one of the "minority" political parties existing in the peasant regions to-day must be numbered among the most powerful and efficiently controlled national organizations in all Europe. And I may add, on the authority of their leaders, that neither the weapon of assassination, nor imprisonment and ill-treatment of members, will intimidate those who are thus demanding justice and freedom to live their own lives.

To remark that such a condition of affairs cannot continue indefinitely without serious trouble is to state the obvious. Various remedies, ranging from a stricter regard for minority rights to the creation of a new Danubian "confederation"—to embrace Austria, Hungary, Czechoslovakia, Croatia, and perhaps Rumania, thus recreating that "natural economic unit" shattered by the war in Central Europe—have been proposed for ending conditions which are a disturbing factor to the peace of the continent. The Italian Government has taken a leading part in formulating plans for an economic *rapprochement* in that region.

Proposals advanced by interested governments, intent upon reviving "balances of power" in forms favourable to themselves, are unlikely to do more than touch the fringe of the essential problem as seen by the peasants themselves. More interesting than recent diplomatic moves instituted by Rome, Berlin, and Vienna is the contemplation of the new Europe which would dawn were the peasant hosts consulted on the delicate question of revising the Versailles-manufactured maps of Eastern Europe.

The strongest peasant organizations existing in Europe to-day are the illegal Croat Peasant Party, the Ukrainian National Democratic Organization in Eastern Galicia, the Bulgarian Peasant Party, the National Peasant Party of Rumania, and the famous Macedonian Revolutionary Organization. Having talked with the leaders of every one of those parties, and with hundreds of peasants of no party leanings, in all the countries concerned, it is possible to forecast the frontier lines of a new Eastern Europe bearing little resemblance to the plans of this or that government—a Europe the coming of which would be hailed by millions of peasants as the birth of freedom and justice.

That Europe would, firstly, create a dramatic change in the frontiers of Soviet Russia, Poland, and Rumania (not to mention certain ill-digested plans attributed to Herr Hitler for Germanic expansion in Eastern Europe), by the emergence of a national democratic Ukrainian state, containing forty millions of peasants of that nationality, living on the lands that have been Ukrainian since the dawn of time.

The boundaries of this new peasant nation, with its capital at Kiev, would stretch from Przemysl, in Poland, to the River Don in Russia, taking in the Podkarpatska Rus region of Czechoslovakia, the Northern Bukovina, and parts of Bessarabia. It is probable, however, that the Ukrainians might choose to make the Carpathian mountains the south-western frontier of a free Ukraine, leaving the Podkarpatska Rus region to become an autonomous unit within Czechoslovakia.

That area was the cradle of the Ukrainian race, and there the Ukrainian people dwell in 1934. Of that territory, totalling 735,000 square kilometres, Soviet Russia would contribute 582,000 square kilometres, comprising the territory at present known as the Ukrainian Socialist Soviet Republic, and the Ukrainian territories in the Central Black Earth soil region and northern Caucasus. Poland would contribute 120,000 square kilometres in Eastern Galicia, Volhynia, and Polissia, and Rumania 16,000 square kilometres. The return of Podkarpatska Rus from Czechoslovakia to a united Ukraine, amounting to 15,000 square kilometres, would, if decided upon, complete the new nation.

The vast majority of Ukrainian peasants living outside the borders of Soviet Russia eagerly look forward to the day when the Greater Ukraine will be established, and if more guarded terms must be used in speaking of the wishes of that majority of the Ukrainian people who to-day dwell under the Sickle and Hammer, it may be pointed out that, despite persecution, the Separatist movement, centred on Kiev, has never ceased to preach the same ideal within the frontiers of the Ukraine under Soviet Russia. Further, the prompt formation of a Ukrainian government at Kiev in 1918 may be cited as clear evidence—indeed, the last free verdict possible— of where lie the wishes of the Ukrainians living under the U.S.S.R. Moscow realizes this, even if apologists of the Soviets outside Russia do not. Hence the persistent fear which haunts the Kremlin, and finds expression in frequent "heresy hunts" among the minor officials and population of Ukraine—the fear of a free Ukraine.

A substantial slice of Transylvania, and the Magyar regions of Czechoslovakia and Yugoslavia, would return to Hungary, from which country wise statesmanship would never have separated these regions, but with provision for the safeguarding of the Rumanian minority which would thus be created in Transylvania. Some form of "dualism" would be demanded by the Slovaks as the price of their continued adherence to the Czechoslovakian state; this being the real aim of all but a handful of extremists in that land.

In a Rumania reduced to manageable, and just, proportions, the peasantry would demand the inauguration of a truly democratic régime, which would lift their nation to the standard of integrity and welfare that has been attained by Bulgaria, their poor neighbour to the south;

a state in which the provision of adequate railway facilities, roads, and co-operative credit and selling organizations is regarded as of more importance than air forces, uniforms—or corset shops where army officers may safeguard their figures !

In return for thus acting as an object lesson to a peasant-ruled Rumanian state in such matters as local government, education, hygiene, and agricultural credits, Bulgaria would receive the Dobruja, the rich wheatlands of which would help to redress the balance tilted against the Bulgarians in 1919.

By this same touchstone of peasant opinion, Yugoslavia, as that country exists to-day, would disappear. The "nation of Serbs, Croats, and Slovenes" never has existed as anything but a political expression, and it lingers on as "ramshackle" as that combination which excited the derision of Europe in the days of the Austro-Hungarian Empire.

Once the wishes of its 90 per cent of peasants were consulted, the Old Kingdom of Serbia would reappear on the maps, with a new Croat-Slovene nation to the north, having Zagreb as its capital, and combining within its borders all of those two races, numbering six millions. Montenegro would reappear as an independent kingdom.

One other territorial change would have to be achieved before the Balkan peoples had settled the major problems which vex that region to-day, and are ripe for that "confederation of Balkan peoples" which many believe to be the forerunner of a Peasant International. The violent ghost of Macedonian intransigence, which has haunted the lonely hills and valleys of that region for a century, must be laid by the creation of an independent Macedonia, formed by the amalgamation of these regions of Yugoslavia, Bulgaria, and Greece inhabited by the Macedonian people. Lest any reader regards this suggestion as a counsel of perfection, let me hasten to add that leaders of the Macedonian Revolutionary Organization—men who have been "on the run" for years, and who have backed their principles with their lives—assured me that nothing less than a free Macedonia will satisfy their people. That Macedonian state might remain loosely linked with Bulgaria—their nearest kinsman, but only freedom for Macedonia can banish the danger of constant terrorism and diplomatic friction in the Balkans.

Such are the desires of the peasant peoples. The fact that those peasant millions are not likely to be consulted in the event of a revision of frontiers in these predominantly agricultural regions, or that this outline of their views runs directly counter to powerful political influences, does not make the outline of what may be called "the Europe the peasants want" any the less interesting, nor is it without significance that millions of humble cultivators regard the revision of national frontiers as the first, indispensable step towards a greater measure of security, justice and fair treatment in the peasant lands.

Ever since the beginning of the fourteenth century, when the clearance of the primeval forests in Central Europe was completed, and husbandry began to expand to the East, these vast territories have been the domain of the food-producer, the herdsman, and the lonely shepherds. For over 500 years generations of peasants have toiled, first as serfs, and later as smallholders living under conditions little better than serfs, working long hours for the bare means of existence, and nursing within their hearts the dreams of a new day.

To-day—in 1934—one great reform has changed the peasant lands, and another is destined to change them even more drastically in the near future. The sweeping land reforms which followed the European War transformed millions from labourers on the big estates to peasant owners. Over vast stretches of Europe where land-hunger had been a chronic disease for generations it was cured, or substantially alleviated, overnight.

The second factor which makes the peasant all-important to modern Europe is the age of mass-production, which predicates mass-sales. That hundred millions of impoverished peasants in Eastern Europe represents the largest almost untapped reservoir of potential demand existing outside China or Africa ; already it is far more

S

articulate and nearer to political power than the nameless millions of either Asia or Africa. And already it has been demonstrated beyond reasonable doubt that there can be no assured prosperity for Western Europe while the agriculturists of that continent are clothed in skins and rags and trade eggs for matches.

The figure of the giant peasant, typifying all peasants, which looms over the factories of Western Europe is compounded, not of fears of a "Green International", which will wreck the future peace and orderly development of our continent, but of the great mass of future consumers whose purchasing power will save it.

To-day the peasants are awake. Their thoughts are on the march. If the mountains of debts which they owe have not proved a catastrophe for them it is because they are already strong enough, and watchful enough, to cause governments to fear their strength. It is a growing strength, but not one that Europe need fear. For the peasant is, above all things, conservative and constructive. He is a builder, not a wrecker. Patient, inured to hardship, docile, those peasants have yet managed to outlast all the empires which reared their misbegotten shapes upon the shoulders of the countryman. Out of their poverty they have created boundless wealth, financed wars, and enabled bureaucracies to flourish. They have elevated the education of their children into a passion, and in many parts created co-operative organizations through which to express their economic power. Their political parties can wreck governments; and are to-day defying some of the most powerful and chauvinistic oligarchies in Europe.

Their weapons remain the same—the spade, the hoe, the reaping-hook. The peasant, rightly understood, is the greatest passive resister in all history. If governments are wise, they will remember that fact, and give heed to the views of those toiling millions whose eyes are beginning to look out beyond their own valleys and hills— to see, as though it were their own country—the endless oceans of farmlands stretching to other horizons beyond.

THE END

INDEX

INDEX

Agricultural crisis, effects of, 66
 sqq., 181 sqq., 240 sqq.
Atanasoff, Professor, 67
Austria :
 agricultural imports into, 30
 agriculture, position of, 28
 agricultural production in, 28
  sqq.
 depression, effects of, 30
 infant mortality in, 17
 Lower Austrian Bauern-Bung, 36
 land, redistribution of, 21, 27
 livestock, numbers of, 28
 Nazi Party, activities of, 31,
  37 sqq.
 peasants, conditions of, 31 sqq.
 prices in, 31
 sugar-beet production in, 35
 timber industry in, 33
 tourist industry, importance of,
  33 sqq.
 Tyrolese peasants in, 32 sqq.
 Vienna, importance of as market,
  36, 39
 wine-growing in, 37 sqq.

Bata, Thomas, 18, 45
Bessarabia :
 agricultural prices in, fall of, 133
 agricultural production in, 132
 autonomous government, suppression of, 130, 202
 future of, 270

Bessarabia—*continued*.
 history of, 127, 202
 Kishinev, characteristics of, 130
  sqq.
 land, redistribution of, 110, 130
 livestock in, 132
 peasants, conditions of, 132 sqq.
 population, distribution of, 124,
  128 sqq.
 political conditions in, 124 sqq.,
  134 sqq., 264, 267
 roads in, 114, 131
 Ukrainians in, 127 sqq., 202
Bukovina :
 agricultural production in, 150
 Austria, conditions under, 141,
  157, 265 sqq.
 economic conditions in, 148 sqq.,
  153 sqq.
 educational facilities in, 144
 employed agricultural labourers
  in, 149
 future of, 270
 land, redistribution of, 110, 149
 land values, fall in, 252
 peace settlement, effects of,
  142, 202, 265 sqq.
 peasants, taxation of, 137, 154
 racial groups in, 141, 202
 Rumanian colonists in, 150 sqq.,
  266
 theatrical censorship in, 138
  sqq.
 Ukrainian Church in, 145 sqq.

For Product Safety Concerns and Information please contact our EU
representative GPSR@taylorandfrancis.com
Taylor & Francis Verlag GmbH, Kaufingerstraße 24, 80331 München, Germany

www.ingramcontent.com/pod-product-compliance
Lightning Source LLC
Chambersburg PA
CBHW070554270326
41926CB00013B/2314